ASSIGNMENTS

IN

TRIAL PRACTICE

FIFTH EDITION

Joseph D. Howe
Judge
Superior Court of Arizona

Walker J. Blakey
Professor of Law
University of North Carolina

LITTLE, BROWN AND COMPANY
Boston   1986   Toronto

Copyright © 1962, 1964, 1971, 1975 by Little, Brown and Company

Copyright © 1986 by Joseph D. Howe and Walker J. Blakey

All rights reserved. No part of this book may be reproduced in any form or by any electronic or mechanical means including information storage and retrieval systems without permission in writing from the publisher, except by a reviewer who may quote brief passages in a review.

Library of Congress Catalog No. 86-080929

ISBN 0-316-37576-4

Fifth edition

Printed in the United States of America

ALP

CONTENTS

Introduction v

Acknowledgements vii

Ground Rules for the Course viii

Assignment 1A Marsh v. Fitch (Lee Simpson) 1

Assignment 1B Beatty v. McGuire (Frank Anthony) 19

Assignment 2A Charles v. Kay (Irma Charles) 26

Assignment 2B Grubbs v. Passmore Securities Corp. (Karl Kaline) . . . 35

Assignment 3A Charles v. Kay (Irma Charles) 51

Assignment 3B Charles v. Kay (Willis Hood) 52

Assignment 4A State v. Dirandum (Officer Holmes) 55

Assignment 4B Olson v. Raines (Chester Milford) 60

Assignment 5A State v. Dirandum (Daniel Dirandum) 66

Assignment 5B Bates v. Dunn (David Bates) 67

Assignment 6A Sanders v. Bennett (charge) 74

Assignment 6B State v. Devereaux (charge) 75

Assignment 7A Sanders v. Bennett (summation) 77

Assignment 7B State v. Devereaux (summation) 78

Assignment 8A State v. Brawley (Bertha Lyman) 79

Assignment 8B Sommers v. Ames Transfer Co. (Sgt. Winters) 95

Assignment 9A State v. Brawley (Cameron Himes, M.D.) 103

Assignment 9B Sommers v. Ames Transfer Co. (Sgt. Winters) 107

Assignment 9C State v. Devereaux (Thomas DeGowin, M.D.) 109

Assignment 10A Oliver v. Ballew (three or four witnesses) 110

Assignment 10B Lynch v. Ames Insurance Co. (five witnesses) 122

Assignment 10C Myers v. Davis (three witnesses) 143

Assignment 11A Fortune v. Bilder (Hope Hollow). 158

Assignment 11B State v. Devereaux (Irene Gossage) 164

Assignment 12A Pyle v. Ace Storage Corp. (pleadings and pre-
                trial practice) 169

Assignment 12B Birch v. Asher Associates, Inc. (pleadings and
                pre-trial practice) 177

Assignment 12C Day v. Dawson Cleaners (pleadings and pre-
                trial practice) 191

Negotiation Assignment 196

Assignment 13A Pyle v. Ace Storage Corp. (William Weld deposition) . . 198

Assignment 13B Birch v. Asher Associates, Inc. (Albert A. Birch
                deposition) 199

Assignment 13C Hearsay Review Problems 200

Assignment 14A Parry v. Ames and Western R.R. Co. (Harry
                Timmons deposition) 202

Assignment 14B Beatty v. McGuire (James McGuire deposition) 207

Assignment 15A Gates v. Williston Hotel Corp. (Harold Frank) 209

Assignment 15B State v. McGuire (Frank Anthony) 219

Assignment 15C Interview of a Witness 222

Appendix A   Record of Sanders v. Bennett 223

Appendix B   Record of State v. Devereaux 289

Appendix C   General Instructions to Witnesses 319

INTRODUCTION

This book presents a series of substantial trial practice problems. Although the instructor may decide to assign the entire class to be prepared to perform any of these problems, these materials have been designed for use in a trial practice course in which a few students will act as counsel and perform the assignment during the first part of the class session. The instructor will allow approximately an hour of this performance. During the remainder of the class all members of the class will participate in a criticism of this performance. The Ground Rules set out at the beginning of the book describe in some detail the procedure for the course.

The focus of this course will be on trial tactics and techniques, not upon the substantive and procedural law underlying the problems in the assignments; but it will frequently be necessary for student counsel to research underlying substantive and procedural law before they can decide what opportunities there are for trial tactics and techniques. All assignments are set in Ames, the fifty-first state. The individual assignments and Ground Rule 8 and 9 give some indication of relevant Ames law, but, as Ground Rule 10 states: "Except as otherwise indicated, points of substantive law and rules of evidence involved in an assignment are to be regarded as matter of first impression in Ames unless the instructor announces that Ames has just adopted the Ames Rules of Evidence which are identical to the Federal Rules of Evidence (or a state evidence code designated by the instructor)."

Although we have added a second criminal law expert witness assignment (Assignment 9C) and a hearsay review assignment (Assignment 13C), most of the changes in this edition have been made in order to enable the instructor to use either the common law of evidence or an evidence code.

"Secret instructions" for all witnesses are included in the Instructors' Manual, and the instructor should give photocopies of those instructions to each witness. All of the possible exhibits are now included in the student's assignments book on "tear-out pages" so that they can be taken out and used as exhibits in the performances.

The instructor may modify any of the ground rules or assignments. In order to facilitate modifications by the instructor, we have set forth some of the most likely ones as "Alternative Assignments." These alternatives are not to be followed unless the instructor assigns them. When alternatives are assigned, all of the rest of the problem remains the same except insofar as the problem is changed by the alternatives assigned or by the instructor.

The text for the course is Keeton, _Trial Tactics and Methods_, second edition (hereinafter cited as _Text_). Each student should complete a first reading of the entire _Text_ before the first class performance. This first reading is merely for orientation with respect to the kinds of help which the _Text_ can provide, and it need not be a painstaking study. Particular sections of the _Text_ are assigned for study along with each of the assignments in this book.

ACKNOWLEDGEMENTS

We must thank a great many people who have contributed to the development of these materials. The first edition of Assignments in Trial Practice consisted of materials prepared by Robert E. Keeton, Richard H. Field, Leonard G. Ratner, Robert W. Meserve, James D. St. Clair, Lewis H. Weinstein, and Jerome P. Facher, Instructors in Trial Practice at Harvard Law School. Contributions to the development of those materials were also made by the Teaching Fellows and their faculty advisor at the Harvard Law School, who created two model trials upon which Assignments 1A, 6A, and 7A were based.

The second edition was edited by Leon Letwin, and the third and fourth editions by the present authors. Contributions to the development of the new assignments in the third edition were made by Messrs. Keeton, Field, St. Clair, Weinstein, Facher, and also by James P. Lynch, Jr., and David S. Nelson, all of whom were Instructors in Trial Practice at Harvard Law School. Assignment 10C is adapted from materials created by Judge Keeton for the National Institute for Trial Advocacy and is used by arrangement with the Institute. We received assistance with Assignment 10B from Mrs. Zia C. Schostal of the North Carolina Bar, and with Assignment 1B from Mr. Andrew Ross of the Ohio Bar and Judith R. Ross. Our principal typist for the fourth edition was Mrs. Eileen P. Jago.

The illustrations in this edition have been prepared by Dr. Georgia Tangi and Charlot Martin. We received assistance in preparing this edition from Mark Edwards, Diane White, Reuben F. Boone, Cynthia A. Baddour, Jon McCachren, and Brian Clarkson while they were students at the University of North Carolina School of Law. Finally, we must thank the typists for this edition, Bonita Summers, Sharon Brooks Laney, Paul Sherer and Danny Reid.

Joseph D. Howe

Walker J. Blakey

GROUND RULES FOR THE COURSE

1. The first part of the two-hour class period will normally be devoted to a performance by student counsel of some phase of trial or preparation for trial of the case assigned for that day. This performance should take one hour or less, leaving approximately an hour for critique. If you do not have an assignment as counsel, you are nevertheless expected to study both the assignment in the text and the materials concerning the case assigned for the day, in order that you may participate intelligently in the critique. As you observe the performance, take notes on matters worthy of comment, including matters you would have handled differently and matters student counsel have handled well.

2. During the entire course, each student may have several special assignments as counsel. Some members of the class will also have an assignment as a witness. The purpose of the latter type of assignment is to provide instructional value to the person serving as a witness, as well as to aid in the development of the assignment for others. The witness should read the General Instructions found in Appendix C. He will also be given additional materials to help him prepare for his role. He will be expected to be ready to describe and criticize, during the class critique, any significant aspects of the performance of counsel in their relations with him prior to the class exercise. Since the number of witness assignments is limited, preference will be given to volunteers. If you wish to receive such an assignment, so advise your instructor during the first or second week of the course.

3. At the first meeting of the class, counsel and the witness will be designated for several assignments. Thereafter the instructor will, at appropriate intervals, designate counsel and witnesses for later assignments. If any student is aware that he will be unable to act as counsel or witness at some particular time during the course, he should give the instructor notice as early as practicable. Students may exchange assignments only with the consent of the instructor.

4. The special assignments for "firms" designated by letter in the class materials are ordinarily given to partnerships composed of two students, and the responsibility and opportunities for participation in each assignment should be divided between them. Since equal division will normally be impracticable, one should take the larger role in their first class assignment and the other in their next.

5. If the two members of a firm cannot reach agreement as to any choice which faces them as counsel, the judgment of the one serving as leading counsel for the assignment should control, but the wisdom of his choice will be subject to discussion during the critique.

6. Insofar as possible, preferences of students will be observed in assigning partnerships. Students desiring to work together should notify the instructor as soon as possible.

7. Unless otherwise indicated, each case is pending or is to be filed in the Superior Court of the Commonwealth of Ames, County of Thayer.

8. The rules of civil procedure in Ames are the same as the Federal Rules of Civil Procedure (hereafter cited as Federal Rules), with such modifications as are necessary to make them applicable in a state court. You should be thoroughly familiar with the Rules affecting trial and pre-trial procedures, especially the Rules dealing with depositions.

Ames rules of criminal procedure are set forth as needed in the individual assignment materials.

9. Unless otherwise indicated, act on the following assumptions:

(a) The unlimited rule as to scope of cross-examination, rather than the federal rule, is in effect in Ames. Cross-examination may therefore extend to matters not touched in direct examination.

(b) Ames has enacted the Uniform Business Records as Evidence Act.

10. Except as otherwise indicated, points of substantive law and rules of evidence involved in an assignment are to be regarded as matters of first impression in Ames, unless the instructor announces that Ames has just adopted the Ames Rules of Evidence which are identical to the Federal Rules of Evidence (or a state evidence code designated by the instructor).

11. Unless otherwise indicated, assume that the only available witnesses who can give admissible testimony are those disclosed in the file materials distributed with the assignment. If you wish to use other testimony that you consider would surely be available in such a case as the one on trial, ask the instructor before the class meeting for permission to assume the availability of such testimony.

12. When you have a special assignment as counsel, make a short typewritten outline covering (1) your theory of your client's case and its points of strength and weakness, (2) your objectives in the phase of the case assigned for performance during the class period and their relationship to your theory of the case and overall plan for trial, and (3) the risks to your case against which you must guard, during the phase of the case assigned for class performance. Hand this outline to the instructor at the beginning of the class period or at whatever time the instructor directs, such as "by 5 p.m. the day before class." You may be asked at the beginning of the critique to explain some of the points referred to in your outline. You may also be asked to state your views as to whether your objectives were achieved and whether, as a matter of hindsight, there are specific things you would have done differently if given another chance.

13. Often the witness who is to testify at a forthcoming session will be available for interview in advance by counsel for one or both sides. Unless instructed otherwise, counsel for each side are free to request such an interview of the witness if they consider it proper and wise to do so. Whether such requests are honored is, of course, up to the witness. The witness will have been given instructions about this and about the basic lines of his testimony. When you are assigned as counsel, do not ask the witness about these instructions. Learn what you want to know by interrogating him just as you would an actual witness. He also will have been instructed not to engage in any "off the record" conversations with you, and he will take anything you say to him as being said by you in your role as counsel.

14. Assume that all parties have been given due notice of the taking of any deposition that appears in the course materials.

15. Sometimes counsel approach the bench during trial, with the court's permission, for the purpose of having a conference with the court out of the hearing of the jury. In the trial practice sessions, such conferences must be heard by the class. Therefore when counsel wishes to approach the bench, he will request permission from the court, and if permission is granted he and opposing counsel will take positions at the opposite sides of the courtroom. Members of the class will understand that such movement signifies a bench conference, and that the bench conference is concluded when counsel return to their places. This method will make it possible for everyone to distinguish what is said outside the hearing of the jury from what is said in their hearing.

16. At times, for tactical reasons, you may decide not to make a valid objection to evidence. In all such instances, make a note immediately and be prepared to state during the critique what valid objections you declined to make and why.

17. Conversely, at times you may make a legally valid objection in carrying out your instructions that you regard as tactically unwise. Be prepared during the class session to indicate such occasions with reasons for believing them tactically unwise.

18. In some assignments counsel may decide that the tactically correct examination would be short or nonexistent but want to conduct a longer examination in order to gain experience. They should indicate this to the instructor in their memorandum or otherwise, prepare both examinations, and conduct the examination that they are prepared to defend as tactically the wiser. If time allows, the instructor may then permit them to conduct the longer examination as well for practice and comparison.

19. To conserve time for critique, the trial judge may interrupt proceedings during either direct or cross-examination and instruct counsel to summarize one or more phases of interrogation planned for use during the assigned hearing; in that event, the trial judge may also call on opposing counsel to indicate what objections, if any, they would have made.

20. Unless otherwise announced, an instructor will serve as trial judge for each assignment involving court proceedings. The judge's actions, as well as those of counsel, are subject to comment during the critique.

21. The roles of court reporter and court clerk will be performed by students. The instructor will designate a court reporter and a court clerk (or a single individual to play the role of a clerk-reporter) for the first session. Thereafter, it will be the responsibility of these individuals to designate their successors in these roles for the following assignment, and they in turn will designate their successors. The function of the clerk will be to swear witnesses; that of the reporter, to mark exhibits. Each will perform such additional duties as may be assigned by the instructor.

22. When you have a special assignment, you are not permitted to visit an earlier meeting of another section on the same assignment. Such visiting would interfere with the development of the assignments by individual effort and would often make the class session less valuable both to the student counsel and to the observers. When you do not have a special assignment for the week, you are permitted to attend another section in lieu of your own for good reason, such as illness or a conflicting engagement.

23. With respect to those assignments involving direct and cross-examination, students not given the special assignment for the class session may wish to arrange among themselves for an extracurricular performance in which they take the roles of counsel and judge. The instructor will cooperate with any such group of students by providing special instructions to the volunteer witness whom the students are using. Such voluntary exercises should occur prior to the class session to enable the participants to gain the maximum benefit from both the exercise and the critique during class.

24. All statements of witnesses in this book and in the special materials are typewritten for legibility, but all parts of a witness' statement except for the signature should be assumed to be in the handwriting of the person who obtained the statement from the witness. The signature should be assumed to be the handwritten signature of the witness.

25. The instructor may assign an additional team or teams from the class to prepare a written critique of the performance during a class session.

26. Dates of recent events in these materials are frequently stated in a dating code in which 19Y1 means one year ago, 19Y2 means two years ago, 19Y3 means three years ago, and so on.

27. In the event of a conflict between a ground rule and any special instruction in the assignment book, the special instruction governs.

Assignments in Trial Practice

ASSIGNMENT 1A

Study Chapter I and §§ 2-25, 2-34 through 2-38, 4-6, 4-7, and 9-7 of the Text.

The special assignment involves the direct and cross-examination of Lee Simpson, a photographer employed by plaintiff's lawyers in the case of Marsh v. Fitch, and such use as the parties wish to make of any parts of the deposition of Morris Dennis bearing on the photographic evidence.

Firm A (Counsel for plaintiff): Conduct the direct examination, placing in evidence whichever of the four Photographs 1-4 you think wise and as much interpretive testimony as is desirable.

Firm B (Counsel for defendant): Conduct the cross-examination. Also, if you think it tactically wise to do so as the circumstances develop, try to get in evidence, during the cross-examination of Simpson, Photograph A and any of Photographs 1-4 not offered by plaintiff. The defendant's photographer who took Photograph A is unavailable, as is Morris Dennis, who it is stipulated now lives in Florida, several hundred miles from Ames.

Plaintiff seeks damages on the theory, among others, that defendant libeled plaintiff by referring to him as a hit-and-run driver. Plaintiff admits driving the car that hit the defendant's nephew, a pedestrian, on a lonely country road near Austin, Ames, at about sundown on September 17, 19Y2, and departing from the scene of the accident without leaving any identification. Plaintiff claims, however, that he did this because he was going for help, leaving the unconscious person unmoved, as he thought first-aid procedure required. Plaintiff passed the house nearest the scene of the accident, and later telephoned from the second house. One of the issues of fact is whether plaintiff deliberately passed the first house in flight, thereafter changing his mind and deciding to stop and telephone, or instead failed to see the first house and failed also to see the driveway and mailbox to the house.

It has been stipulated that the hour of sunset in Austin, Ames, on September 17, 19Y2, was 6:51 p.m., Eastern Daylight Time, and that the Weather Bureau Records for Austin, Ames, show that September 17, 19Y2, was an overcast day, but without rain.

Assignments in Trial Practice

Excerpts from Deposition of Morris Dennis

Taken at the Instance of Defendant's Counsel on October 26, 19Y1

Q. (1-27 Summarized). I live on a farm on Hedgehollow Road about eight miles from Austin Centre; I have owned this farm for about forty years. In the early dusk of September 17, 19Y2, Colonel Fitch ran into my place and asked to use the telephone, explaining that his nephew had been injured in an auto accident on the curve near my farm, that the nephew was unconscious, and that the Colonel needed to call the police. He did not stay after making his call. I did not accompany the Colonel because I am 71 and also a little lame as a result of a broken hip I suffered two years ago.

My farm is about 200 yards from the center of the curve where the accident occurred; it is on the north side of the road at a point where it runs almost due east and west. The house, a one and one-half story bungalow, is about 100 yards from the road and 25 feet high. The barn is 25 yards behind the house, farther away from the road. It is a small barn -- about 30 feet high. The house is about 50 feet by 30 feet and the barn is about 50 feet by 20 feet.

In front of the house near the road is a grove of shade trees and evergreens, two dozen or so, none of them over 25 feet high and 10 inches in diameter. Near the house are four or five fruit trees and one quite large shade tree. There is also a lot of underbrush along the roadside.

Q. 28. In your opinion, can the house be seen from the road?

PLAINTIFF'S COUNSEL: I object to the opinion evidence.

DEFENDANT'S COUNSEL: Mr. Dennis, you may answer the question.

A. Could you repeat the question?

DEFENDANT'S COUNSEL: Mr. Reporter, could we have the last question again? (Question 28 was read.) A. I'm sure it can. So far as I know, no one has ever had any trouble finding it.

PLAINTIFF'S COUNSEL: I object. It's irrelevant and not responsive.

Q. 29. State whether or not your house lights were on at that time. A. I don't remember. It's quite possible that they were.
Q. 30. How wide is the driveway? A. About 10 feet.
Q. 31. What does the surface of the driveway consist of? A. Mostly sand and gravel.
Q. 32. Is there a mailbox on your property? A. Yes. I have an R.F.D.

mailbox.
Q. 33. Where is it located? A. It's a few feet back off of Hedgehollow Road, maybe about 10 feet east of the driveway.
Q. 34. What color is it? A. It's white.
Q. 35. How high above the ground is it? A. Oh, I'd say about 4 feet.

Cross-Examination by Plaintiff's Counsel

X. 1. Now, you testified, Mr. Dennis, that people had no trouble finding your place. A. That's right.
X. 2. You are frequently visited by friends, are you? A. Well, pretty often. And family too.
X. 3. Your friends and family know where you live, don't they? A. Of course.
X. 4. It would be fair to say, wouldn't it, that most of the people who visit you know where your place is and know what to look for when they're trying to find your place? A. Well, I suppose so.
X. 5. Your mailbox is back off the road a number of feet? A. Yes.
X. 6. There's quite a bit of underbrush in the area of the mailbox, isn't there? A. Some.
X. 7. In fact the mailbox is partly hidden by underbrush, isn't it? A. I think so.
X. 8. Has the mailbox been moved since that day Colonel Fitch's nephew was injured? A. No sir, it's been there for years.
X. 9. And has your driveway been moved since that date? I mean have you had any work done on it to broaden or narrow it or move it one way or another? A. Heavens no, it's been like that for years.
X. 10. Have any of the trees or bushes in the area of the mailbox been cut down since the date of this accident? A. No. Not so far as I know.
X. 11. Have any trees or bushes or other things been added to the area of the mailbox since the date of the accident? A. Not that I know of.
X. 12. Would it be accurate to say that except for seasonal changes, the mailbox and the area immediately surrounding it now look substantially the same as they did on the day of the accident? A. Yes.

Photographs

Plaintiff's lawyers employed a photographer, Lee Simpson, to take photographs of the mailbox from the direction in which plaintiff approached as he was driving by the house on the date of the accident. These photographs were taken on September 25, 19Y1, and Lee Simpson has furnished to plaintiff's lawyers a memorandum as follows:

Photograph No. 1. Taken on an extremely overcast day at 5:56 p.m., Daylight time, September 25, 19Y1. Camera placed at northerly edge of pavement facing west, at a location 50 feet east of Dennis

Assignments in Trial Practice

mailbox. Height of camera lens 5 feet.

Photograph No. 2. Taken on an extremely overcast day at 5:58 p.m., Daylight time, September 25, 19Y1. Camera placed at northerly edge of pavement facing west, at a location 30 feet east of Dennis mailbox. Height of camera lens 5 feet.

Photograph No. 3. Taken on an extremely overcast day at 6:00 p.m., Daylight time, September 25, 19Y1. Camera placed at northerly edge of pavement facing west, at a location 15 feet east of Dennis mailbox. Height of camera lens 5 feet.

Photograph No. 4. Taken on an extremely overcast day at 6:07 p.m., Daylight time, September 25, 19Y1. Camera placed at northerly edge of pavement facing north, at a location 10 feet south of Dennis mailbox. Height of camera lens 5 feet.

The location and height of the camera were determined by instructions from a member of plaintiff's counsel's firm. All other technical decisions relating to the photographic process were made by the photographer.

Morris Dennis, who is friendly to defendant, observed the photographer's activities and notified defendant. Defendant's lawyers then sent out a photographer to take some additional photographs. This was done on October 5, 19Y1. Only one photograph, reproduced here as Photograph A, was taken. Defendant wishes to have it in evidence to show the obvious break in the underbrush alongside the road at the point where the driveway is located and to show the relation between the mailbox and driveway. The photographer's memorandum to defendant's lawyers concerning this photograph is as follows:

A. Time: 2:10 p.m. Daylight time, October 5, 19Y1.
Place: Looking northerly from southerly edge of Hedgehollow Road toward Dennis mailbox and driveway. Distance of camera from mailbox, 30 feet south. Height of camera lens 5 feet. Light conditions: Excellent; clear, bright day.

Pre-trial Conference

At the pre-trial conference, the judge explored the possibility of securing stipulations between the parties as to the admissibility of various exhibits, including photographs. No such stipulations were secured, though as part of the procedure, the parties exchanged copies of all of the photographs reproduced herein and now have them in their files.

Defense Preparation for Cross-Examination

After obtaining copies of Photographs 1-4, defense counsel conferred with their photographer to prepare for cross-examination of plaintiff's photographer. They showed their photographer plaintiff's pictures, described the factual issue to which the photographs were relevant, and inquired whether the pictures were accurate.

They learned the following. Had plaintiff's photographer wished to do so, he could have utilized a number of techniques to produce relevant distortion, i.e., give an impression falsely favorable to the plaintiff.

(1) He could minimize the apparent contrast between the mailbox and the foliage and between the driveway and the foliage:

> (a) by use of a colored filter (perhaps green) in taking the picture;
>
> (b) by the type of film developer used;
>
> (c) by the technique of film developing;
>
> (d) by the contrast grade of paper on which the prints were made;
>
> (e) by the printing technique.

(2) He could distort the apparent distances between objects, such as driveway, foliage, and mailbox. For example, he could use a long-focus lens to shrink perspective, or a wide-angle lens to exaggerate it.

While defendant's photographer is unable to say whether such distortions are present in Photograph 1-4 merely by inspecting them, he thinks it fair to assume that Simpson will deny that there are any.

The Trial

The first witness for plaintiff was a surveyor, whose map of the area was identified, admitted in evidence as Exhibit 1, and explained. The second witness is the photographer employed by plaintiff's lawyers. Although plaintiff's lawyers might have preferred to call him at a later point in the trial, the photographer insists that it would be most inconvenient for him to appear later, and plaintiff's lawyers have decided to accommodate him.

As a matter of tactics each firm might decide not to make any objections to the admission of the photographs. In this assignment, however, we are primarily concerned with learning how to get photographs into evidence over determined opposition. Accordingly, the lawyers will make every objection that they consider to be valid as matters stand at the moment the objection is made, with one exception -- defendant's counsel need not object to any photograph which they intend to offer in the event plaintiff does not.

Assignments in Trial Practice

The critique will include discussion of not only the performance of trial counsel (the students assigned as Firms A and B) and the tactical advisability of their objections, but also the manner in which the photographic evidence was developed before they came into the case.

ALTERNATIVE ASSIGNMENT 1A-1

The instructor may limit this assignment to the performance of the direct examination. If this is done there will be no cross-examination, but defense counsel will still be able to request a voir dire.

ALTERNATIVE ASSIGNMENT 1A-2

The instructor may assign as defense counsel everyone in the class who is not assigned as plaintiff's counsel. As plaintiff's counsel attempt to introduce the evidence, the other members of the class should make every objection they consider valid on the state of the record at the moment they make the objection, whether or not they consider it tactically sound to make the objection.

ALTERNATIVE ASSIGNMENT 1A-3

The instructor may provide that the witness is not to be interviewed before class, and then allow the first 15 minutes of the class session for an in-class interview.

ALTERNATIVE ASSIGNMENT 1A-4

The instructor may assign everyone in the class to prepare both sides of the assignment. During the class session the instructor will call upon different members of the class to perform portions of the assignment on either side. The class session will begin with a 15-minute witness interview.

Assignments in Trial Practice

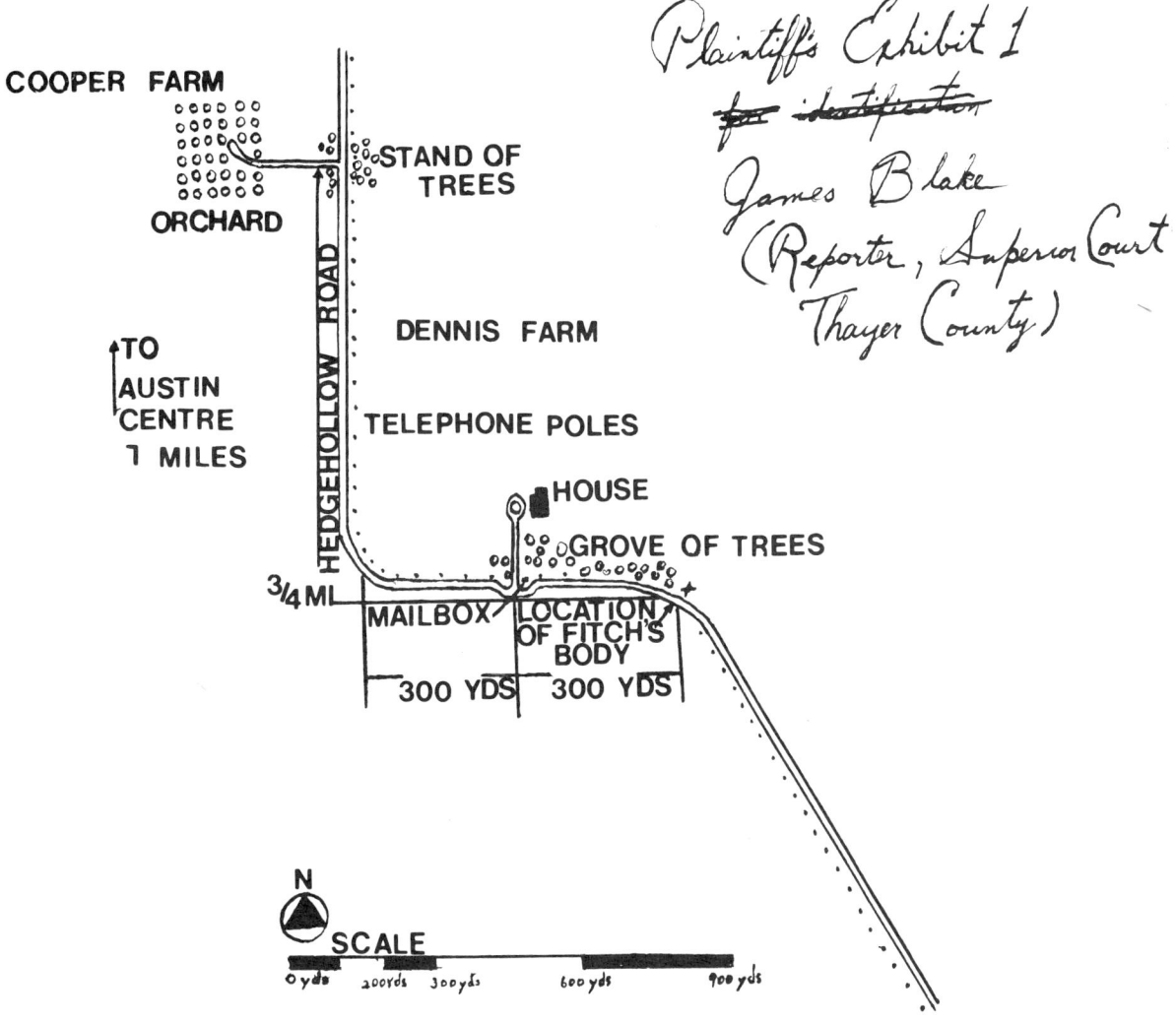

MAP OF A PORTION OF THE SOUTHEAST
QUARTER SECTION OF AUSTIN TOWNSHIP
PREPARED BY *William Bird*

Assignments in Trial Practice

Photograph No. 1

Assignments in Trial Practice

Photograph No. 2

Assignments in Trial Practice

Photograph No. 3

Photograph No. 4

Assignments in Trial Practice

Photograph A

Assignments in Trial Practice

ASSIGNMENT 1B

Study Chapter I and §§ 2-25, 2-34 through 2-38, 4-6, 4-7, and 9-7 of the Text.

This special assignment involves the direct and cross-examination of Frank Anthony, a witness for the plaintiff in the case of Beatty v. McGuire.

Firm A (Counsel for plaintiff): Conduct the direct examination of Frank Anthony. Attempt to lay the foundation for the introduction of the photograph which Anthony found in the barber shop and to introduce that photograph along with as much interpretive testimony as is desirable.

Firm B (Counsel for defendant): Oppose the introduction of the photograph. Conduct cross-examination if you think it tactically wise to do so.

The plaintiff, John Beatty, has brought this action against the defendant, James McGuire, in order to reform or cancel a $2,500 promissory note made out to a David Hill and signed by the plaintiff. The note is now in the possession of defendant McGuire, who claims that Hill endorsed the note to him and that he is a holder in due course of the instrument. If McGuire is a holder in due course, he is entitled to enforce the note regardless of whether Hill obtained the note by fraud. There are several points on which the plaintiff has challenged James McGuire's claim to be a holder in due course, but the only one with which we will be concerned in this assignment is that the plaintiff contends that David Hill and the defendant James McGuire are the same person. If the plaintiff can show that the defendant, while using the name David Hill, committed fraud in order to obtain the promissory note, the plaintiff will be entitled to have the note canceled.

Under Ames law this action is one in equity, but the judge can use a jury to determine issues of fact. The evidence involved in this assignment is being presented to such a jury.

Statement of Plaintiff John Beatty to His Counsel on March 14, 19Y1

I am 72 years old and retired. I own a small house in Beale, Ames, where I have lived alone since my wife's death two years ago. I have an old furnace which occasionally needs repairs but which heats the house.

On March 5, 19Y1, a man appeared at my door who identified himself as a city furnace inspector and showed me an official looking identification card. He went down to the basement and the furnace stopped. About half an hour later he came back up and told me that the furnace had broken down while being inspected and that I would have to replace it immediately. He talked about how expensive this would be and how long it would take to order a new furnace. He then suddenly suggested that he had recently inspected a house where they had taken out a perfectly good furnace that I could use, and offered to go see if he could buy it for me.

He left before I could say yes or no and came back two hours later with a small furnace in the back of a pickup truck driven by the other man. I didn't take a good look at the other man because I was looking at the furnace they unloaded and brought into the house. It was small, old, and dirty. Before I could object to any of that, he told me I owed him $2,500 for the furnace and installation.

The other man went out to the truck while we argued over whether or not I had told him to buy the furnace and whether or not it was big enough. After about an hour of argument I signed a promissory note on a blank note form he had with him for $2,500, payable at $50 a month.

He told me his name was David Hill, and I made the promissory note out in that name. We kept on arguing, however, because he insisted that he was going to take my old furnace away for me. He insisted that this was a favor to me, but he insisted on doing it despite my objections.

At this point my nephew, Frank Anthony, rang the bell. While I was letting him in and answering his questions about what was happening, the man who said his name was David Hill must have slipped out the side door, for the truck drove off and he was gone. My nephew did not see the man who called himself David Hill, but he had questioned the truck driver before he rang my bell.

On March 10, 19Y1, I received a telephone call from a James McGuire of McGuire's Heating in Austin, Ames, who said that he had my note and that I should send my $50 a month to him. I asked my nephew to go see them. He can tell you about his visit, but he came back all excited about seeing a picture of the truck driver and took me back with him to see McGuire. This James McGuire turned out to be the man who said he was David Hill. He denied it and said he didn't care what had happened between Hill and me, and that I still owed him the money, but he *is* the man who said he was Hill.

Statement of Frank Anthony to Plaintiff's Counsel on March 14, 19Y1

On March 5, 19Y1, I drove up to my uncle's house in Beale, Ames, a little before 5:30 p.m. and noticed that a truck was parked in his driveway. I asked the driver what he was doing and he answered that he was delivering a furnace. I was surprised and asked some questions, but he answered them all by saying he didn't know, so I went up to the door and rang the bell. I found my uncle inside and a junky, dirty, little furnace in the kitchen but I didn't see the man who had been talking to my uncle.

I called a furnace repairman who quickly fixed my uncle's furnace. He showed us how the electrical connections had been deliberately cut.

On March 10, 19Y1, I went to Austin to see this James McGuire, who wanted my uncle to pay him on that note. He insisted that my uncle would have to pay. I was too angry when I left him to ask him if I might use his telephone. I therefore went into the Davis Barbershop next door and used the telephone there. While I was thanking the barber, I noticed that he had a number of photographs on his walls and in his display cases. One of those was a picture of the truck driver. It had been taken when he was a few years younger. I asked the barber who was in the picture, and he told me that the man in the picture was named George McGuire and that he had his picture up because George McGuire had been one of the better bowlers in the neighborhood before most of the people living in that neighborhood moved away. He hadn't seen George McGuire in several years, but McGuire's brother, James McGuire, still ran a heating business next door.

I thanked him and drove to Beale to pick up my uncle for a confrontation with James McGuire. My uncle identified James McGuire as the man who called himself David Hill, and I thought everything was cleared up, but McGuire denied everything and insisted my uncle would have to pay.

Additional Statement of Frank Anthony to Plaintiff's Counsel on March 21, 19Y1

At counsel's request I went back to the Davis Barbershop to get the picture I had seen there. The barbershop was closed and I learned that the barber, who was named Edward Davis, was now dead. I finally located his widow, who let me go into the barbershop and take the picture which I am now turning over to the counsel.

Information Available to Defense Counsel

Defense counsel have learned through settlement negotiations the general nature of the statements by the plaintiff and his nephew to plaintiff's counsel, but defense counsel do not have the statements themselves.

Excerpts from the Deposition of Defendant James McGuire Taken at the Instance of Plaintiff's Counsel on August 17, 19Y1

Q. 71. Is Exhibit A a picture of your brother George McGuire? A. Yes, but it's several years old.
Q. 72. What difference does that make? A. I don't think you could tell George from that picture.
Q. 73. How had he changed? A. Well, he's heavier and he's just older.
Q. 74. When was this picture taken. A. Oh, at least five, six years

Assignments in Trial Practice

ago.
Q. 75. What is George's address? A. I don't know.
Q. 76. Why don't you know? A. Well, I just haven't heard from him in a few years.
Q. 77. What does he do for a living? A. I don't know. He used to drive a cab.
Q. 78. Was he ever in the heating business? A. Yes. When our dad was alive we both worked for him. And later George did some work for me but that was at least five years ago.
Q. 79. Did he work for David Hill? A. No. I don't think George lives in Ames anymore.
Q. 80. Why don't you think he lives here? A. If he did I'd run into him.
Q. 81. What is David Hill's address? A. I don't know.
Q. 82. Why did you accept a $2,500 note signed by a stranger from a man whose address you didn't know? A. Oh, I knew David. I just didn't know any address for him. He did business door-to-door from his pickup truck.
Q. 83. What was his business? A. He bought and sold used furniture, used furnaces, and things like that. He could do business from his truck because he always found his customer before he bought the goods.
Q. 84. You seem to know a lot about his business. A. I wouldn't say that.
Q. 85. How do you know your brother wasn't working for him by driving his truck on March 5, 19Y1. A. I saw the guy who was driving the truck that day and he wasn't my brother. He didn't even look like him.

The Trial

The first witness at the trial was the furnace repairman who testified that he easily repaired Beatty's original furnace by replacing electric wires that had been cut. The furnace repairman also testified that the furnace he found in the kitchen would have been too small for the Beatty home even if it were new, and that it was a worn-out piece of junk that was not worth over $100 if it was worth anything.

The second witness was the plaintiff John Beatty, who testified in accordance with his statement and identified the defendant, James McGuire, as the person who had claimed to be a furnace inspector named David Hill. On cross-examination, however, Beatty was totally unable to explain how he could identify McGuire. Plaintiff's counsel have therefore decided that they must use Frank Anthony's story about the barbershop picture to bolster the identification.

Assignments in Trial Practice

The Photograph Which Frank Anthony Found in the Barber Shop

Exhibit A
Deposition of James McGuire

David Douglas
Court Reporter

Assignments in Trial Practice

ALTERNATIVE ASSIGNMENT 1B-1

The instructor may limit this assignment to the performance of the direct examination. If this is done there will be no cross-examination, but defense counsel will still be able to request a voir dire.

ALTERNATIVE ASSIGNMENT 1B-2

The instructor may assign as defense counsel everyone in the class who is not assigned as plaintiff's counsel. As plaintiff's counsel attempt to introduce the evidence, the other members of the class should make every objection they consider valid on the state of the record at the moment they make the objection, whether or not they consider it tactically sound to make the objection.

ALTERNATIVE ASSIGNMENT 1B-3

The instructor may provide that the witness is not to be interviewed before class, and then allow the first 15 minutes of the class session for an in-class interview.

ALTERNATIVE ASSIGNMENT 1B-4

The instructor may assign everyone in the class to prepare both sides of the assignment. During the class session the instructor will call upon different members of the class to perform portions of the assignment on either side. The class session will begin with a 15-minute witness interview.

Assignments in Trial Practice

ASSIGNMENT 2A

Study §§ 2-24 through 2-28 and all of Chapter IV of the Text except sections included in Assignment 1.

The special assignment, in the case of Palmer M. Charles v. William O. Kay & Gold Fisheries Co., is the presentation of a portion of the testimony bearing on the identification of the truck that struck the Charles car. The witness Irma Charles is available to testify in person. Testimony from other witnesses, subject to the limitation described below, may be offered from their depositions.

Firm A (Counsel for plaintiff): Conduct the direct examination of Irma Charles. Omit any testimony by her as to the circumstances of the accident and her personal observations of the hit-and-run vehicle (including her observation and recording of its registration number). You will note that this is the testimony covered up to the asterisk in her statement to plaintiff's counsel of May 26, 19Y1, which appears below. This testimony will be the basis of a forthcoming assignment, 3A.

For the purpose of this assignment, assume that Mrs. Charles has already testified as to the matters you have been directed to omit. Assume further that this testimony was consistent with her May 26 statement to plaintiff's counsel.

Omit, also, any testimony about the nature and extent of her husband's injuries and disability.

Offer any other available evidence bearing on identification of the truck and the driver of the truck that struck the Charles car.

Firm B (Counsel for defendants Kay and Gold Fisheries):

1. Attempt by all valid means to prevent admission of testimony tending to connect defendants with the accident on which the suit is based.

2. Cross-examine Irma Charles concerning the matters covered in the direct examination. Observe the same limitations concerning the subject matter of inquiry as those stated above in the directions to Firm A.

One of the two students designated as Firm B will represent Kay and the other will represent Gold Fisheries. It will be assumed that they are practicing independently, not as members of the same firm, and they will cooperate or not as they see fit. The attorney representing Kay has been employed to do so by the insurance company with which Kay carries an automobile liability policy of adequate limits to cover the present claim. The attorney representing Gold Fisheries has been employed to do so by a second liability insurer, which carries a "fleet policy" covering Fisheries' trucks. This policy does not cover an individual driver unless he is acting in the scope of employment for Gold Fisheries.

As a matter of tactics, each firm might make decisions inconsistent with the directions given above. In this assignment, however, we are primarily concerned with learning how to get evidence admitted over determined opposition. Accordingly, counsel will make every objection that they consider to be valid as matters stand at the moment the objection is made; they will not make objections they consider to be without merit. Be sure to consider the appropriate Ground Rules, including 17.

Suggestion to All Counsel

Consider carefully the possibility that certain evidence may be admissible against one defendant and inadmissible against the other. If you are counsel for one of the defendants, concentrate on providing paramount protection for the particular interest of your client, rather than thinking only about the common interests of the defendants against the plaintiff. If you are counsel for the plaintiff, take account of any possibilities you see for getting evidence admitted against one defendant even though it is inadmissible against the other.

Some Relevant Ames Law

1. Ames case law recognizes the customary common-law exceptions to the hearsay rule.

2. Under Ames common law, a master is liable for negligent acts of his servant committed within the scope of employment. Subsequent admissions of such conduct by the servant, however, are inadmissible against the master unless the admission itself was within the scope of employment.

3. A 1971 Ames case, Gordon v. Black Transit Co., 112 Ames 407, quoted with approval the following excerpt from the first edition of McCormick, Evidence § 193 (1954).

> . . . when the witness calls the number of a business establishment and asks for a particular kind of employee . . . and is connected with someone who identifies himself as such, this is evidence that he holds this position, and generally . . . whoever holds himself out in the telephone conversation as qualified to transact business within the scope of the ordinary affairs of the concern, is presumed to be authorized to speak for the employer.

Assignments in Trial Practice

Complaint

Palmer M. Charles, plaintiff, claims personal injuries and damages to his automobile resulting from a collision with a truck negligently operated by a hit-and-run driver. Allegedly the truck was owned by defendant Gold Fisheries Company and operated by Kay, in the scope of employment for Gold Fisheries. Damages sought are $2,621 for property damage to the car and $40,000 for personal injuries against defendants, jointly and severally.

Statements of Palmer M. Charles Taken by Plaintiff's Counsel on June 15, 19Y1

(Mr. Charles made a substantially similar report to a police investigator, and this information is therefore available to defendant's counsel).

I am 32 years of age. On May 23, 19Y1, I was driving easterly on the turnpike between Beale and Austin, Ames. My wife Irma, age 26, was in the back seat, and her brother John H. Castle, age 22, was in the front seat beside me. We had been visiting my wife's family and were bringing John back to Austin to stay with us a few days. At about 11:30 p.m. we were proceeding through Northboro, about 40 miles west of our destination in Austin. John was asleep. My wife had been asleep in the back seat earlier, but was awake at this time. The weather was good and the roads were dry. Repairs were being made on the westbound side of the turnpike, and westbound traffic was detoured into one of the eastbound lanes; we were proceeding east in the other (the southerly) eastbound lane, at a speed of about 35 m.p.h. The posted speed limit was 40 m.p.h. My lights were on low beam.

A truck traveling easterly came from the rear of my car and as it was passing cut right in front of me so that the right side of the truck from the door back struck the left front fender of my car. I was then slowing down for the intersection. The truck was going fast, maybe 45 to 50 m.p.h. There were cars coming in the opposite direction. After the impact I lost control and my car moved off the road to the right a few feet and then diagonally to the left, colliding with the rear end of the car just in front of me. A man by the name of Hood was driving that car; he was headed easterly and had pulled up to a stop to enter Williston Street. The truck did not stop. It was a big van. I could not tell any more about the truck. There was a great deal of truck traffic on the turnpike. John was not hurt; he did not wake up until we hit the Hood car. At some point during the accident, my wife was thrown down between the front and back seats but was not hurt. I suffered three broken ribs. (Other comments about injuries, hospitalization, medical treatment, and loss of earnings deleted.)

Statement of Willis Hood Taken by an Investigator for
Gold Fisheries' Insurer on May 27, 19Y1

My name is Willis Hood. I live in Northboro and I operate the Amoco Station (Ames Oil Company) located at Williston and Scott Streets in Northboro.

On May 23, 19Y1, at about 11:30 p.m., I was preparing to turn left onto Williston Street, near the Northboro-Westboro line. I came to a stop to let a westbound car pass. My left-turn blinker light was on. Just after the westbound car passed, I was about to make my left turn when I heard a loud horn blast from behind. I stopped immediately. The next thing I knew, a truck was passing on my left, and another vehicle was crashing into me from behind. Because of the crash I did not get more than a glimpse of the truck, and I could not identify it from what I saw. The truck proceeded on down the turnpike without stopping.

I have read the foregoing one-page statement and it is true and correct.

/s/ Willis Hood

Assignments in Trial Practice

Excerpt from Statement by Willis Hood to Plaintiff's Counsel on June 19, 19Y1

When the truck went by, I was able to see the letter and the first two numbers of the registration, Ames registration A-43. I remember the numbers because I thought about the fact that I grew up in an apartment numbered A-43.

/s/ Willis Hood

Stipulation of All the Parties

The records of the Registry of Motor Vehicles in Langdell include files on 100 vehicles with numbers beginning A-43. A-4327 was the registration of the Gold Fisheries truck the plaintiff alleges was involved in the accident. A-4389 was the registration of a van-type 19Y2 Ford truck, owned by Zenith Appliance Company of Zenith, Ames (on the extreme northerly border of Ames, 200 miles from Northboro). Among the registrations beginning A-43 there was no other truck of this type and style. It is also stipulated that Officer Krupke died after his deposition was duly taken, signed, and filed.

Excerpts from Statement of Irma Charles Taken by Plaintiff's Counsel on May 26, 19Y1

As we approached the point of impact, I saw the truck before it hit us. I was seated on the left side of the rear seat. The truck made a loud noise coming alongside. I looked back and to the left, through the window on the left side, and saw the truck as it was just at the back of our car. I watched it from then until the moment of collision. It was very close to us. It cut right in and struck the left front side of our car. It was a van-type truck. As it went by, I got the registration number, Ames registration A-4327. The number plate was on the rear where lights shine on it, though I don't remember whether it was in the center or on the side. I saw it as it was going by, when the rear of the truck was not yet past the front of the car, and just as the truck cut in. After the collision with the Hood car, when our car came to rest, I got an envelope out of my purse and wrote down the number. I believe I still have the envelope somewhere around our house.

On May 25, following the accident I called the Registry of Motor Vehicles in Austin and they told me this registration number was on a truck owned by Gold Fisheries Company. I wrote down the name of the company on a memorandum pad I had at the telephone table. Then I looked up their telephone number in the directory and wrote it down on the same piece of paper. I believe that I still have that memorandum too. I dialed the number. Someone answered saying, "Hello, Gold Fisheries." I said I wanted to talk with the driver of the truck with registration number A-4327. The man who answered told me to wait. Then another man

came to the phone and asked me what I wanted. He said his name was Bill
O. Kay. I remember the name because I thought he was kidding when it
sounded like he was saying "O.K." I asked him if he was operating the
truck with number A-4327 on Saturday night, and he said he was. I said,
"Well, why didn't you stop when you hit us?" and he said he didn't know
he hit anybody.

Assignments in Trial Practice

Excerpts from Deposition of William O. Kay Taken at the Instance
of Plaintiff's Counsel on August 17, 19Y1

Q. 21. Now, one of the trucks owned by Gold Fisheries was registered under the number A-4327, was it not? A. Yes.
Q. 22. And it was so registered throughout the month of May, 19Y1? A. Yes.
Q. 23. You were the person who ordinarily drove that truck? A. Not always.
Q. 24. But you ordinarily drove it? A. Usually.
Q. 25. What hours during the day was the truck normally used? A. During working hours: between 5:00 a.m. and about 3:00 or 4:00 in the afternoon.
Q. 26. You were driving that truck on May 23, 19Y1? A. Yes.
Q. 27. Yes, in fact, you drove it that night, didn't you? A. No sir. I drove it that morning until about noon.
Q. 28. What did you do with it after noon on that day? A. I left it in the garage and didn't see it again until the morning of May 25.
Q. 29. On May 25, you took the truck to an auto body repair shop, didn't you? A. Yes.
Q. 30. What was the name and address of that shop? A. Welbilt Body Shop on Webster and Amory Street.
Q. 31. Why did you go there? A. Because I had heard it said that I was involved in an accident on the night of May 23rd in the truck. I wanted evidence that there was no damage at all to the truck, in case someone decided to go after me. Mr. Lane at the body shop looked the truck over and agreed with me.
Q. 32. Then you knew on May 25 that it had been suggested that you were driving the vehicle and had been involved in an accident on May 23rd? A. Yes. Someone had told me that.
Q. 33. And that someone was Mrs. Charles during a phone conversation with you on May 25, isn't that so? A. No, sir. Somebody at work told me that.
Q. 34. Who? A. I don't really remember. There was quite a bit of talk about this incident around the shop, but I don't remember who told me.
Q. 35. In your conversation with Mr. Lane at the body shop, tell me what each of you said. A. I told him someone claimed the truck had been in an accident on the night of the 23rd. I told him he could see there was no damage on the truck. I told him there must have been a mistake, since I hadn't been driving the truck on that night, and he agreed it was probably a case of mistaken identity. He said it certainly didn't look to him like the truck had been in any accident.
Q. 36. It is your testimony that you never had a phone conversation with Mrs. Charles? A. That's right.
Q. 37. What is the phone number of Gold Fisheries? A. 926-1555.
Q. 38. How long has it been that? A. Oh, at least for the past 8 to 10 years.

Excerpts from Deposition of Officer Willard Krupke Taken at the
Instance of Plaintiff's Counsel on August 24, 19Y1

A. (1-18 Summarized.) My name is Willard Krupke. I've been with the Northboro Police Department for the past twelve years. I investigated an accident at the intersection of Williston Street and the Northboro Turnpike during the night of May 23, 19Y1. I prepared a diagram of the scene (plaintiff's deposition Exhibit 1) which I attached to my report. The diagram represents a composite from the statements I got from various witnesses. I didn't arrive at the scene of the accident until about 25 to 30 minutes after the accident.

Q. 19. Who gave you the information as to the points of impact on the truck and on the Charles car? A. Mr. Charles.

Q. 20. And is that information accurately portrayed on Exhibit 1? A. Yes, it is.

Q. 21. As part of your investigation, did you discuss this accident with William O. Kay? A. Yes, I did.

Q. 22. When and where did you have such conversation? A. I spoke to him by phone on the evening of May 27, 19Y1. I called him at his home.

Q. 23. Tell us, please, what you said to him and what he said to you. A. I told him that we had a report to the effect that he had been involved in this accident on the Turnpike on the night of May 23 -- as the driver of a Gold Fisheries truck. He said that he figured as much and said he bet he knew who'd told me that. He said it was Mrs. Charles, the wife of the man who'd been injured. He said she'd already made the same ridiculous charge in a phone call to him, that it wasn't true, and that he wished she'd quit making trouble for him.

Q. 24. Officer Krupke, were criminal charges ever brought against Kay? A. No, it seemed a borderline case for prosecution.

Q. 25. Did you inspect the Fisheries truck bearing registration number A-4327 to see whether there was damage on it indicating an accident? A. Yes, I did.

Q. 26. What did you observe? A. Well, there were scratches and dents at a number of different places on the truck, but I couldn't identify any of them for sure as being of recent origin or indicating a serious accident.

Q. 27. On what date did you conduct this examination of the truck? A. May 27, 19Y1.

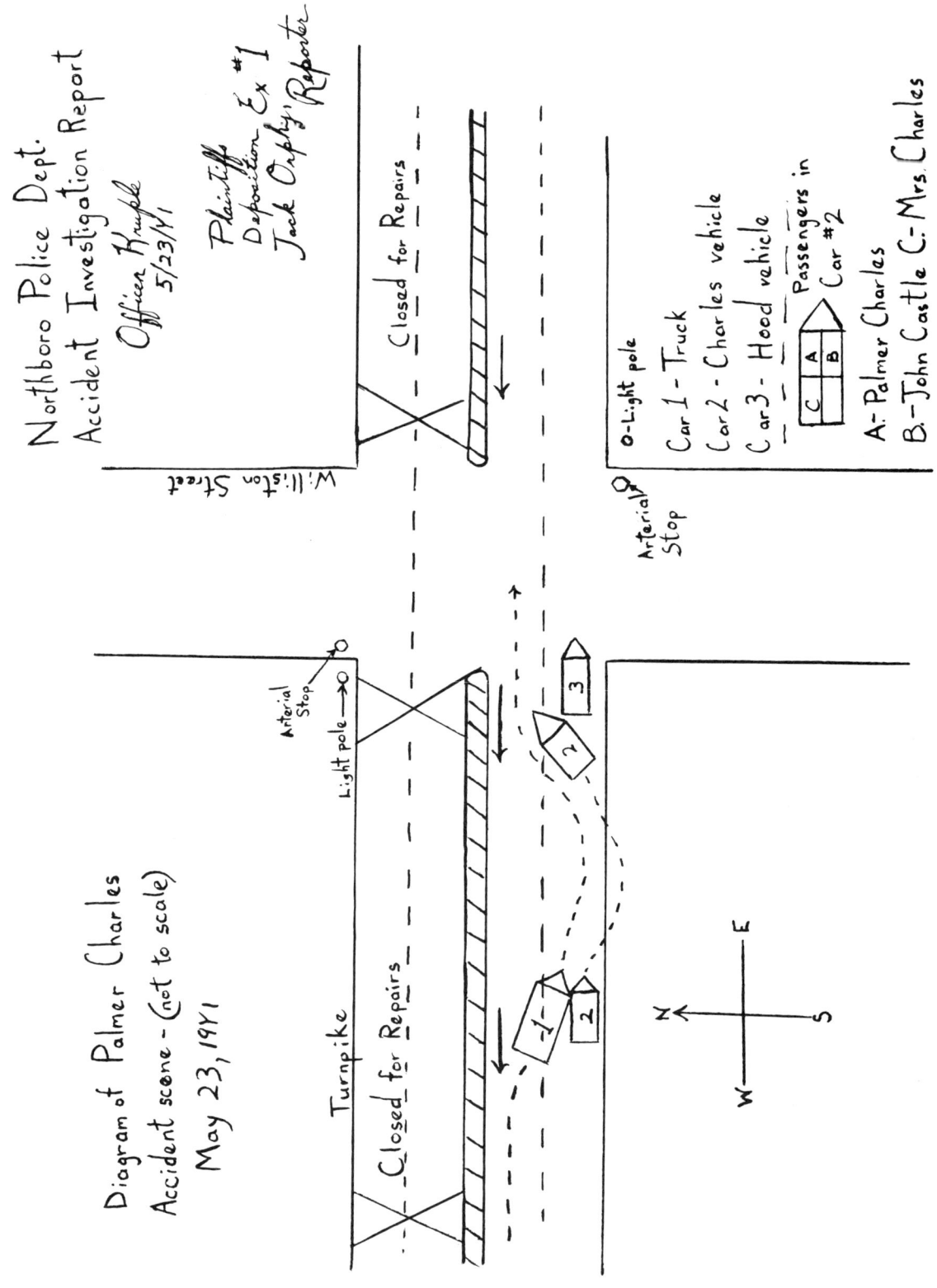

ASSIGNMENT 2B

Study §§ 2-24 through 2-28 and all of Chapter IV of the Text except sections included in Assignment 1.

The special assignment involves the direct and cross-examination of the witness Karl Kaline in the case of Grubbs v. Passmore Securities Corp., and such use as the parties wish to make of excerpts from the deposition of Paul L. Parker, who, it is stipulated, lives in New Jersey, just across the state line from Ames City, Ames.

Firm A (Counsel for plaintiff): Conduct the direct examination, placing in evidence all documentary evidence (except Document 4) which can be successfully offered with the aid of the testimony of this witness, and placing in evidence the testimony about Anson's telephone call to Parker, if possible. Elicit only that testimony that goes to lay the basis for offering the documents and the telephone call. Do not assume that documents must be offered in the order they are reproduced below.

Firm B (Counsel for defendant): Attempt to prevent the introduction by plaintiff's counsel of the documentary evidence and telephone call; cross-examine, attempting to introduce Document 4.

As a matter of tactics, each firm might make decisions inconsistent with the directions given above. In this assignment, however, we are primarily concerned with learning how to get documents and conversations into evidence over determined opposition. Accordingly, the lawyers will make every objection they consider to be valid as matters stand at the moment the objection is made; they will not make objections they consider to be without merit. See Ground Rule 17.

The Pleadings

The complaint alleges that plaintiff, Grubbs, held Anson's note for $12,000 which was not paid at maturity; that Anson executed a confession of judgment for the amount of the note but requested plaintiff not to file and enter the confession of judgment; that for the purpose of inducing plaintiff not to file and enter the confession of judgment, Anson delivered to plaintiff (through his attorney, Karl Kaline) a letter from defendant Passmore (Document 3), a copy being attached to the complaint, which promised to pay plaintiff $12,000 upon certain conditions; that defendant had knowledge of the purposes for which the writing was delivered to plaintiff and that the defendant knew that plaintiff, in reliance upon the letter, would refrain from filing and entering the confession of judgment against Anson; that in reliance on defendant's promise, plaintiff refrained from filing and entering the confession of judgment; and that the conditions mentioned in the letter were satisfied but the defendant has refused to pay the $12,000.

Assignments in Trial Practice

The first defense of the answer is that the complaint fails to state a claim for relief because it shows on its face that the alleged agreement lacked consideration. The answer admits that the letter (Document 3) was prepared by Paul L. Parker, vice-president of defendant corporation, acting within the scope of his authority, and admits delivery of the letter of March 4, 19Y1, but either denies the other allegations of the complaint or alleges a lack of knowledge or information sufficient to form a belief. As an additional defense, the answer pleads that the alleged agreement was without consideration because (1) defendant company expected to have funds belonging to Anson and pursuant to Anson's directions, solely as an accommodation, and without consideration, had agreed to deliver such funds to plaintiff, and (2) Anson thereafter revoked such directions.

Defendant's Motion to Dismiss

Defendant moved to dismiss the complaint under Federal Rule 12 for failure to state a claim for relief. The corporation argued that even if it had knowledge

(a) of Anson's purpose in delivering Passmore's promissory letter, and

(b) that plaintiff would rely on said promise, those facts would be irrelevant and would not establish consideration.

The court denied the motion. In its opinion, it cited Ames cases holding that such knowledge might be highly relevant either in establishing consideration or in laying the basis for invoking promissory estoppel. Although the complaint did not specifically allege promissory estoppel, the court read the complaint as sufficiently broad to embrace this theory. The court therefore indicated it would probably consider as relevant any evidence that Anson had communicated to defendant his intention to use Passmore's promise to secure plaintiff's forbearance.

Assume that the Ames Statute of Frauds is not applicable to this case.

Documentary Evidence Available for the Trial

In view of the results of the pre-trial proceedings, plaintiff's counsel wants to use the documentary evidence appearing below in support of his claim that defendant made a promise to pay the $12,000 as consideration for plaintiff's forbearance, and that such forbearance occurred in reliance on the promise.

Assignments in Trial Practice

Document 1 (Confession of Judgment)

SUPERIOR COURT OF THE COMMONWEALTH OF AMES
County of Thayer

Ernest Grubbs,

<u>Plaintiff</u>,

against

Samuel R. Anson,

<u>Defendant.</u>

It is hereby stipulated by and between the attorney for the plaintiff in the above entitled action and the defendant therein in person, that judgment in this action in favor of the plaintiff, Ernest Grubbs, for the sum of $12,000.00 with interest from October 22, 19Y2, against Samuel R. Anson, the defendant therein, may be entered and docketed at any time in the Thayer County Clerk's Office without further notice to the defendant.

The defendant herewith acknowledges that he made and delivered to the plaintiff his promissory note for $12,000.00 in consideration for a loan in said sum of which the following is a copy:

$12,000.00   July 22, 19Y2

Ninety days after date I promise to pay to the order of Ernest Grubbs

Exactly $12,000.00 & Cts.   Dollars

Payable at Industrial Bank of Commerce, 56 East 42 St., Ames City

Value received   Due Oct. 22nd 19Y2

The defendant stipulates that he has never repaid said sum and is justly indebted to the plaintiff for the said sum of $12,000.00 with interest from October 22, 19Y2.

The defendant further stipulates that he voluntarily appears in this action and that he has no defense or offset of any kind whatsoever with respect thereto.

Assignments in Trial Practice

The defendant further stipulates that his default in answering or otherwise pleading with respect to this cause of action may herewith be noted and that a judgment in the amount hereinabove set forth may be entered and docketed at any time without further notice.

Dated March 3, 19Y1

/s/ Karl Kaline
    Attorney for Plaintiff

/s/ Samuel R. Anson
    Defendant in Person

Commonwealth of Ames
County of Thayer

On this 3rd day of March, 19Y1, before me personally appeared Samuel R. Anson to me known and known to me to be the person mentioned and described herein, and who executed the foregoing instrument, and he duly acknowledged to me that he executed the same.

/s/ Ruth L. Sellers
Notary Public in the Commonwealth of Ames

SEAL

Assignments in Trial Practice

Document 2 (carbon)

March 4, 19Y1

Mr. Ernest Grubbs
99 West 40th Street
Ames City, Ames

Dear Sir:

At the request of Mr. Samuel R. Anson, we hereby agree to pay to you, for the account of Mr. Anson, the sum of Twelve Thousand ($12,000.00) Dollars ~~but not to exceed the value of collateral hereafter referred to less the amount of bond premium charges against such collateral, if any payment to be made~~ within thirty (30) days after certain Bonds No. 16-2548/9-64 issued by the United States Fidelity and Guaranty Company for Samuel R. Anson have been cancelled and all the collateral now pledged to secure said bonds has been released by the United States Fidelity and Guaranty Company and returned to us.

Very truly yours,

PASSMORE SECURITIES CORPORATION
By /s/ Paul L. Parker
~~Vice President~~

~~Confirmed:~~
~~Ernest Grubbs~~

Deposition of Paul L. Parker
Exhibit A
Joe Zeff, reporter

Document 3 (original)

Passmore Securities Corporation
Williston Building
Ames City, Ames 00352

March 4, 19Y1

Mr. Ernest Grubbs
99 West 40th Street
Ames City, Ames

Dear Sir:

    At the request of Mr. Samuel R. Anson, we hereby agree to pay to you, for the account of Mr. Anson, the sum of Twelve Thousand ($12,000.00) Dollars within thirty (30) days after certain bonds No. 16-2548/9-64 issued by the United States Fidelity and Guaranty Company for Samuel R. Anson have been cancelled and all the collateral now pledged to secure said bonds has been released by the United States Fidelity and Guaranty Company and returned to us.

                                Very truly yours,

                                PASSMORE SECURITIES CORPORATION

                                By /s/ <u>Paul L. Parker</u>
                                    <u>Vice-President</u>

Deposition of Paul L. Parker
Exhibit B
Joe Jeff, reporter

Document 4
Allan L. Charter
Counsellor at Law
Williston Building
Ames City, Ames 00352

734-7494

August 12, 19Y1

Karl Kaline, Esq.
230 Scott Avenue
Ames City, Ames

Dear Mr. Kaline:

I have discussed your letter of August 1, 19Y1, with Mr. Parker of the Passmore Securities Corporation, and I referred to your letter of June 8, 19Y1, wherein you quote verbatim a copy of the letter agreement signed by Passmore Securities Corporation, and I am quoting from that agreement:

At the request of Mr. Samuel R. Anson, we hereby agree to pay to you, for account of Mr. Anson, the sum of Twelve Thousand ($12,000.00) Dollars within thirty (30) days after certain Bonds No. 16-2548/9-64 issued by the United States Fidelity and Guaranty Company for Samuel R. Anson have been cancelled and all the collateral now pledged to secure said bonds has been released by the United States Fidelity and Guaranty Company and returned to us.

Mr. Parker, of Passmore Securities Corporation, advised me that at that time they did expect to have some funds of Mr. Anson's and that is why they promised to pay you, at Mr. Anson's request, but they do not have any funds of Mr. Anson's at the present time. He further advised me that there was no consideration given to them for their promise to pay you, at the request of Mr. Anson. They claimed they were merely going to turn over funds to you at the direction of Mr. Anson. Since that time Mr. Anson has revoked his order to pay you.

Assignments in Trial Practice

In order to clarify the situation I would appreciate knowing if you feel my client received any consideration for their promise to pay you the funds, at the request of Mr. Anson. I was not aware of the events leading up to this agreement, but just by reading the agreement itself, I cannot understand how my client could be liable, if there was no consideration for their promise.

                Very truly yours,

                /s/ <u>Allan L. Charter</u>
                    Allan L. Charter

Assignments in Trial Practice

Deposition of Karl Kaline Taken at the Instance of
Defendant's Counsel on September 15, 19Y1

(Summarized.) I represented Ernest Grubbs in various legal matters for several years before March, 19Y1. I knew nothing of the Anson transaction until a few days before March 3, 19Y1, when Mr. Grubbs placed the note in my hands for collection. The note was in the amount of $12,000, dated July 22, 19Y2, and executed by Samuel R. Anson in favor of Mr. Grubbs. He instructed me to bring suit unless I got effective assurance from Anson that prompt payment would be made.

I communicated with Anson by telephone and made an appointment in my office for March 3. Anson appeared on that day, without counsel, and freely admitted his indebtedness. He explained that his assets were temporarily tied up. I served him with a summons and complaint in an action by Mr. Grubbs against him to recover the amount of the note. I then said that I wanted him to sign a confession of judgment for the amount he owed. He agreed. I called in my secretary, Mrs. Ruth Sellers. I dictated to her the confession of judgment I wanted him to sign. I was busy so I told Mrs. Sellers to take care of the details -- that is, type up the document, have Anson sign it, then to notarize it and return it to me when it was completed.

While she was typing it up, Mr. Anson was sitting in the outer waiting room. I was working on other matters in my office. About a half hour later, Mrs. Sellers returned to my office with Mr. Anson and with the document (Document 1) and said, "Here it is, Mr. Kaline. It's been signed by Mr. Anson." I thanked her and she went back to work. I then signed the document in Anson's presence.

Anson then asked for further time to raise the money. I refused and said I would have to enter judgment on the confession forthwith. Anson then explained that he was under indictment in a federal court in Detroit for mail fraud in connection with the sale of securities, but he said that the trouble would be cleared up shortly, and he would then be able to make payment from the proceeds of securities held by the United States Fidelity and Guaranty Company as collateral for its bail bond in the criminal case. Anson expressed fear that his credit standing would be badly damaged by filing of the judgment.

Finally, Anson said that he could get a promise from Passmore Securities Corporation to pay Grubbs $12,000 when this collateral was released. I agreed to forbear from filing the judgment if Anson would promptly furnish such an undertaking from Passmore. Anson said that he would do so the next day. Up to this time I had no previous dealings either with Anson or Passmore. Anson made some explanation of his own relations with Passmore. I do not remember the details, but I got the impression that Passmore was in some way involved in the mail fraud matter.

I next saw Anson on the afternoon of the following day, March 4, in my office. He brought the original and carbon copy of Document 2. When I saw the document, I was angry with Anson because they had stuck in the condition about limiting the maximum amount of the payment to the value of the securities. I didn't know anything about the securities and, in any case, I wasn't interested in gambling on their value. I wanted a flat promise to pay $12,000 when the securities were released. I told Anson this. I also told him that I saw no reason why Grubbs should sign the document. I then crossed out those parts of the letter I disapproved. I told Anson I would go ahead and file the judgment unless they gave me a letter in the form we had agreed.

At that point, Anson said he would call Mr. Parker at Passmore to try and get it straightened out right away. He used my telephone to dial a number he read out of a little black address book. Anson was standing close to me and I could see the page on his address book. I saw Parker's name and a telephone number. I do not recollect the number. I assume, however, that was the number he dialed. I did not hear the voice on the other end of the telephone. Mr. Anson, as nearly as I recall, first asked for Mr. Parker on the telephone. He didn't get him directly and said "Sam Anson is calling"; then somebody got on the telephone and he said, "Paul, this is Sam; I am over in Mr. Grubbs' lawyer's office, a Mr. Kaline, with the letter that I promised to give to him and that you gave me. He doesn't like the letter and he says first of all he doesn't want to get involved with anything dealing with the value of the security. Secondly, he doesn't want to get involved with having the premiums deducted from the $12,000, and thirdly he sees no necessity for Mr. Grubbs signing the letter. I have to have this letter right away, the way Mr. Kaline wants it. I have shown you the confession of judgment that I signed and unless you give me the letter the way Mr. Kaline wants it he will enter the judgment, and my understanding with him was that he would get $12,000 when the bail bonds would be cancelled and the collateral returned to Passmore. On that basis he is willing not to enter the judgment. If you don't give it to me clearly that way, he is going to enter the judgment. I will be over right away." Before he hung up, Anson read Parker the exact portions of the letter I wanted deleted.

After the phone call, Mr. Anson told me everything was O.K. He said he'd bring back the letter revised as I wanted it the next day. I told him if he did, the deal was still on. I'd hold off on filing his confession of judgment.

The following day, March 5, he brought Document 3 to me. We didn't discuss the matter any further. I never had any personal conversations with anyone from the Passmore Corporation except for a phone call from Mr. Parker in response to a demand letter I'd written to Passmore on June 8. All he said was that he was going to take the matter up with his attorneys. Mr. Grubbs never had any contact with Passmore in this matter. He dealt entirely through me. No one from Passmore Corporation was ever present during any of my dealings or Mr. Grubbs' dealing with Mr. Anson.

I am not personally representing plaintiff in this matter because I assumed I'd probably be a principal witness. I've not been paid for my services in connection with the proceeding. I expect to bill for my time spent as a witness and in preparation for this trial, on an hourly basis.

With reference to Document 4, I do not know Allan L. Charter well enough to recognize his signature on the letter, but I assumed when I got the letter that it was from him. My letter of August 1, 19Y1, referred to in the letter of August 12 purporting to be from Charter, was addressed to Passmore Securities Corporation. It was a demand for payment of the $12,000 as promised in their letter of March 4, 19Y1. Likewise, the letter of June 8, 19Y1, was addressed to Passmore Securities Corporation and was a demand for payment of the $12,000. About a week after I posted the letter of June 8, 19Y1, I received a telephone call from a person identifying himself as Paul L. Parker, Vice-President of Passmore Securities Corporation, acknowledging receipt of the letter of June 8 and stating that he would have to take the matter up with the attorneys for Passmore Securities Corporation. I received no further response, and then I wrote my final demand letter of August 1, 19Y1. I have no doubt that Charter was, as he purported to be, counsel for Passmore, but I have no positive information to that effect.

I admit that I did not reply to the letter of August 12, 19Y1, from Charter. I agree to have the original of that letter available when this case is called for trial. I certainly was not admitting there was no consideration for defendant's promise. I just concluded I would have to sue and that there was no point in writing more letters.

I have not been able to locate Anson. Counsel for Passmore furnished me with a California address for him, but he could not be found there. I've checked with people in California, however, and I'm told that the record shows bankruptcy proceedings against Anson in California.

Assignments in Trial Practice

Deposition of Paul L. Parker Taken at the Instance of Plaintiff's Counsel on September 15, 19Y1

Q. (1-58 Summarized.) I am Paul L. Parker, Vice-President of Passmore Securities Corporation. During 19Y2 Samuel Anson had a dispute with us over the amount of commissions we owed him for sales of securities he'd made in our behalf. In January, 19Y1, he became involved in a federal mail fraud charge and was placed under arrest. He got in touch with us and told us that bail had been set at $15,000. He had sought a bail-bond from the United States Fidelity and Guaranty Co., but they apparently wanted some collateral before they'd write the bond. Anson owned no property to offer as collateral. He asked us to put up the money we owed him so he could make bail. We agreed to post securities, valued at about $12,000, as collateral for the bail-bond. We further agreed these securities would be his payment in full on the disputed claim for commissions. It was understood that when the criminal case was all over and the collateral returned to us by U.S.F. and G., we would transfer the securities to his name in settlement of his claim.

Q. 59. When did you next discuss the matter of these securities with Anson? A. That was on March 4, 19Y1.

Q. 60. What was said by each of you?

DEFENDANT'S COUNSEL: I object. No foundation.

Q. 61. When and where did this conversation take place? A. Sometime on the morning of March 4, 19Y1, I believe. He came to my office.

Q. 62. Who was present during this conversation? A. Just the two of us.

Q. 63. Tell us substantially what each of you said. A. He asked that I give him a letter on behalf of Passmore Corporation agreeing to pay Grubbs $12,000 when the securities held by U.S.F. and G. were returned to us. I said, "O.K. It's your money and we'll do whatever you say with it."

Q. 64. And did you draft such a letter? A. I did.

Q. 65. And you gave it to Anson? A. Yes. I gave him the original and a carbon copy, each signed. Anson was to have Grubbs sign the copy and then return it to me for my file.

Q. 66. And he took those with him? A. That's right.

Q. 67. Now when did you hear from Anson regarding this letter? A. He phoned me later on March 4, 19Y1, at my office.

Q. 68. You recognized his voice? A. I did.

Q. 69. What was said during that conversation? A. He told me that Mr. Kaline, the attorney for Grubbs, didn't want any statement in the letter about limiting the maximum amount we'd pay to the value of the securities. He also said Kaline didn't want any space on the letter for Grubbs to sign it. I said, "All right, we'll go along with it. Come by this evening. I'll have the revised letter prepared by the time you get here."

Q. 70. How was it that you agreed to remove the clause limiting your agreement to pay to the value of the securities? A. Well, the securities were worth more than $12,000 and we were pretty confident the value would hold up. Besides, we wanted to help Anson. He'd had a pretty rough couple of months.
Q. 71. You wanted to help Anson? A. Yes.
Q. 72. And you know that a revised letter of the type Anson requested would help him? A. Well, he said so.
Q. 73. And he explained, didn't he, that it would help him because Mr. Kaline would refrain from filing a certain confession of judgment against Anson if you supplied the revised letter? A. No, Anson didn't tell me about the details. I wasn't trying to pry.
Q. 74. You didn't know why he wanted the letter? A. Only because Mr. Kaline was pushing him for such a letter from us. I didn't know why.
Q. 75. Did you at any time get any other phone calls from Anson relating in any way to this transaction, to the $12,000, or to your letter or letters to Mr. Grubbs? A. No, that was the only one.
Q. 76. Anson told you in that phone conversation that he was calling from Mr. Kaline's office, didn't he? A. No, I don't think so. My recollection is that he said he was calling from Mr. Grubbs' office. So far as I know he never called me from Mr. Kaline's office.
Q. 77. Then Anson returned both the original and copy of the letter to you? A. Yes, he did.
Q. 78. I show you what has been marked plaintiff's Exhibit A (Document 2) and ask you if that is one of the documents which Anson returned to you. A. Yes. That is the carbon copy.
Q. 79. Now, do you know who made the inked changes on Exhibit A? A. No I don't. It came back that way.
Q. 80. Exhibit A is a carbon, is it not? A. Yes.
Q. 81. Do you have the original of which Exhibit A is a copy? A. Yes, It's in our files.
Q. 82. I show you what has been marked plaintiff's Exhibit B (Document 3) and ask what it is. A. That is the revised letter I prepared in response to Mr. Anson's request.
Q. 83. What did you do after preparing it? A. I signed it and turned it over to Mr. Anson.
Q. 84. You knew, of course, he was going to deliver it to Mr. Kaline, as Mr. Grubbs' attorney? A. Of course. That's what it was for.
Q. 85. Now, did you in fact make payment to plaintiff in accordance with the terms of the letter? A. No.
Q. 86. Why not? A. Well, some time in April, Anson was convicted and fined on this mail fraud charge. He told us he had changed his mind -- that he wanted the securities so he could pay his fines. He said we should forget about paying Grubbs. We figured it was his money. He was entitled to it. So when we got the securities back from U.S.F. and G. -- that was on April 22, 19Y1, we transferred them to Anson as we had promised.
Q. 87. You felt your agreement to pay Mr. Grubbs was not binding on

you? A. That's right. We never asked or got anything by way of consideration from anyone for that letter to Grubbs. We did it as an accommodation.

Q. 88. You knew, didn't you, that Mr. Grubbs had held back on filing a confession of judgment in the amount of $12,000 against Anson because of your letter? A. No sir. We knew nothing about Grubbs' reasons or Anson's reasons in connection with the letter. I figured that was none of my business, and Anson never told me or anyone else at Passmore Corporation so far as I know.

ASSIGNMENT 3A

Study §§3-6 through 3-28 and 9-13 through 9-17 of the Text.

The special assignment in the case of Palmer M. Charles v. William O. Kay & Gold Fisheries Co. is the direct and cross-examination of Mrs. Irma Charles, a witness called by plaintiff. The materials for this case are set forth in Assignment 2A.

Before conducting the direct examination, plaintiff's counsel will be asked to state what witnesses (if any) they would have called before Mrs. Charles and in what order. For the purpose of this assignment, assume that the proceedings conducted in Assignment 2A have not been held.

Firm A (Counsel for plaintiff): Conduct the direct examination. Limit the examination to evidence bearing on Mrs. Charles' personal identification of the truck at the time of the accident and, to the extent you think desirable, her testimony tending to establish the truck driver's negligence. You will note that these are the matters preceding the asterisk in Mrs. Charles' statement at page 28, supra.

Firm B (Counsel for defendants Kay and Gold Fisheries Company): One of the two students designated as Firm B will represent Kay and the other will represent Gold Fisheries. It will be assumed that they are practicing independently and not as members of the same firm, and they will cooperate or not as they see fit. The attorney representing Kay has been employed to do so by the insurance company with which Kay carries an automobile liability policy of adequate limits to cover the present claim. The attorney representing Gold Fisheries has been employed to do so by a second liability insurer, which carries a "fleet policy" covering Fisheries trucks. This policy does not cover an individual driver unless he is acting in the scope of employment for Gold Fisheries.

Assignments in Trial Practice

ASSIGNMENT 3B

Study §§3-6 through 3-28 and 9-13 through 9-17 of the Text.

The special assignment in the case of <u>Palmer M. Charles v. William O. Kay & Gold Fisheries Co.</u> is the direct and cross-examination of Willis Hood, a witness called by plaintiff. The basic materials for this case are set forth in Assignment 2A.

Before conducting the direct examination, plaintiff's counsel will be asked to state what witnesses (if any) they would have called before Hood and in what order. For the purpose of this assignment, assume that the proceedings conducted in Assignment 2A have not been held.

<u>Firm A</u> (Counsel for plaintiff): Conduct the direct examination eliciting whatever testimony you regard as tactically wise, in the light of your reasonable expectations as to the testimony of the witnesses who would have preceded Hood.

<u>Firm B</u> (Counsel for defendants Kay and Gold Fisheries Company): One of the two students designated as Firm B will represent Kay and the other will represent Gold Fisheries. It will be assumed that they are practicing independently, and not as members of the same firm, and they will cooperate or not as they see fit. The attorney representing Kay has been employed to do so by the insurance company with which Kay carries an automobile liability policy of adequate limits to cover the present claim. The attorney representing Gold Fisheries has been employed to do so by a second liability insurer, which carries a "fleet policy" covering Fisheries trucks. This policy does not cover an individual driver unless he is acting in the scope of employment for Gold Fisheries.

Plaintiff's counsel should be prepared to state whether they would have called Hood as a witness, and why, had they been given the choice.

<u>Supplementary Statement of Willis Hood Taken by an Investigator for Gold Fisheries' Insurer on August 12, 19Y1</u>

(A substantially similar statement has since been obtained by plaintiff.)

On May 23, 19Y1, at about 11:30 p.m., I was on my way home from a movie. I was alone. I had been going east on the Austin-Beale turnpike for about two miles, and was preparing to turn left at the intersection with Williston Street in Northboro. When I reached Williston Street, I came to a full stop in order to permit a westbound car to pass. Just after it passed I was about to start up again and make my left turn when I heard the noise of a truck approaching from behind, sounding a loud blast on the horn. As a result, I did not move my car. The truck whipped on past, and the next thing I knew my car was hit from behind by a car behind me. It was a good solid blow, and did some damage to the car behind me, but did not hurt me or my 19Y2 Buick, other than to put a couple of minor dents in the bumper. I haven't made a claim against anyone for these damages and I don't intend to.

I gave my name to a police officer who came to the scene. About the end of May, 19Y1, an investigator came around to see me. He was representing Gold Fisheries Company, and I gave him a statement. About three weeks after the accident, a lawyer who said he was representing Mr. Charles came around and asked me some questions. Both when I talked with the investigator and the plaintiff's lawyer, I said I got only a glimpse of the truck as it passed me, and that it appeared to be consistent with the appearance of the Gold Fisheries van-type truck, with which I am familiar, and that if I had to say one way or the other I would say that it was the Gold Fisheries truck. At that time, however, I was not sure of my opinion on that matter.

Subsequently, in July, 19Y1, I was driving along on Williston Street one morning when a truck approached me from behind in a noisy way, sounding a blast on the horn, and I was startled because it sounded just like the hit-and-run truck did that night on May 23. I turned to see the truck and realized that it was this Gold Fisheries truck. The horn was a little unusual, since the two tones were more in harmony than is usually the case. It was a 19Y2 Chevrolet van-type truck. I observed lettering on the back of the truck that identified it as a Gold Fisheries truck. (I did not observe lettering on the back of the truck at the time of the accident; things just happened too fast.) In view of this experience of hearing the sound of that horn again, I am now sure that it was the Gold Fisheries truck that passed me on May 23 on that turnpike. Prior to now I have not told anybody about this incident of July, 19Y1, except my own lawyer. I asked my lawyer if I ought to tell some of the lawyers in the case about it, and he said not to bother because the insurance companies nearly always settle these hit-and-run cases anyway. I probably wouldn't have volunteered this information to you if I hadn't been asked.

I am a former employee of Gold Fisheries. I worked for them before the 19Y2 Chevrolet truck in question was ever bought. I quit early in 19Y3 after an argument over some shortages on my truck.

When I worked at Gold Fisheries, there were two sets of keys for each truck, both sets being kept in the office except when in use. Although a driver was not supposed to have the key after working hours, occasionally somebody would, by habit developed in the driving of his own car, put a key in his pocket and walk off with it overnight instead of returning it to the office. The trucks were parked in an open parking lot adjacent to the business building. Gold Fisheries had three trucks at the time I was employed there and at the time of the accident.

The truck which was involved in the accident was not one of those which Gold Fisheries had at the time I was working for them.

At the present time I am operating an Amoco station (Ames Oil Company) located on Williston and Scott streets in Northboro.

Assignments in Trial Practice

ASSIGNMENT 4A

Study §§2-15 through 2-23, 2-29 through 2-33, 3-1 through 3-5, and 3-7 of the Text.

This assignment is based on the case of State of Ames v. Daniel Dirandum. Dirandum stands accused of the murder of one George Childs, the motive allegedly being that Childs was "running around" with Dirandum's girl friend, Ethyl Sinclair.

At preliminary hearing, the magistrate found probable cause to bind the defendant over for trial on a charge of first degree murder. At the trial, the prosecutor has introduced testimony of Irving J. Morg, M.D., the state's pathologist, who found the cause of death to be strangulation; of Mrs. George Childs, estranged wife of the decedent, who identified the body from photographs shown her in court, and who said she had left her husband because of his running around; and of Ethyl Sinclair, who implicated her boyfriend (the defendant) as the murderer. Now, the prosecutor calls to the stand Officer John Holmes, of the Austin, Ames, Police Department, who made the arrest and initial interrogation of the defendant. Holmes did not testify at the preliminary hearing and he has declined to talk to defense counsel about the case.

Firm A (Counsel for the prosecution): Conduct the examination of Officer Holmes, attempting to introduce evidence about the arrest and initial interrogation of Dirandum which has culminated in an admission by Dirandum that he killed Childs. Be prepared to discuss what considerations would be involved in making a decision whether to offer such evidence, were you free to make the decision. Pick up special materials from the instructor.

Firm B (Counsel for the defense): Attempt to keep the admission out of evidence by making all appropriate motions and objections, and by conducting whatever cross-examination of Holmes you feel necessary and proper. Be prepared to discuss whether you would offer Dirandum's testimony on the issue of voluntariness of his admission, and what considerations would be involved in arriving at your decision.

Defendant's Statement

The defendant, Daniel NMI Dirandum, has given his lawyers the following statement, the substance of which is known to the prosecution through negotiations by the attorneys looking toward the possibility of Dirandum's entering a plea of guilty to a reduced charge:

When I was arrested I had been asleep about three hours. I didn't realize what was going on until these cops were pounding on my door, and had cuffs on me and hauled me out to the paddy wagon. I remember one

Assignments in Trial Practice

cop -- some Mexican name, I think -- was stuffing me in the back end of the wagon, and I asked him point blank if it would go easier on me if I confessed, and he said he'd see about it when we got to the station. But as soon as we got to the station, he bugged out somewhere, and I never saw him again.

Anyhow, the other cop -- name of Holmes, I think -- shoved me into the booking area where I emptied my pockets and they took everything I had, including my watch, so I couldn't tell what time it was. But I'm sure it was around 2 or 3 in the morning by that time, and I was really out of it. Anyway, they wash the fingerprint ink off me and turn me back over to this Holmes, who takes me into some sort of creepy office. All I remember is a desk and a lamp with a metal shade hanging from the ceiling. There was another cop in there who told me I could have some coffee if I confessed, and started playing the Mutt & Jeff routine with me -- you know, this new cop (plainclothes type) was the good guy with the coffee and all, and Holmes was the jerk. So Mr. Nice Guy goes nicely out for the nice coffee, and the uniform Jerk gets tough and sez he's gonna let me stew awhile before I get my coffee. Well, I'm sort of out of it, but I am sure nobody told me I could have a lawyer or anything like that. I mean, I been through this before, and I know they're supposed to tell me these things, so I sorta watch for it. Like I say, before I get any coffee, the Jerk throws me in some rat hole cage where I suppose they were keeping an eye on me. It was real crummy, believe me, and I got to wanting outa there real bad, and I grabbed the bars in the door and was getting ready to start hollering to be let out when my buddy Holmes the Jerk comes back and asks me why I killed Childs, so I told him the truth -- namely, that the dirty bastard was running around with my Ethyl and please get me out this goddamn cage and get me a lawyer.

So, Holmes, acting real pleased, turns me over to some other cop who put the cuffs on me and takes me to the phone where I call you. I never got my coffee.

Other Witnesses

<u>Officer Edward Marquez</u>, who with Holmes made the arrest, has left the Austin Police Force, and is now stationed overseas with the United States Marines.

<u>Detective Sergeant Joseph C. Moriarty's</u> police report, in its relevant portions, is set out below. The prosecutor has a copy of the report, but none has been available to the defense.

Assignments in Trial Practice

APD Form 7   AUSTIN POLICE DEPARTMENT

Officer's Report

Officer: Det. Sgt. J. Moriarty Badge #007
                    Case: Daniel Dirandum No. 13756
                          WM
                          Murder

[First part of report omitted.]

Left residence of victim's wife approx 2330 hrs 3 Mar 19Y1, and radio dispatcher advised that officers HOLMES and MARQUEZ had apprehended subject and subject was being booked in. Arr. APD approx 2345 hrs, talked with Officer HOLMES. We took subject to my office where HOLMES read him his rights from card. Subject understood rights but declined comment. I left for coffee while HOLMES took subject to detention cell. Shortly thereafter subject stated to HOLMES that he, the subject, had in fact killed the victim, stating the reason was that the victim had been playing around with subject's girlfriend. No threats or promises made to subject at any time.

[Rest of report omitted.]

                                          NFI
                                          J. Moriarty
                                          4 Mar 19Y1 1100 hrs.

FBI Report

FBI records show the following information. It should be assumed that the prosecutors can obtain a certified copy of the record of any of these items:

DANIEL DIRANDUM:
FORGERY, arrested July 3, 19Y9, by Austin, Ames Police Department.
AUTO THEFT, ASSAULT, arrested July 12, 19Y9, by Austin, Ames, Police
  Department.
JUVENILE DELINQUENCY, July 13, 19Y9, Thayer County Juvenile Court, Austin,
  Ames.
AUTO THEFT, arrested December 12, 19Y7 by Austin, Ames, Police Department.
OPERATING MOTOR VEHICLE WITHOUT CONSENT, convicted on guilty plea
  January 25, 19Y6, Thayer County Court, Austin, Ames. Six months
  probation.
RAPE, arrested January 12, 19Y4 by New Town, Ames, Police Department.
KIDNAPPING, arrested January 12, 19Y4 by New Town, Ames, Police
  Department.
BURGLARY OF INHABITED DWELLING, arrested March 20, 19Y4 by Austin, Ames,
  Police Department.
ASSAULT AND BATTERY, convicted on guilty plea, July 30, 19Y4 in New Town

Assignments in Trial Practice

County Court, New Town, Ames. 30 days (suspended) and $100.00
BURGLARY OF INHABITED DWELLING, indictment July 10, 19Y4 by Thayer
   County Grand Jury.
PETIT LARCENY, arrested August 1, 19Y4 by Austin Police Department.
PETIT LARCENY, convicted on guilty plea August 2, 19Y4. Three months.
BREAKING AND ENTERING, convicted on guilty plea August 10, 19Y3.
   Sentenced to one year, Ames State Prison.
ASSAULT AND BATTERY, arrested August 30, 19Y2 by Austin, Ames, Police
   Department.
ASSAULT AND BATTERY, convicted on guilty plea September 1, 19Y2 in Thayer
   County Court, Austin, Ames. 30 days and $200.00.

Some Ames Law

Fieton v. State, 87 Ames 53, 59, 32 N.S.2d 1013, 1015 (1967): The United States Supreme Court has made it plain that any confession taken by the state from a person accused of crime must be enveloped in a cocoon of procedural safeguards. In Miranda v. Arizona, 384 U.S. 436, 478-479 (1966), the Court said:

> To summarize, we hold that when an individual is taken into custody or otherwise deprived of his freedom by the authorities in any significant way and is subjected to questioning, the privilege against self-incrimination is jeopardized. Procedural safeguards must be employed to protect the privilege, and unless other fully effective means are adopted to notify the person of his right of silence and to assure that the exercise of the right will be scrupulously honored, the following measures are required. He must be warned prior to any questioning that he has the right to remain silent, that anything he says can be used against him in a court of law, that he has the right to the presence of an attorney, and that if he cannot afford an attorney one will be appointed for him prior to any questioning if he so desires. Opportunity to exercise these rights must be afforded to him throughout the interrogation. After such warnings have been given, and such opportunity afforded him, the individual may knowingly and intelligently waive these rights and agree to answer questions or make a statement. But unless and until such warnings and waiver are demonstrated by the prosecution at trial, no evidence obtained as a result of interrogation can be used against him.

The Supreme Court has thus delineated two primary requisites: (1) objective procedural safeguards and (2) subjective waiver of rights by the accused. But these requisites apply only to the circumstances of custodial interrogation. Here the evidence amply demonstrates that Officer Clancy had just placed the defendant under arrest and had formally advised him of the rights set forth in the above-quoted portion of the Miranda opinion when the defendant, in Officer Clancy's words, "blurted out" the statement in issue. There was custody, but no interrogation. The trial judge committed no error in admitting that statement into evidence. . . .

Fieton v. McGurney, 89 Ames 530, 39 N.S.2d 32 (1969): (PER CURIAM): The petition [for a writ of habeas corpus] is denied. When petitioner was last before this court [in Fieton v. State, supra] we held that his incriminating statement was properly admitted because the evidence adequately demonstrated that it was given voluntarily and was not the product of interrogation. That holding need not be changed by the subsequent passage of the federal Omnibus Crime Control and Safe Streets Act [18 U.S.C. §3501] whose retroactive applicability we need not decide. That Act by its terms applies only to federal courts; our legislature has enacted nothing similar to it; and subsection (d) of the Act emphasizes the admissibility of statements given under circumstances just such as those in the case at bar.

Ames Statutes Annotated, Title 3 (Crimes and Criminal Procedure), §3500: After a witness called by the State has testified on direct examination in the trial of any criminal prosecution, the court shall, on motion of the defendant, order the State to produce and deliver directly to the defendant for his examination and use any statement of the witness in the possession of the state which relates to the subject matter as to which the witness has testified.

Rothwell v. State, 77 Ames 297, 305, 15 N.S.2d 650, 653 (1960): This state has both adopted and adapted, wherever appropriate, the Federal Rules of Criminal Procedure. . . . Not infrequently, where those Rules dovetail with certain federal statutes, our legislature has followed suit and has enacted similar dovetailing legislation. We have here such a case: Federal Criminal Rule 16(a), dealing with the production of certain items, specifically incorporates by references the so-called "Jencks Act," 18 U.S.C. §3500. In 1959, our legislature passed a "little Jencks Act" now codified as 3 A.S.A. § 3500, in the construction of which we may turn to the federal enactments for guidance. . . .

Assignments in Trial Practice

ASSIGNMENT 4B

Study §§2-15 through 2-23, 2-29 through 2-33, and 3-1 through 3-5 of the Text.

The special assignment is the direct and cross-examination of the witness Chester Milford in the case of Evan Olson v. Timothy Raines.

Firm A (Counsel for plaintiff): Conduct the direct examination, offering whatever testimony you consider useful in relation to the issue of the defendant's negligence.

Firm B (Counsel for defendant): Conduct the cross-examination.

Pleadings

Olson, a resident of Thayer, Ames, alleges that while he was driving east on Route 30 in Ames on February 19, 19Y1, his car was struck by a westbound vehicle negligently operated by Raines, a resident of Pennsylvania. Olson prays for a judgment of $57,645 for personal injuries and damage to his car. Raines admits the collision, denies negligence, denies the amount of damage, and pleads contributory negligence as a complete bar (Ames does not have a comparative negligence statute).

Excerpts from Deposition of Evan Olson Taken at the Instance of Defendant's Counsel on November 6, 19Y1

(Summarized.) I live in Thayer, Ames, and am a barber. On the 19th of February, 19Y1, I was involved in an automobile accident at a point on Highway 30 about three miles east of Little America, Ames. The accident occurred somewhere between 10 and 11 in the morning, maybe 10:20 or 10:30. The driver of the other car was Mr. Raines.

The day was nice with the temperature about 20 degrees. Within a half mile or mile from the scene of the accident there were continuous slick spots at different times. I was driving with chains on the rear wheels. My car was a 19Y2 Ford. I was driving on my side of the road at the time of the collision, possibly two feet from the right-hand side of the highway. The road was a good highway of blacktop construction.

I was proceeding east and observed a car approaching from the opposite direction. Suddenly he went out of control; that is, he just loomed up in front of me sideways in my lane. The event occurred about 25 feet away from me. He went into what looked like a spin, just the glimpse I got of it; he just went out of control and spun, the front end of his car coming first, but it was coming sideways. With reference to the center of the road, his car was pointed back toward his side of the road. He came possibly 8 or 10 feet on my side of the road. The only thing I can remember is trying to turn to the right. I don't think I got very far. The left front of my car and the left side of his car collided just about in front of the front door, I think, on his car.

My car did not skid in any way prior to the time of the collision and it was not out of control. I stayed at the scene of the accident for some time but can not say how long it was before the ambulance got there. I was somewhat dazed. I had received a blow on the forehead.

Statement of Chester A. Milford
Taken by Plaintiff's Counsel on February 26, 19Y1

My name is Chester Ambrose Milford. My address is No. 6 Nathaniel Lane, Langdell, Ames. My business address is 916 Beale Blvd., Langdell. I have been a plumbing contractor since 19Y5. Prior to that I was a police officer with the Langdell Police Department for 6 years.

While on a business trip on February 19, 19Y1, at about 10:30, I came upon the scene of an accident on Route 3 near Little America, Ames, involving cars operated by Timothy Raines (hereinafter called Car #1) and Evan Olson (hereinafter called Car #2). I more or less took charge of caring for the injured and controlling traffic until a police officer arrived.

I had seen Car #1 (Pennsylvania license) earlier that morning. It passed me once between Rock Springs and Green River about 2 miles east of Green River and again about 3 miles west of Green River. Both of us were going west on Route 30. Car #1 was going about 35 or 38, while I was traveling at about 20 or 25 m.p.h. The first time he came up rapidly where the road was very icy. The second time he passed me he was going faster -- probably 45, maybe 50. No other cars passed me between that point and the scene of the accident.

I talked with the driver of Car #1 at the scene of the accident. I asked him what happened. He shrugged his shoulders and said, "I don't know. I was going too fast, I guess." About an hour later traffic had backed up in both directions and the crowd wanted through. There was no highway patrolman present. Mrs. Raines was lying in such a position that to allow traffic to go through would have been dangerous and I did not want Mrs. Raines or anyone else moved. No traffic could move between the cars. Mr. Raines said in the presence of these people there, and I can't tell you who they were, "Maybe if we moved her just a little bit, maybe some of these people are in a hurry like I was."

I have read the foregoing statement and it is true and correct.
/s/ Chester A. Milford

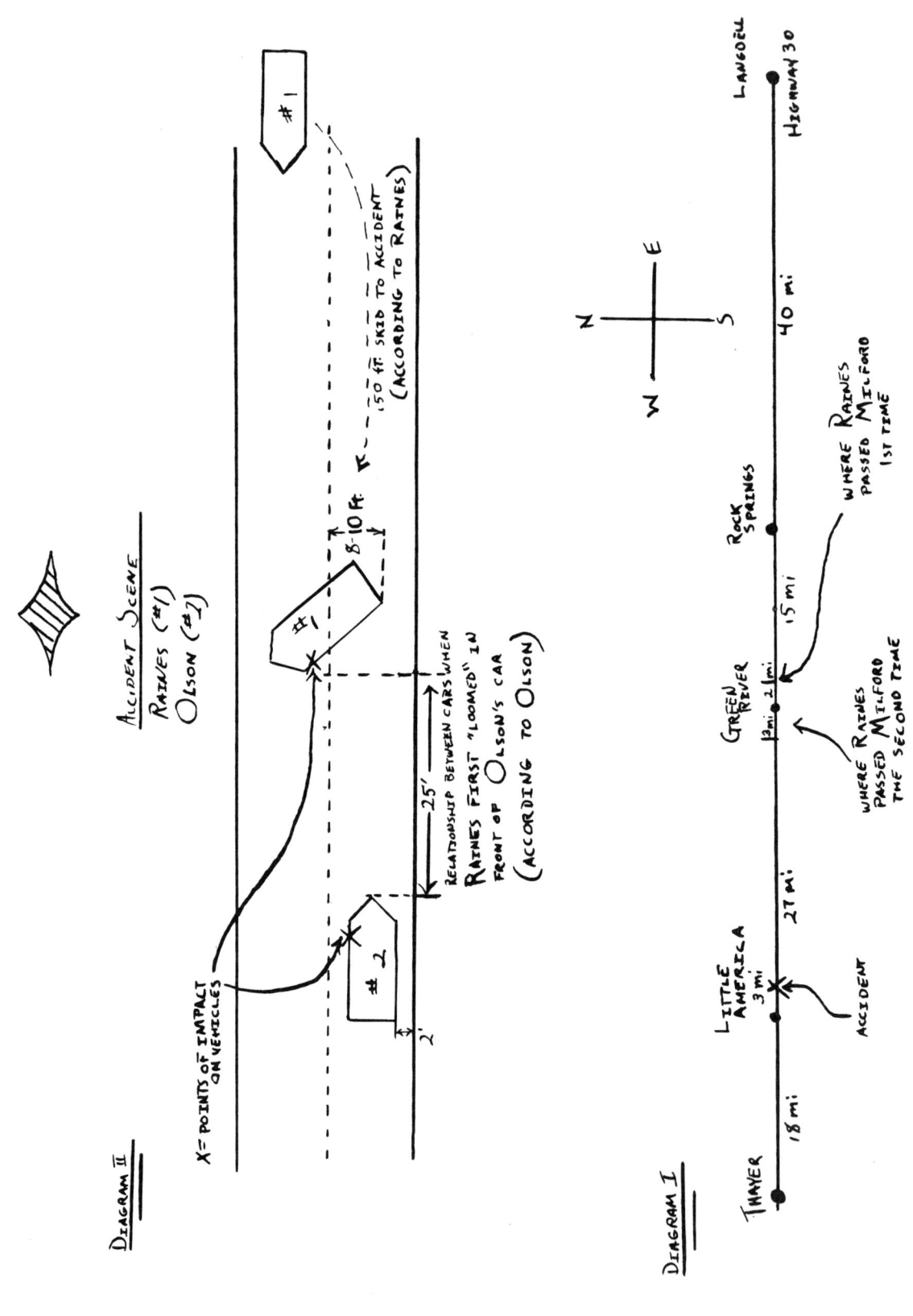

Assignments in Trial Practice

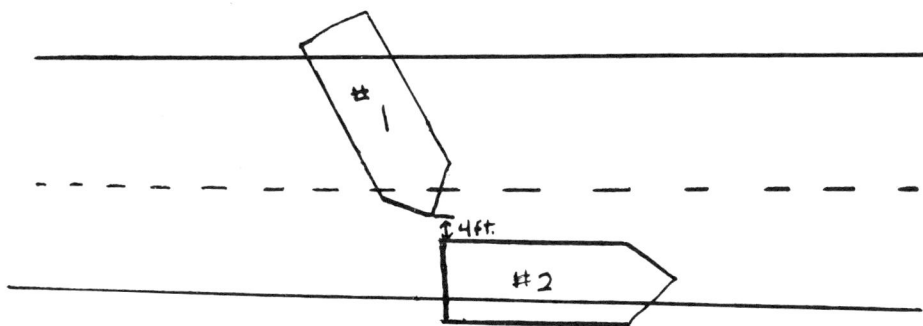

Diagram III from the investigation notes of Officer Trainor, prepared on February 19, 19Y1.

Memorandum of J.J. Harrington, Insurance Company Investigator, to Defendant's Counsel Dated March 1, 19Y1

(The existence of this memorandum is unknown to plaintiff's counsel).

Milford is an intelligent witness and a smooth talker. He would like to be a witness -- he was grasping for something he could say that would be important. He volunteered during my interview of him (see statement below) that the Raines car had passed him twice at earlier times on the morning of the accident -- once before they reached Green River and a second time just west of Green River. He said Raines was going about 35 or 40 each time (speed limit is higher, but he said there was glare ice in spots all the way). He seemed to want this in the statement at first, but was willing to leave it out when I explained that it was too remote to be admissible in evidence.

You will note that Milford's statement says he was alone. He seemed evasive when he said it, and my other investigation had indicated that he had a female companion. Not wanting to antagonize him, I completed the statement as he gave it and got his signature on each page. Then I pressed him about being alone, and he became very angry. He said, "I still say I was alone, and that's the way it's going to be." I said, "Your business is your business, even if it's monkey business."

Milford protested that I had him all wrong, and said: "Wouldn't you protect an innocent person in an above-board situation which might be misconstrued?" I mollified him by saying I certainly would, and we parted on apparently good terms.

Assignments in Trial Practice

This interview occurred on March 1, 19Y1.

/s/ J.J.H.

Statement of Chester A. Milford Taken by Defendant's
Investigator J.J. Harrington on March 1, 19Y1

(Plaintiff's counsel obtained a copy of this statement through discovery proceedings.)

My name is Chester A. Milford, 916 Beale Blvd., Langdell, Ames. I have had experience as a police officer in the past and have investigated dozens of accidents.

I do a substantial amount of traveling throughout Ames. On February 19, 19Y1, at about 10:20 or 10:30 a.m., I came upon an accident between two cars on Route 30 about three miles east of Little America, Ames. I was alone at the time. I later identified the two drivers as Timothy Raines and Evan Olson. The weather was clear, visibility good. The road was icy in spots. There was no fresh snow.

The road runs in an east-west direction at the point of the accident. When I came upon the scene, the two right wheels of the Olson car (eastbound) were off the hard surface, and the two left wheels were still on. It was on the south side of the road facing east, almost exactly parallel on the edge of the hard surface. The Raines car was slightly to the rear (west), and at a 45-degree angle with the front end facing the Olson car. There was only about three or four feet between the cars -- not enough room for another car to go through. The rear end of the Raines car was just off the hard surface. The road at this point was 20 feet wide, but the highway was blocked by the cars.

I was not near enough to the accident to see it occur. Traffic was not heavy, and I could not say exactly how long after the accident I arrived. As I arrived, I noticed a man in a sailor's uniform helping Mrs. Raines out of the right rear door. This suggested to me that the accident had just taken place, but both cars had come to rest before I saw them, and I can only speculate as to when the accident occurred. In accordance with my understanding of first-aid procedure, I insisted that Mrs. Raines be moved as little as possible, and she was placed on some blankets beside the Raines car.

About three or four minutes after I reached the scene, I had a conversation with Raines. Raines appeared to be unhurt and in full possession of his faculties. I asked him what happened, and he said, "I don't know. I just lost control when the car skidded." I did not have any conversation with Mr. Olson. He was not in condition to talk.

There was glare ice at the scene of the accident.

I had snow tires on my car. I did not have chains on at the time, although I carry chains with me.

Soon the blocked highway caused a pile-up of traffic in both directions, and I took charge, directing other motorists to walk to the east and the west and flag down approaching cars. I refused to allow the Raines car to be moved, because this could not be done without moving Mrs. Raines.

/s/ Chester A. Milford

Assignments in Trial Practice

ASSIGNMENT 5A

Study §§ 2-1 through 2-14, 9-1 through 9-6, and 9-9 through 9-12 of the Text.

This assignment is based upon the case of State v. Daniel Dirandum. The special assignment is the direct and cross-examination of the defendant Daniel Dirandum during a non-jury hearing concerning the admissibility of Dirandum's statement to the police. All the materials are set forth in Assignment 4A.

For the purposes of this assignment assume that only Officer Holmes has testified in support of admissibility and that the trial judge has reserved his ruling until after the defense presents its voir dire evidence.

If Assignment 4A is performed, counsel assigned for 5A should take careful notes on Officer Holmes' testimony during 4A. If assignment 4A is not performed, the instructor will provide a summary of the testimony which Officer Holmes will be assumed to have given.

Firm A (Counsel for defendant): Conduct direct examination of the defendant, Daniel Dirandum.

Be prepared to discuss whether you would have used the defendant as a witness during voir dire if you had been permitted to make a choice.

Firm B (Counsel for the state): Conduct appropriate cross-examination of Dirandum.

Assignments in Trial Practice

ASSIGNMENT 5B

Study §§ 2-1 through 2-14, 9-1 through 9-6, and 9-9 through 9-12 of the Text.

This assignment is based upon the case of David Bates v. Jonathan L. Dunn. Assume that on the first day of the trial before a jury, counsel for plaintiff offered only the testimony of plaintiff, summarized below, and then rested. Defendant thereupon moved for directed verdict, and the motion was denied. Court was then adjourned for the day. The events of this assignment occur on the following morning.

Firm A (Counsel for plaintiff): When you come into the courtroom the morning after resting your case, your client hands you the note reproduced at the end of this assignment, saying it contains a very important message which he wrote out rather than waiting to tell you orally because he was afraid there might not be time to talk. The class period performance will commence as of the moment after you read the note and receive advice from the clerk that the judge will be delayed for about fifteen minutes because he is hearing an application for a temporary injunction in chambers. You are to do the following during the class period:

1. Interview your client about the matter referred to in the note he has handed you. (This is to occur as if you were taking advantage of the fifteen minute delay in resumption of trial to conduct this interview. You will not have an opportunity to see your client before the class period, though this note is being given to you with the assignment to allow you time to consider the problem.) DEFENSE COUNSEL WILL LEAVE THE ROOM DURING THIS PORTION OF THE PERFORMANCE.

2. State what action, if any, you would take in view of the information obtained from your client in the note and the interview, and be prepared to explain during the critique. THIS OCCURS WHILE DEFENSE COUNSEL ARE STILL OUT OF THE ROOM.

3. Proceed on the assumption that, regardless of what your own preferred course of action might have been, the senior partner of your firm has advised you to put Bates back on the stand and straighten matters out as best you can. It is left to you to work out the method of doing this. This is your central task.

Firm B (Counsel for defendant):

1. Cross-examine the plaintiff on the subject matter of the direct examination during the class period, exploiting as best you can the fact that part of his testimony on direct examination was untrue. You will not be permitted to go into matters covered in the previous day's testimony except to the extent they are directly tied in with the

subject of the direct examination during the class period. It is, of course, unrealistic to believe you would have access to Bates' note to his own counsel, and you are to assume you do not for purposes of the class exercise. However, you would realize that Bates might appreciate the fact that he is about to be exposed when he spots Delbert in court. You, therefore, suspect that Bates may admit his "oversight" to his attorneys and that Delbert's testimony will not come as a total surprise to them.

2. On the assumption that no further testimony (either from Bates or any other witness) is offered by plaintiff before your decision must be made, state whether you would rest without introducing evidence on behalf of defendant, and be prepared to give reasons for your decision during the critique.

3. State what, if any, effect plaintiff's actions during the class period would have on your decision in response to paragraph 2.

Background of the Case

Jonathan L. Dunn, an underwriter of Lloyd's, London, issued to David Bates, doing business in Gray, Ames, as Bates & Company, wholesale jeweler, an insurance policy in the sum of $40,000 against loss of, or damage to, described jewelry arising from any cause whatsoever, with certain exceptions. One clause of the policy excepts from coverage any:

> Loss of, or damage to, property insured hereunder whilst in or upon any automobile unless, at the time the loss occurs, there is actually in or upon such vehicle the Assured or a permanent employee of the Assured, or a person whose sole duty it is to attend the vehicle.

Bates claims that jewelry valued at $75,000 and included within the descriptions in the policy, was stolen from a car in Dayton, Ohio, on January 8, 19Y1. He had rented the car from a Lease-Ur-Wheels garage. Bates telephoned the underwriter at 3:15 p.m., January 8, reporting that a case containing the jewelry (which he was using as samples in calling on retailers) was stolen from the car while it was in the custody of Lease-Ur-Wheels for a few minutes, as he was arranging for a parking attendant to drive him to one of the downtown jewelry stores where parking was unavailable.

The Pleadings

Plaintiff filed suit against the defendant in March, 19Y1. The allegation as to the theft stated simply that the jewelry was stolen on January 8, 19Y1, from the Lease-Ur-Wheels vehicle while it was properly attended, within the meaning of the insurance policy. The complaint did not indicate the precise geographic location of the theft.

Defendant's answer alleged lack of knowledge or information sufficient to form a belief as to the truth of the averment of loss of jewelry by theft. A separate paragraph of the answer alleged that if the plaintiff lost jewelry on January 8, 19Y1, the loss occurred while the jewelry was in or upon an automobile at a time when there was not in or upon the automobile the assured or a permanent employee of the assured, or a person whose sole duty it was to attend the vehicle.

An Ames Decision

The only prior Ames decision involving interpretation of the type of policy quoted above is <u>Harbin v. Brien</u>, 43 Ames 2d 307 (1956). In that case, the lower court, after a non-jury trial, entered judgment for plaintiff, finding that an attendant who had agreed to attend the vehicle and was nearby when the theft occurred was actually "in or upon" the vehicle. The appellate court affirmed by memorandum opinion saying only that (despite contrary law elsewhere) in this state the burden of proving that the loss occurred while the property was in an automobile was upon the insurer; but when the insurer established that fact, the burden of proving that the vehicle had been properly attended at the time of the loss fell upon the insured. This burden, held the court, had been discharged by plaintiff. The briefs in that case disclose that plaintiff argued the following:

(1) In the phrase "actually . . . upon such vehicle," the word "upon" makes no sense as applied to a car unless it means "near to," as in the statement, "He came upon the stalled car unexpectedly." Therefore, a person is "actually . . . upon such vehicle" if he is standing near to it while assigned the duty of attending it.

(2) "Sole duty" does not mean the person has no other duty at any other time. Thus an attendant who agrees to guard a vehicle, is, until he is relieved or makes other arrangements, under the "sole duty" to attend it.

Summary of the Testimony of David Bates during Trial
Direct Examination

My name is David Bates. I live at 642 Langdell Blvd., Apt. 8, in Gray, Ames. I own the Bates and Company firm, which is a wholesale distributor of jewelry. The business is located at 410 Main Street in Gray. We travel the eastern half of the country, calling on our retail jewelry accounts. [The insurance policy and the proof of loss were identified and offered in evidence.]

In January, 19Y1, I made a business trip to Dayton, Ohio. I carried a stock of jewelry with me in two sample cases. On January 8, I had occasion to go to an appointment in Springfield, Ohio. I left Dayton at 8:30 a.m. in a car rented from the Lease-Ur-Wheels Company, located on

Assignments in Trial Practice

Second Street in Dayton. The car was a two-door Chevrolet. I returned the car to the rental company just before 3 o'clock in the afternoon.

As I got there, the garage attendant (whose name I later learned to be Johnston) waved me in. I made the left turn, drove the car into the garage, and stopped. I told Johnston that he should obtain a driver to take me and my jewelry cases to one of the stores on Main Street where I had an appointment. I gestured toward the back of the car, and I said, "There are two cases in the back of the car. You stay with them." He said "O.K.", if I would promise to come right back. I said I would. I stepped out of the left side and Johnston got into the driver's seat. I crossed the exit lane. He drove away and brought the car to a stop at the rear portion of the garage. After I paid the bill, I left the office and went to the car. The attendant whom Johnston had obtained for me was standing at the car. As I started to enter the car, I immediately noticed there was only one sample case, instead of the two. We immediately called the police. The stolen case and jewelry have never been recovered.

Cross-Examination

I went to the Dayton garage about 8:30 in the morning on January 8. I rented a car there to drive to Springfield. Before I started the trip, the cases were on the floor, behind the front seat -- one case behind the right and one behind the left. One case contained diamond-mounted jewelry and the other case contained mountings. The value of the case containing the mountings is between $18,000 and $19,000. The value of the case which held the diamonds is close to $76,000. Each case was about the size of an attache case. I'm sure the two cases were in the car when I drove back into the Dayton garage later that afternoon. I remember putting them in the car as I left Springfield, and I did not leave the car until I reached the Dayton garage. I started the trip alone, drove to Springfield alone, and returned alone. My call in Springfield was at the Manley Jewelry Company. I worked with the owner of the store. I showed him what he was interested in. I left Springfield about 2:00 p.m. to return to Dayton.

Statement of Roger Johnston Taken by Defendant's Investigator on January 9, 19Y1

I am employed by the Lease-Ur-Wheels Company on Second Street in Dayton, Ohio. I have been working for the company about twenty months. I am the garage manager. I was at the front entrance of the garage about 3 p.m. on January 8, yesterday. The garage was very busy at that time. I saw a car waiting to make a left turn into the garage; it was one of the rental cars, a new Chevrolet. I gave a signal to him and he made a left turn and came into the garage. He stopped right in back of a truck that was parked in front of him, a white laundry truck. About one to two feet of the Chevrolet extended onto the sidewalk. When the Chevrolet came up and stopped, I went to the car and opened the door; the driver started to come out of the car. He asked me to get a driver to take him over to Main Street. During our conversation I was standing on the outside of the left door when it was opened. He asked me to watch his car for him, but I didn't realize he had valuable jewelry in it.

After the conversation had ended, he went into the office. I then stuck my head into the window and jotted down the speedometer reading of the car. I continued around to the rear of the car and raised the lid and checked the spare of the car, and then continued on around the right side of the car noting if there was any damage to the automobile. The inspection took about a minute. After that I went to the white laundry truck and took down its speedometer reading and proceeded on back to the back end of the driveway outside the office, at the far end of the driveway, just off to the left of the driveway. It was about fifty to sixty feet from the Chevrolet to the office. Every once in a while I glanced back at the Chevrolet car. After I had filled in the inspection card, I turned the card in to the office through a window we had for that purpose. I then went back to the car. All this probably took around a minute or a little more. When I got back to the Chevrolet, I got into the car and noticed that the right door was ajar. I closed it and drove the car to the back part of the garage. I called an attendant to drive Mr. Bates over to Main Street and went back to my regular duties, looking over at the Chevy every once in a while.

In a minute or two Mr. Bates came over to the office and said a case of jewelry was missing from the car. He called the police from the office. While I was standing in front of the office, I did not see anybody open the door of the car, nor did I see anything that took place around the Chevrolet car. I did not see anyone remove one of the jewelry cases from the car at any time, though I suppose there would have been time for someone to do so. The garage was pretty busy during that time of day. People were continually walking in and out of the garage.

The above statement is true.   /s/ Roger Johnson

Assignments in Trial Practice

Additional Evidence Available to the Defense

Later in the afternoon of the alleged theft, Sam Traill, defendant's investigator, examined the Chevrolet which had been rented to plaintiff. He discovered in the crack between the front seat cushion and backrest a gasoline credit card receipt, dated January 8, 19Y1, for payment of $10 to the Last Chance Service Station, located on the main highway between Springfield and Dayton, just outside Springfield. The receipt contained a notation, "Right front tire and spare shifted." The investigator went to the Last Chance Service Station, found that Thomas R. Delbert had done the work and prepared the receipt, and obtained from him the following statement.

Statement of Thomas R. Delbert Taken by Defendant's Investigator on January 9, 19Y1

On the afternoon of January 8, 19Y1, about 2:15 p.m., two men stopped in a late model, two-door Chevrolet, which I recognized as a Lease-Ur-Wheels rented car. The driver was in a hurry and told me to shift the right front tire and spare because the right front tire was making a thumping sound and he was afraid he wouldn't make it back to Dayton. As I worked on the car, both of the men stood off a little way, watching and talking in a low tone. I could not hear what they were saying. They were in the station just long enough for me to shift the tires -- only about 5 or 10 minutes. I have never seen either of them before or since. I'm pretty good at remembering faces and I think I'd recognize the driver if I saw him again.

/s/ Thomas R. Delbert

Note Given by Mr. Bates to His Attorneys in Court on the Morning of the Second Day of Trial

I saw in the corridor a few minutes ago a man who I think was an attendant at a service station where I stopped to have a thumping tire shifted from the right front to the spare as I was returning from Springfield to Dayton on the day of the theft. I'm afraid they may have him to testify that I was not alone. I am sorry that I did it, but I lied about being alone. I picked up a hitchhiker at the edge of Springfield, just before I noticed the tire trouble. He introduced himself as a business school student, and I indicated that I was in the wholesale jewelry business. He expressed great interest in the opportunities in the jewelry trade, both retail and wholesale, and we talked on that subject most of the way to Dayton, including the period of our stop at the service station. I don't remember for sure, but I probably told him during the course of our discussion about the jewels in the car. I do not know any way of identifying the young man; I do not even recall what school he was attending. I left him off in Dayton at the main highway that goes through to the west. I didn't mention this before because I thought it would confuse the situation, since I did not think it possible that he had anything to do with the theft of my jewelry case. I don't know how they found out about this, but it may be that I left the service station receipt in the rented car.

Now that I think about it, it is possible that the hitchhiker took the case when he left. He had a suitcase that he had flung in the rear seat when he got into the car. I didn't watch too carefully as he got out. I had driven off onto the shoulder of the road to let him out, but part of my car was still on the road and I was watching the traffic. I'm sure I saw both cases when I left the service station. I assumed they were still there when I entered the garage in Dayton but I'm not 100% sure I actually looked. I never got out of the car between the service station and the garage. The reason I lied was that I was very excited when I reported the theft to my insurance agent and I was afraid my policy might not cover me if I had taken on a hitchhiker when the jewelry was in the car.

Assignments in Trial Practice

ASSIGNMENT 6A

Study Chapters V and VI of the Text.

This assignment concerns the jury charge in Sanders v. Bennett. A memorandum of law concerning the case and a record of trial proceedings appears as Appendix A, infra.

Firm A (Counsel for plaintiff).

Firm B (Counsel for defendant).

Not later than two weeks before the class meeting on this assignment, requests for instructions to the jury are to be submitted by counsel for each party to the instructor. These will be duplicated and distributed to class members so as to permit preparation in advance of the class meeting.

The class session will commence with a conference in which the trial judge will indicate generally the content of his intended charge (as would ordinarily be done before the attorneys' summations to the jury). Counsel will be given an opportunity to make additional or modified requests for instruction. It will then be assumed that the summation has occurred (though it will in fact not take place until the following class session). The trial judge will then proceed to give his oral charge to the jury. Upon completion of the charge, counsel will make such objections to the charge as they consider appropriate. Critique by the class will follow.

Note to counsel assigned for Assignment 7A: The conference that opens Assignment 6A would normally be followed by your summation. It is suggested you take careful notes of the judge's views in this preliminary conference since they will, of course, be applicable to your summation in Assignment 7A.

ALTERNATIVE ASSIGNMENT 6A-1

The instructor may limit the subject of requests for instructions to the coercion issue.

ALTERNATIVE ASSIGNMENT 6A-2

The instructor may require everyone in the class to submit written requests for instructions on the coercion issue.

Assignments in Trial Practice

ASSIGNMENT 6B

Study Chapters V and VI of the Text.

This assignment concerns the jury charge in State v. Devereaux. A memorandum of law concerning the case and a record of the trial testimony, partly summarized, are set forth in Appendix B, and should be supplemented by the materials in assignment 11B, relating to the witness Irene Gossage. The student should assume for purposes of Assignments 6B and 7B that the substance of Mrs. Gossage's statement of June 15 (to the prosecution) has been admitted into evidence, and that her statement of July 30 (to the defense) was introduced as a defense exhibit for impeachment purposes.

Firm A (Counsel for the state of Ames).

Firm B (Counsel for defendant Devereaux).

Not later than two weeks before the class meeting on this assignment, counsel for each party are to submit to the instructor their respective requests for instructions to the jury. These requests will be duplicated and distributed to class members so they may prepare in advance for the class meeting.

The class session will commence with a conference in which the trial judge will indicate generally the content of his intended charge (as would ordinarily be done before the attorneys' summations to the jury). Counsel will then be given opportunity to submit requests for additions to or modifications of the instructions. Depending upon the procedure felt most appropriate by the instructor, the class may proceed directly to summations under Assignment 7B, with critique by the instructor to follow; or the instructor may opt to proceed as if argument had been given, and instruct the jury immediately following the in-chambers discussion of jury instruction requests. If he takes the latter option, counsel should prepare to make such objections to the charge at the close thereof as they deem appropriate.

Note to counsel for Assignment 7B: If the instructor has opted to follow normal trial order and hold the summations immediately after the arguments on jury instructions, you should take careful note of the judge's views on the instructions so that you may adapt your summations accordingly. Similarly, if Assignment 11B (examination and cross-examination of Irene Gossage) is scheduled to take place before your summation, you should take notes of her testimony and incorporate it into the remainder of the trial record provided in Assignment 7B.

ALTERNATIVE ASSIGNMENT 6B-1

The instructor may limit the subject of requests for instructions to the attempt issue.

ALTERNATIVE ASSIGNMENT 6B-2

The instructor may require everyone in the class to submit written requests for instructions on the attempt issue.

Assignments in Trial Practice

ASSIGNMENT 7A

Study Chapter VII of the Text.

The special assignment will be the summation in Sanders v. Bennett. A memorandum of law concerning the case and a record of trial proceedings appears as Appendix A, infra.

Firm A (Counsel for plaintiff).

Firm B (Counsel for defendant).

It will be assumed that the summation is being made before the court charges the jury (though in point of fact, the charge was given during the preceding assignment); it will, however, be assumed that counsel have been advised by the trial judge (in the preliminary conference held during the preceding assignment) of the general content of his planned charge. These previously expressed views are applicable to the present assignment.

Each party will be allowed 30 minutes. The two attorneys for each party may divide their time as they choose. Both attorneys for the defendant will speak before either of the attorneys for the plaintiff.

ALTERNATIVE ASSIGNMENT 7A-1

The instructor may assign both the jury charge and the summation in Sanders v. Bennett for the same class session. In that event, the class session will begin with the conference with the trial judge concerning the content of his intended charge, and counsel will then give their summations before the judge charges the jury. In this combined exercise, each party will be allowed only 20 minutes for summation.

Assignments in Trial Practice

ASSIGNMENT 7B

Study chapter VII of the Text.

The special assignment will be the summation in State v. Devereaux. A memorandum of law concerning the case and a record of trial proceedings appears in Appendix B. The record is to be supplemented by the materials in Assignment 11B (examination and cross-examination of Irene Gossage). If the Gossage assignment is scheduled for performance prior to this summation, counsel should have taken careful notes of the witness's actual testimony so as to incorporate it into the materials here. If the Gossage assignment has not been performed prior to this summation, counsel should presume that the substance of Mrs. Gossage's statement of June 15 (to the prosecution) has been introduced testimonially, and that her statement of July 30 (to the defense) was introduced as a defense exhibit for impeachment purposes.

Firm A (Counsel for the state of Ames).

Firm B (Counsel for defendant Devereaux).

Assume that the summation here precedes the court's charge to the jury (although the charge may have been given during performance of Assignment 6B). Counsel has, of course, been advised by the court during performance of Assignment 6B concerning the instructions the court intends to give the jury, and counsel is bound here by the court's advice there.

Each party will be allowed 30 minutes. The two attorneys for each party may divide their time as they choose. Order of argument should be as follows: state's opening, defendant's answering, state's rebuttal.

ALTERNATIVE ASSIGNMENT 7B-1

The instructor may assign both the jury charge, and the summation in State v. Devereaux for the same class session. In that event, the class session will begin with the conference with the trial judge concerning the content of his intended charge, and counsel will then give their summations before the judge charges the jury. In this combined exercise, each party will be allowed only 20 minutes for summation.

ASSIGNMENT 8A

Study §§2-6, 20, 24, 25, 32, 33 and 3-5, 6, 10, 22, 25 of the Text.

This assignment involves the direct and cross-examination of the witness Bertha Lyman in the trial of State of Ames v. Ina Mae Brawley. Miss Brawley has been charged with manslaughter for stabbing her half-sister, Geraldine Jelks. The stabbing occurred in the Polecat Bar and Grille in East Austin, Ames, during the early morning hours of October 17 last year.

Firm A: You, as trial counsel in the Austin County Attorney's office, have been assigned to handle the trial of this case. Your special assignment is to decide whether to call Bertha Lyman as a witness for the prosecution, and, if you decide to call her, proceed with direct and re-direct examination. If you do not call Miss Lyman, summarize to the court the evidence you have presented to demonstrate you have proved a prima facie case and demonstrate that a defense motion for a directed verdict should be denied. If the defense chooses to call Miss Lyman as a defense witness, conduct the cross-examination.

Firm B: You are trial counsel for the defense. Chief defense counsel Emerson A. Brewster has ultimate responsibility for decisions of strategy; otherwise, you're in charge. If Bertha Lyman is called by the state, conduct appropriate cross-examination. If she is not called by the state, decide whether you will call her as a defense witness, and be prepared to justify your decision with Mr. Brewster. (Assume that for quite valid reasons you have determined not, under any circumstances, to place the defendant herself on the witness stand.)

If neither Firm A nor Firm B chooses to call Miss Lyman, the instructor will indicate which firm will proceed on the assumption that they are acting under directions of their leading counsel to call Miss Lyman.

Assume that unless otherwise indicated all dates in the following materials refer to last year.

Defendant's Statement

On October 23 the defendant, Ina Mae Brawley (who had been released on bond the day after her arrest), appeared with her attorney, Emerson A. Brewster, at the offices of the Austin County Attorney. There she dictated the following statement:

Date: October 23   Time: 10:30 a.m.
Place: Austin County Attorney's Office, Austin, Ames
Present: Ina Mae Brawley

Assignments in Trial Practice

Emerson A. Brewster, Attorney for Miss Brawley
Frank G. Hubbell, Investigator, Austin County Attorney's Office
Mary Berg, Court Reporter

My name is Ina Mae Brawley. I live at 458 Vermont Avenue, E. Austin, Ames. My age is 39. I am five foot four inches tall and weigh 135 pounds.

Since 1966 me and my half-sister, Geraldine Jelks, have been running the Polecat Bar and Grille in E. Austin. We also have been living together for a long time. Usually we worked the bar and grill together, but the past two years or so we would sort of split shifts waiting the tables and we hired a person to do the cooking and bar tending. Sometimes I would go down and wait the tables and sometimes Gerry would and sometimes we were both there during busy times.

On October 16, I went down to the place at about three in the afternoon and waited on tables. Bertha -- Bertha Lyman, that's our cook -- was there. Gerry was supposed to come in about seven p.m. and help with the supper hour and the bar, but she didn't show up until about 11 and she was pretty drunk, you know what I mean? She didn't do no work and instead plopped down at one of the tables and started drinking beer. I told her she ought to do some work, but she got nasty about it, and so I dropped the subject. There was some customers around and I didn't want any scene. I went into the kitchen and worked awhile back there.

By one o'clock Bertha and me had the place pretty well cleaned up and was sitting in the kitchen visiting. About this time Gerry come into the kitchen. You could tell she had been drinking pretty heavy. Anyway she said she wasn't going to take orders from me or anyone else. I told Bertha to go on home that I would have to handle this myself and she left. Then all of a sudden Gerry started to come for me and I backed up to the kitchen table and told Gerry to keep away from me. I said, "Gerry, please leave me alone." I must have picked up the knife at that time, but I don't remember ever having it in my hand. Anyway, it all happened right then. Gerry suddenly ran at me and began scratching and clawing at me and suddenly she jumped back and then I saw the blood and I screamed and ran out of the kitchen. I don't remember anything more except Bertha came back and I remember Gerry lying on the floor and blood all over and then the police came and some ambulance people and I ended up in jail.

I certify that the above is a true and accurate transcription of the statement made by Ina Mae Brawley at the date, time, and place shown.

/s/ Mary Berg, Court Reporter

Preliminary Hearing

On October 27 preliminary hearing was held in Austin County Magistrate's Court. The state proceeded against the defendant on a charge of manslaughter. Its theory was that the stabbing was perpetrated during an altercation in which the defendant was the aggressor (or that she had used excessive force to defend herself) and that she acted while in the heat of passion. State's attorney Lee Silverman presented testimony of George Swoboda, Kenneth Creelman, James A. Reidy, Cameron Himes, M.D., Bertha Lyman, and Harry Brubaker. He placed in evidence the defendant's extra-judicial statement (reproduced above) and rested. The defense offered no evidence. It moved to dismiss the charge, arguing that the extra-judicial statement, as the only available direct evidence of the actual stabbing, compelled dismissal on grounds either of self-defense or of accident. The magistrate denied the motion, found probable cause to believe the defendant committed the crime as charged, and bound her over for trial.

The following are summaries of preliminary hearing testimony, taken either directly from the transcript or from witnesses' statements which were, in substance, identical to their testimony.

Testimony of Austin Police Officers George Swoboda and Kenneth Creelman

The morning of October 17 we were on routine patrol in E. Austin, Ames. At 1:15 we were dispatched by radio to the Polecat Bar and Grille on Factory Avenue to investigate an assault call which had been relayed by the AAA-Amex Ambulance Service. We arrived at the bar at approximately 1:20 a.m. A Triple-A Amex ambulance was parked in front. We proceeded directly into the establishment, observing activity back behind the bar in the kitchen. When we entered the kitchen, we observed a female subject lying on the floor in the position outlined in Exhibit A. The two ambulance attendants were readying a litter near the subject. They said it was a knife wound and that the subject was still alive. We instructed them to get her to the hospital, and they loaded her onto the litter and left the premises.

There were two other women present. Their names were Bertha Lyman, an employee at the bar, and Ina Mae Brawley, who was the owner of the place. The Brawley woman seemed to be hysterical. Miss Lyman was more in control of herself, and Creelman talked to her and then advised her she could go home. Swoboda radioed headquarters for assistance.

In our investigation we observed that there was considerable blood on the floor in the area where the victim had fallen. The floor was also covered with broken glass, some of which appeared to be from beer or wine bottles and some appeared to be from drinking glasses. The nearby area of the kitchen was in disarray, with two small chairs and a footstool tipped over on the floor, giving the appearance that a scuffle had taken place for several minutes before the stabbing occurred. On a small work table near the serving window (position "K" on Exhibit A), we also observed a large kitchen knife covered with what appeared to be blood. At this time the lab technicians, photographer, and other investigating officers arrived, so we turned the premises over to them. We place Ina Mae Brawley under arrest and took her to the station.

At the police station, the subject, Ina Mae Brawley, was booked in and advised of her rights. She said she wanted to call a lawyer and she was allowed to make a telephone call. She apparently got advice to keep quiet because she didn't say another word after she hung up the phone. We left her in the custody of the police matron. We then returned to the Polecat Bar, arriving approximately 4:15 a.m. There we made measurements of the premises which we used, with the assistance of Walter Reisel, the police artist, to make up Exhibit A. We cleared the premises at approximately 6:00 a.m.

Police laboratory technician James A. Reidy testified that blood samples taken from the kitchen knife and from the floor of the bar were of the same type as that of the decedent, Geraldine Jelks.

Direct Examination of Cameron Himes, M.D.

(Summarized.) I was at the hospital during the early morning hours of October 17 and was called to the emergency entrance when Geraldine Jelks, the decedent, was brought in. She was in severe shock having suffered an abdominal knife wound. I called to set up emergency surgery, but Miss Jelks died within a few minutes after her arrival. Time of death was 1:45 p.m.

I then performed an autopsy on the decedent and determined the cause of death to be irreversible shock due to loss of blood from a stab wound above the navel. The wound penetrated the abdominal cavity, lacerating the colon, abdominal aorta, stomach, and liver. Routine blood examination revealed the presence of alcohol in a percentage of .26 which would indicate the decedent was in a state of substantial intoxication at the time of death. The decedent was a female Caucasian of about 42 years of age, moderately obese and weighing about 165 pounds. Height 5'5".

Cross-Examination of Cameron Himes, M.D.

(Summarized.) A blood alcohol reading of .26 percent does not indicate such a state of intoxication as would render a person immobile, such as would a reading of, say, .30 or higher. I can express no opinion as to whether the decedent would have been rendered belligerent by her state of intoxication, but as a general rule alcohol acts as a depressant of inhibitions with the result that the drinker may display more emotions -- whether belligerency or for that matter affection -- when drunk than when sober.

It is possible that the decedent could have inflicted the stab wound on herself by running against a knife held by another person if the other person held the knife rigidly. There were no stab wounds other than the one causing death, although there were superficial scratches on the decedent's face and arms. The scratches appeared to be caused by fingernails and probably not by broken glass, though I can express no specific opinion on the point. I did not find particles of glass in the scratches, though the absence of glass particles would not be a controlling factor in determining the cause.

Statement of Bertha Lyman to Investigator Frank G. Hubbell,
Austin County Attorney's Office, 10 a.m. October 17

(The defense obtained a copy of this statement
at the preliminary hearing.)

My name is Bertha Lyman. I am employed as cook and bartender at the Polecat Bar and Grille in E. Austin, Ames. My employer is Miss Ina Mae Brawley, but I worked for Geraldine Jelks, too, when she was alive. Gerry and Ina Mae ran the place together.

On October 16, I worked at the Polecat from 3 in the afternoon up until closing time, which was around 2 in the morning. These were my regular hours.

Ina Mae and me covered the supper hour and Gerry was supposed to help but she never came down until about 11 o'clock that night. You could tell she had been drinking and Ina Mae was sort of irritated at her. I was back in the kitchen when after awhile I heard them going at it out front. I went out there and they was wrestling around -- you know, standing up. There was broken glass on the floor. I think Gerry threw a beer glass at Ina Mae because Ina Mae yelled at me for help, and she was holding her head and she was all wet with beer. It looked to me like Ina Mae was getting the worst of the fight, so I went right over and pulled them apart. Gerry backed away after that, and I sort of held Ina Mae's arm, as I remember, and pretty soon she said she had had it with Gerry's drinking and not coming to work and even though she might get killed she was going to get this thing settled. I believe her exact words were "I am going to have this thing out with Gerry, and either I am going to walk out of here or they will have to carry me out in a box." I really think she was afraid of Gerry, who was really quite a bit bigger, you know what I mean?

As far as I know, Gerry spent the rest of the evening out front drinking. Ina Mae stayed in the kitchen for a couple of glasses of wine, and she waited on the front some when we had a customer out there. She also helped me clean up the kitchen. Each time she came back in the kitchen she was madder about Gerry's just sitting out front with beer and not helping out. Anyway, we finished cleaning up the kitchen about one o'clock, and I remember Ina Mae was sitting at the table with a glass of wine and she told me I might as well go on home that she would be able to handle what business there was and would close up the place. I left the kitchen and about that time Gerry was headed back that way. She was pretty drunk and had a glass of beer in one hand and a bottle in the other. I went on through the restaurant and on outside to my car which was parked beside the building. I was just getting my keys out of my purse when I heard Ina Mae scream for help and call to me and I figured she had got in trouble with Gerry again. Then I saw her running through the restaurant toward the front door and she yelled at me come

85

in quick and call an ambulance. So I went inside and called an ambulance on the pay phone up front. Then I went back into the kitchen following Ina Mae. And there was Gerry on the floor and blood was all over, and Ina Mae was kneeling beside her. Ina Mae got up when I came in. She was really upset and still sort of screaming and moaning and carrying on. I bent over Gerry. She was still alive. She looked up and saw me and said, "Bertha, she didn't mean it. She didn't mean to do it." And then she stopped talking and closed her eyes. I tried to get Ina Mae calmed down, and pretty soon I heard a siren and the men from the ambulance came in and took Gerry right on out and put her into the ambulance and drove away. About that time the police came. I suppose the ambulance people called them. Anyway, there was two of them and they tried to talk to Ina Mae but she wasn't making much sense. They took my name and where they could reach me and said they wanted to talk to me about it. They looked around and picked up the bloody kitchen knife from the table where Ina Mae had been sitting. They made a couple of phone calls and told me I was a very important witness and they did not want me to leave town or anything and that they would talk to me the next day if I didn't want to stay around right then. So I went off home.

The only customer I remember being up front when I went up there the first time was some guy named Harry. He is sort of a lush and hangs around there. He is lying if he says he saw anything; he was passed out cold all night whenever I noticed him. In fact, when Ina Mae shouted for help, I tried to shake Harry to come help me pull the girls apart, but he didn't even move or anything. I don't remember if I noticed him being there when I first left after Ina Mae told me at one o'clock that I could go on home.

I have worked at the Polecat for about a year and I have seen other times when Gerry and Ina Mae didn't get along too well. Usually it was Gerry's fault, but I admit there was a couple of times when Ina Mae said she was going to knife Gerry, except I am sure she was just mad at the time and didn't really mean it. Usually their fights was like the first one -- yelling and sort of shoving each other around. Maybe throwing a glass or something, but nothing serious.

I have read the above statement and it is true.

Witnessed: /s/ Frank G. Hubbell   /s/ Bertha Lyman
Date: 10/17
Time: 10 a.m.
Place: Austin County Atty. Off.

Direct Examination of Harry Brubaker

(Summarized.) My name is Harry Brubaker and I live at 251 Hampshire Street in E. Austin, Ames.

The night of October 16, I was in the Polecat Bar having a couple of beers, which I often do. The place is run by a couple of sisters who are always squabbling, and sometimes it is sort of like having a floor show to watch. There's a big one and a little one and usually one or the other of them will have a couple of belts of booze and then light into the other. Anyway, this night I think both of them was on the sauce and the little one was getting pretty feisty. They got into one of their hassles, shouting and threatening each other, and the little one hauled off and let the big one have it with a beer bottle -- right on the head. Glass and beer all over the place. Well, about this time the cook come charging around the end of the bar and pulled the sisters apart. They was still yelling and trying to grab each other, but after awhile they quieted down and I went back to my suds. I didn't pay no attention to what time it was I left the place, but I think that was the only to-do they had that night.

Cross-Examination of Harry Brubaker

X. (By Mr. Brewster) You're a regular customer at the Polecat, aren't you, Mr. Brubaker? A. Sure am.
X. And you had quite a lot more than just "a couple" of beers the night of the stabbing, didn't you? A. Well, I might have.
X. Did you have anything to drink before you went to the Polecat that night? A. Oh, I guess I probably had a glass of beer with supper.
X. Possibly two beers? A. Possibly.
X. And you arrived at the Polecat at what time? A. Around 8:00 as I recall.
X. You began drinking right as soon as you arrived? A. Well, I ordered a beer.
X. Draft or bottle, Mr. Brubaker? A. Actually, I don't recall.
X. You drank the first beer and ordered another right away, didn't you? A. Yes.
X. And then another-- A. Well, I might have.
X. You continued drinking at least until you saw this fight with the beer bottle between the two sisters, didn't you? A. Off and on.
X. What time was it that you saw the fight? A. Actually, I don't recall.
X. Do you know approximately? Was it 8:30? A. Oh, no, it was later than that.
X. How about after 11:00? A. It might have been.
X. So you had been drinking steadily for at least three hours -- plus what you had drunk for supper -- before you saw the fight you testified about, is that so? A. I guess so.

Assignments in Trial Practice

X. Then it's true, isn't it Mr. Brubaker, that you had a heck of a lot more than just "a couple" of beers that evening --

    Mr. SILVERMAN: Objection, your honor. The question is argumentative and he is badgering the witness.

    THE COURT: Yes, sustained.

X. (By Mr. Brewster) In fact, Mr. Brubaker, you drank that night in the Polecat Bar until you passed out, didn't you? A. Oh, no. Well, I might have dozed off just from it getting late and me being tired.
X. Well, when did you leave? A. Actually, I didn't check the time on that.
X. Were you there when the stabbing took place? A. Not that I know of.
X. -- When the ambulance men arrived? or the Police? A. Oh no, none of that.
X. You were here in court when the waitress, Bertha Lyman, testified, weren't you, and you heard her say that she saw you passed out, and that she shook you to try to wake you up so you could help pull the sisters apart?
A. Yes sir, that's what she said.
X. Do you have any reason to think she might not be telling the truth?

    Mr. SILVERMAN: Objection.

    The COURT: Sustained.

X. (By Mr. Brewster) As a matter of fact, Mr. Brubaker, you have no idea, do you, of which one of those sisters hit the other with a beer bottle during that fight you say you witnessed? A. Well, you know, I'm not too sure, now that you mention it. You know, I was trying to mind my own business. It's just --
X. Just what? A. -- Well, it was after the little one went back into the kitchen and the big one said to the cook, who was picking up some pieces of glass, she said, "If she gets any meaner, they're gonna be carting me out of here in a box." That's what gave me the impression it was the little one that started the fracas.
X. I see. That will be all, Mr. Brubaker.

<u>Statement of Mrs. Mabeline Moreno to Inspector Frank G. Hubbell,
Austin County Attorney's Office, 3 p.m. October 29</u>

    (Mrs. Moreno also talked with the defendant, at whose request she gave a similar statement to defense attorneys.)

    My name is Mabeline Moreno. I live at 45 Parker Place, Austin,
Ames. I have known both Ina Mae Brawley and Geraldine Jelks for many

years, although I would not say I have known them "intimately." They have lived together in East Austin. They are half-sisters and together they run -- they used to run -- the Polecat Cafe.

I read about the preliminary hearing on the case in the newspaper and was surprised to see that the cook -- Bertha Lyman -- seemed to know so little about the case. She had told me a lot more the day I talked to her at the cafe. That was the same day the radio broadcast the news. I went over to the cafe to see if there was anything I could do to help. Bertha was there. She has been their employee for sometime, and seemed quite eager to discuss the case. She told me that she had seen the whole thing; that she had been in the kitchen with Ina Mae, and when Geraldine came in, Ina Mae picked up a wine bottle and broke it on the edge of the table and told Geraldine she was going to get it. Then they got into a tussle and Ina Mae dropped the bottle and grabbed a kitchen knife from the table. Bertha told me that right then she ran outside for fear something horrible was going to happen -- which obviously it did. But when Ina Mae called her, she came back in and found Gerry on the floor. She said she called the ambulance that took Gerry away, and that she had talked to the police and told them the whole story.

I don't know why Bertha would say anything different now; she seemed sincere at the time and I can't see why she would have lied to me about such a horrible tragedy. I have not, however, talked with her since the day I went to the cafe.

Report of Police Laboratory Technician Lawrence Mattacelli, October 17

(Copy given defense counsel in lieu of calling the witness at the hearing.)

Examined kitchen knife taken by me and J. Reidy from the kitchen table at Polecat Bar and Grille approx. 2:30 a.m. October 17. Described as wooden handle, single-edged non-stainless steel blade of approximate (varying) 1" width and length of 8". Both blade and handle covered with blood and smudges. Unable to raise any identifiable fingerprints. Initialed knife "LM" on handles and turned it over to property custodian at 5 a.m.

Report in Prosecutor's File of AAA-Amex Ambulance Operators Albert Nanson and Edward Bennett

(Copy given defense counsel in lieu of calling the witnesses at the hearing.)

We answered an emergency call to the Polecat Bar and Grille at approximately 1:10 a.m. October 17, arriving about 10 minutes later.

Assignments in Trial Practice

Police were arriving just about the same time. We went into back room -- kitchen of the place, and found subject Geraldine Jelks lying on the floor at the right end of the kitchen. We ascertained that she was still alive, placed her on the litter and transported her to Austin General Hospital. The subject said nothing in our presence. We had no conversation with anyone other than to identify ourselves and tell the police we would take the subject to Austin General. Two other women besides the injured subject were at the scene.

<u>Relevant Ames Law</u>

1. §192, Ames Penal Code:

Manslaughter is the unlawful killing of a human being without malice. It is of three kinds:

(1) Voluntary -- upon a sudden quarrel or heat of passion; . . .

2. Some Ames decisions:

Voluntary manslaughter is an intentional homicide in sudden passion or heat of blood caused by a reasonable provocation and not with malice aforethought. <u>State v. Walser</u>, 24 Ames 30 (1894).

In <u>State v. Laverty,</u> 32 Ames 104 (1902), the court approved the following instruction:

> When a man, in killing another, acts under the influence of sudden passion caused by a reasonable provocation but not in necessary defense of his life or in order to prevent great bodily harm, the law does not excuse him because of the provocation, but it does not hold him guilty of murder. Rather, the law recognizes the fact that a man when greatly provoked will lose the control of his reason and under the influence of the passion and excitement caused by the provocation resort to violence of which he would not be guilty in the absence of passion. It therefore attributes killing to the frailty of human nature and not to malice, and while it does not excuse the killing altogether, it reduces it to manslaughter.

Where the defendant is a victim of a simple assault not apparently endangering his life or threatening him with great bodily harm, he is not justified or excused in killing his assailant or in using a deadly weapon. Under such circumstances the homicide will be manslaughter, at least. <u>Proctor v. State</u>, 50 Ames 354 (1937)

3. From L. Hovind, Manslaughter and Mutuality, 16 Austin L. Rev. 7, 9 (1952) (citations omitted):

> [Manslaughter] prosecutions arise in great proliferation from situations of mutual combat. Mutual combat is generally thought to

come about from a conflict giving rise to angry words, thence to an exchange of blows. At this point, the law is not so concerned with "who started it" as it is with reassuring itself that neither party took "unfair advantage" of the other and did not seek out the other for the purpose of gratifying malice. Thus, where the defendant and his victim have at an earlier time fought, but are apparently reconciled before engaging in the fatal combat, the law will not conclude that the first fight provided the grudge basis for the second unless it so appears from the circumstances. If then, under these almost clinical conditions of mutuality the defendant seizes a weapon and dispatches his weaponless comrade, the act will be regarded as homicide in the heat of blood and manslaughter.

. . . The law does become concerned with "who started it" when the defendant pleads self defense. Some courts hold that an aggressor, having ruffled the otherwise smooth waters of mutuality, cannot thereafter kill his adversary and claim self defense. Others say he can but only if he has in good faith withdrawn from the affray and has brought this fact home to his adversary. Then, if the adversary just won't take "no" for an answer and attempts to kill him or do him great bodily harm, the defendant has the same right of self defense as if he had not originally been the aggressor.

4. Ames has adopted, where appropriate, the Federal Rules of Criminal Procedure. It has adapted portions of 18 U.S.C. §3500 in the so-called Ames "little Jencks Act" (3 A.S.A. §3500), the text and judicial discussion of which are set forth in the Assignment 4A materials.

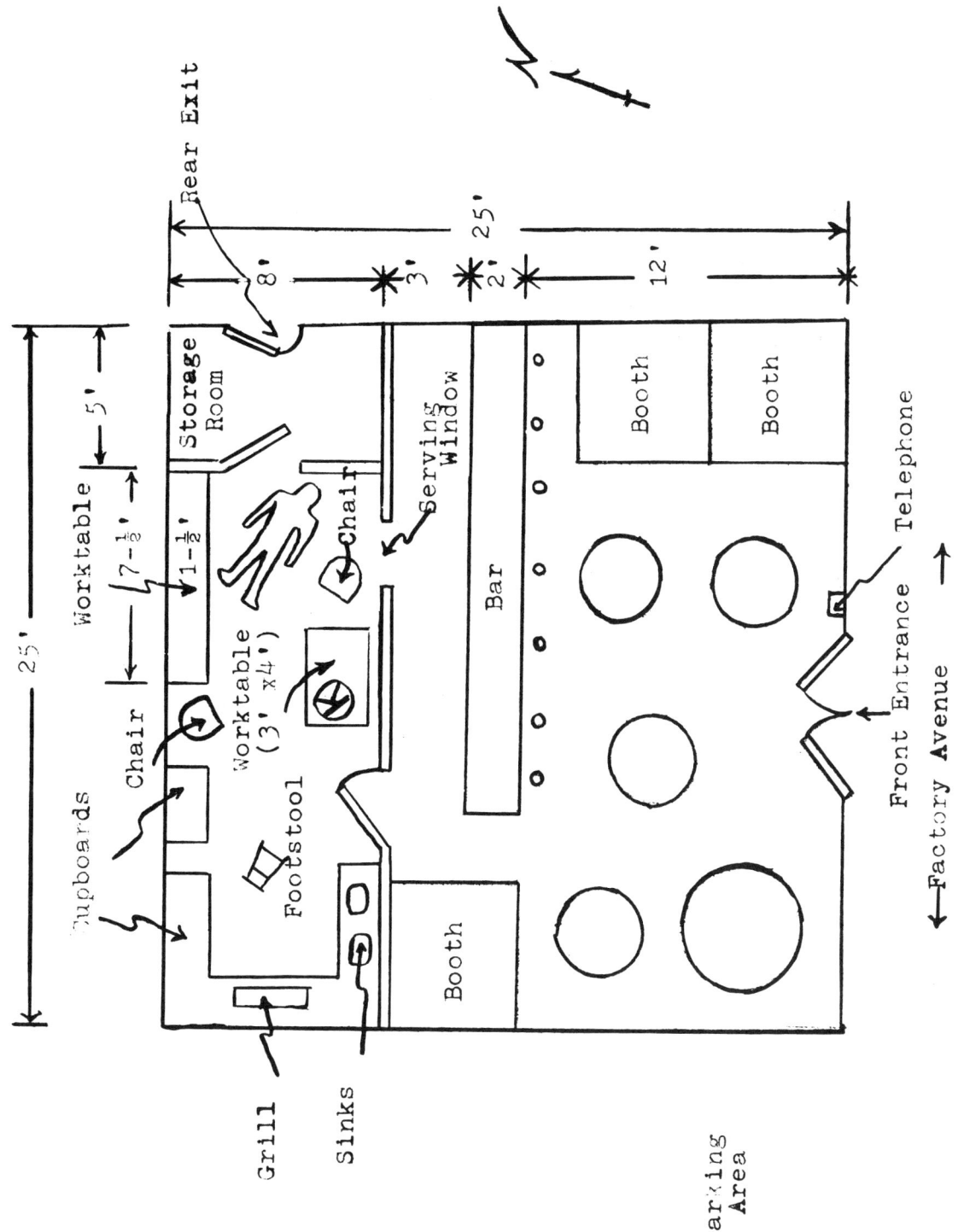

ASSIGNMENT 8B

Review §§4-6, 4-12, and 4-16 of the Text.

The special assignment is the direct and cross-examination of the witness Sergeant Winters in the case of <u>Lois E. Sommers, Administratix of the Estate of Stanley O. Sommers, Deceased v. Ames Transfer Co.</u>

<u>Firm A</u> (Counsel for plaintiff): Conduct the direct examination of the witness. Your objective is restricted to putting in evidence Winters' testimony, insofar as you consider it advisable, as to his "experiment" and any other testimony supporting the conclusion set forth in paragraph A of his statement. Do not go into the opinions expressed in paragraph B of that statement, since these are the subject matter for Assignment 9B. Assume for the purpose of this assignment that you consider the opinions in paragraph B sound and intend to offer them after Winters has testified on the subject matter of today's assignment.

Be prepared to explain whether or not you would use Mr. House as a witness, and if so, for what purpose and at what stage in your case.

<u>Firm B</u> (Counsel for defendant):

1. Attempt to keep out Sergeant Winters' experiment evidence offered during the direct examination except insofar as you think it tactically preferable that it be received (see Ground Rule 16).

2. If it is received, cross-examine Winters as to his experiment. Observe the same limitation as to subject matter as set forth for plaintiff's counsel in the preceding paragraph.

Suggestion to counsel: A central problem in the admissibility of the experiment is whether the circumstances of Winters' observations are sufficiently similar to those that confronted deceased just before the accident to warrant their receipt in evidence. Consider carefully such discrepancies as may exist and their significance.

Pleadings

Plaintiff, as personal representative, sues for $250,000 on account of the wrongful death of her husband in a highway accident occurring at approximately 1:40 a.m., October 16, 19Y1, on U.S. Highway 2 in the Commonwealth of Ames, near Nashua Road. The complaint alleges that as deceased was driving a 19Y2 Ford in an easterly direction on Highway 2, it collided with a tractor-trailer owned by the defendant and then being negligently operated in a westerly direction on Highway 2 by Axel C. King, in the scope of employment for the defendant. Defendant's answer denies the allegations of negligence and damages, admits all other allegations, and pleads the contributory negligence of the decedent as a bar.

Assignments in Trial Practice

Ames Statute

Under Ames law, contributory negligence of the decedent in a wrongful death action is an affirmative defense to be pleaded and proved by the defendant. If established, it is a complete bar to recovery.

Pre-Trial Conference

A pre-trial conference was held prior to trial at which the court pressed for stipulations as to facts not genuinely in dispute.

The following stipulations were made:

1. Plaintiff's Exhibit A, together with the information set forth thereon, may be received in evidence to show the positions of the vehicles after the accident.

2. At the time of the accident, defendant's tractor-trailer was being operated by Axel C. King in the scope of his employment for defendant.

3. The speed limit on Highway 2 in the area where the accident occurred was 55 m.p.h.

Excerpts from Deposition of Axel C. King Taken at the Instance of Plaintiff's Counsel on December 18, 19Y1

(Summarized.) My name is Axel C. King. I am now, and was on October 15-16, 19Y1, working for Ames Transfer Co. On October 15, 19Y1, I took a truck and trailer to Williston to get a load.

I left Williston about 3:00 p.m. I reached the intersection of Highway 2 and Nashua Road about 1:00 a.m. on the 16th. I had become sleepy and decided to pull over. I stopped and started backing up, intending to back over onto the south shoulder of the road where there was plenty of room for my rig.

As I was still backing, I saw the lights of a car coming from the west. I stopped immediately, to wait for the car to pass. I thought my trailer was still entirely on my side (the north side) of the road. I later learned that it was slightly across the center line onto the south half of the road. The oncoming car was moving very fast -- between 70 and 100 m.p.h. It passed my cab about five feet to my left. I never suspected the driver would fail to clear my trailer since there was plenty of room. The next thing I knew, he crashed into the trailer. The car was a total wreck. The driver was killed.

I went to the hospital after the accident. At the time I left the scene, neither vehicle had been moved since the accident. Exhibit A accurately represents the scene immediately after the accident.

Assignments in Trial Practice

The Trial Thus Far

Plaintiff's entire case up to this point in the trial consists of:

1. The pre-trial stipulation.

2. The testimony of Paul A. Trimmer, reported below.

Plaintiff may assume that Caleb House, whose statement appears below, is also available to testify at trial (though the only witness actually available during the class session will be Sergeant Winters.)

You may assume that Trimmer, House, Winters, and King are the only persons available to testify at trial with reference to the negligence issue.

Testimony at Trial of Paul A. Trimmer, Called by Plaintiff
Summary of Direct Examination

At the time of the accident, I had been a highway patrolman for two years. I was trained for two months before going on the job. Prior to becoming a patrolman I was a truck driver, driving all types of vehicles.

I cannot remember all the details of my investigation on the night of October 16, 19Y1, but I have with me the notes I made at the time. Referring to my notes, I find that I was called at home at 1:55 a.m., October 16. I arrived at the scene at 2:15 a.m. When I arrived, the truck-trailer was sitting in the roadway, with headlights and clearance lights on and motor running. The wrecked Ford was just off the south side of the road. Weather was clear. Both vehicles were just east of the intersection of U.S. Highway 2 and Nashua Road. Highway 2 is blacktop.

I found a gouge mark in the blacktop. It was about a foot long. There was a lot of debris, and an antifreeze and oil mixture was strewn from the gouge mark to the position where I found the Ford. The relative location and size of the objects shown in plaintiff's Exhibit A seem accurate to me and are consistent with the measurements I made at the time.

I determined that the point of impact on the Ford was between 2½ and 3 feet from the left side of the car. The gouge mark was made by the Ford at the time of impact.

Mr. King, the truck driver, was at the scene of the accident when I arrived. I took his statement.

The Ford hit the trailer with such force that it knocked the pin loose at the point of connection between tractor and trailer. The front left dual tires on the trailer were blown and the rims were destroyed where the Ford bumper struck. I found a mirror from the Ford 174 feet in an easterly direction from the gouge mark. It had come loose from the right front fender.

I then left the scene of the accident and returned to the station in Langdell to find out who had been in the Ford. After checking that out, I drove back to the accident scene to complete my investigation. Sergeant Winters came along. He conducted an experiment in connection with the accident. I don't recall the details.

When I returned, the vehicles were in the same position as when I had left. The lights on the two light poles near the intersection were burning. The headlights and all the clearance lights on the tractor and trailer were on, and the motor of the tractor was running. It was too early, of course, to get any effect from the approach of daylight. The weather was clear.

Report of Sgt. George Winters to Police Accident File
(Available to both parties.)

I was on duty on the night shift on October 16, 19Y1. Patrolman Trimmer had been sent out to investigate a bad accident between a tractor-trailer and a car on Highway 2 near the Nashua Road.

Trimmer returned from the accident scene at about 3:45 a.m. to check on who had been in the Ford. I decided to accompany him back to the scene since this was the second serious accident we'd had in that area within two months. We left the station at about 4:00 a.m. We drove in a 19Y1 4-door Chevrolet sedan squad car. Trimmer was at the wheel. I was sitting in the seat to his right. Trimmer told me about the accident on the way. As we approached the accident scene, the thought occurred to me to check the distance at which one would first see the headlights of the tractor as well as the trailer lights on the leading edge of the trailer.

I told Trimmer of my plan. I told him I'd tell him to stop as soon as I saw the headlights so we could note the distance to the tractor-trailer. We were proceeding east on Highway 2 in the same direction as the Ford had been driving just before the accident. I first saw the headlights as we came over the crest of a slight rise on Highway 2. I told Trimmer to stop the car. He stopped and then backed up to the point at which I had first been able to see the headlights. I took a mileage reading. It read 37,437.6 miles. I marked this down in my notebook. We then drove directly to the scene of the accident. I had Trimmer stop when the front of our car was in line with the front of the tractor. The odometer reading was then two-tenths of a mile greater than when we had previously stopped. It read 37,437.8. I wrote that down in my notebook. I concluded that the driver of the should have seen the lights from the tractor about two-tenths of a mile west of the accident.

When I had first seen the headlights of the tractor, the only other lights on the tractor-trailer which I could see were the cab lights on the tractor and the flashing left-turn indicator. That was all. I couldn't see any of the lights on the trailer even though they were burning.

After stopping and taking my second reading of the odometer, I thought it would be worthwhile to determine at what point I could first observe the trailer lights as I approached the tractor-trailer. I had Trimmer drive back west about 100 yards and then turn around and come back toward the rig just as I had the first time. I again kept a sharp lookout as we drove east on Highway 2. I was, however, unable to make out the trailer lights, or see any part of the trailer for that matter, until the front end of our car reached a point 50 feet west of the headlights of the rig. I had Trimmer stop the car at this point. This was the first point at which I was able to see any evidence of the trailer lights or any part of the trailer. The sketch below shows the location of the different lights I saw, viewing the rig from the front.

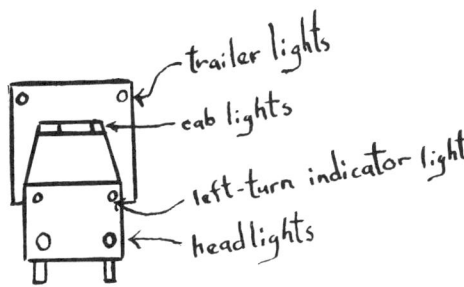

The reason for my inability to see the trailer lights prior to that point probably was that they were rather dim, and also, that the highlights of the tractor tend to blind you until you're pretty close. The rig had all the lights required by state regulation, and they were all found to be in working order.

I got out of the car and measured the distance from the steering wheel of our car to the point of impact on the trailer. It was 101 feet.

A. Based on the above, it is obvious to me that the driver of the Ford could only have seen the portion of the trailer extending over into his half of the road from about 101 feet away from the collision.

B. From the extent of the damage to the two vehicles, I think it quite likely that the Ford was traveling in excess of 55 miles per hour. But even if he'd been going no faster than the speed limit, I doubt that it would have been possible for him to avoid the collision in these circumstances.

I looked over the scene and then left. I made no further measurements or detailed investigation because Trimmer had done the routine investigation.

Dated: October 17, 19Y1

/s/ Sgt. George Winters

Statement of Caleb House Taken by Plaintiff's Counsel on November 26, 19Y1

I live on U.S. Highway 2 about 100 yards west of the scene of the accident. I heard the crash and rushed out immediately. I was the first person there. I saw what had happened and ran back to call the police. I then returned to the scene and stayed around until after the police and ambulance arrived. I know that neither vehicle was moved until after dawn, when they were taken away. The weather was clear all through the night. Before the police arrived, I found a broken whiskey bottle on the highway a foot or two away from the Ford. I could clearly detect the odor of whiskey. I removed this broken glass from the highway and tossed it into the tall grass nearby. It did not occur to me to mention this to the police officer.

As I was running to the scene the first time, I did not notice the lights on the trailer, or any other part of the trailer, until I was up close. As I was going back the second time, after calling the police, I noticed that I could see the trailer lights from a considerable distance up the hill, as I trotted along the shoulder.

/s/ Caleb House

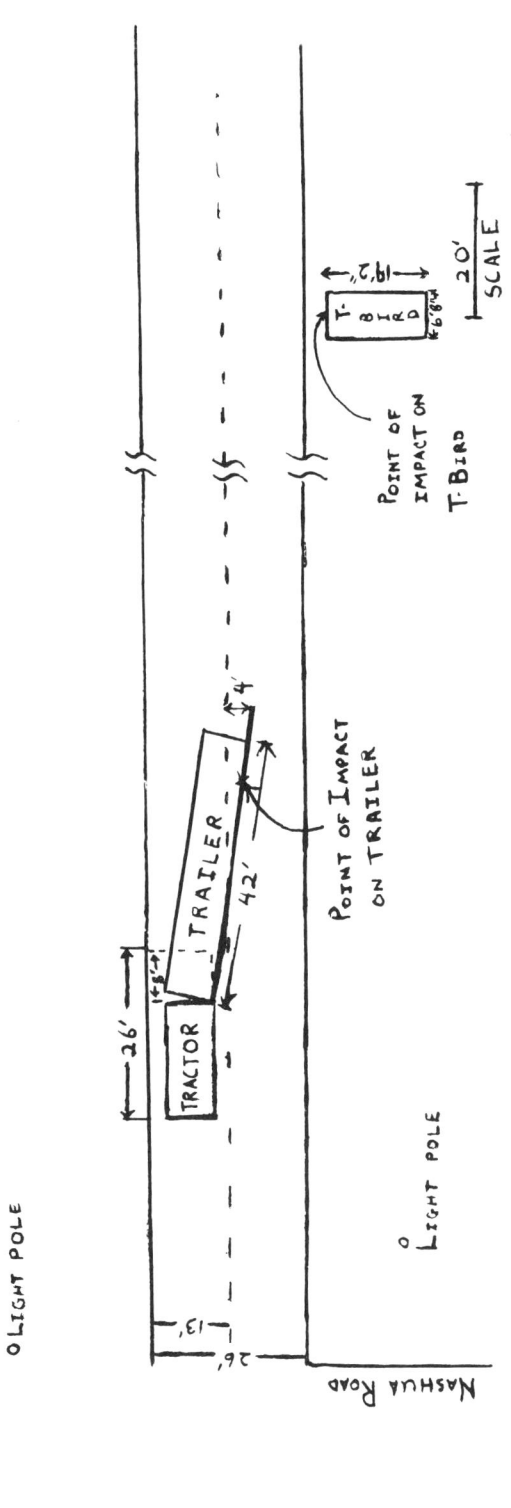

TOP VIEW

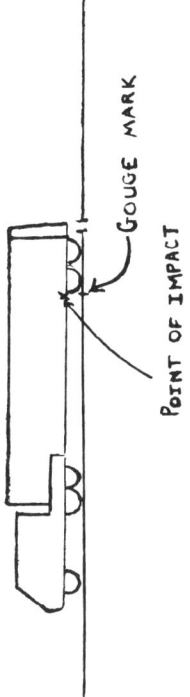

SIDE VIEW

ASSIGNMENT 9A

Study the following sections of the Text:

§§2-15, 2-22, 3-27, 3-29, 3-30 (expert witness);
§§2-19, 3-31 (hypothetical question);
§§2-33, 3-16 (diagram by witness).

This assignment involves the direct and cross-examination of Cameron Himes, M.D., an expert witness in the trial of State of Ames v. Ina Mae Brawley. The trial and the witness's preliminary hearing testimony are described and summarized in Assignment 8A.

Firm A: You represent the state of Ames. Conduct the direct and any appropriate re-direct examination of Dr. Himes.

Firm B: You represent the defendant, Ina Mae Brawley. Conduct appropriate cross-examination of the doctor.

Either side may deem it advisable to present evidence through the use of a hypothetical question. If you intend to use such a question, prepare it in writing and deliver a copy of it to the instructor two days before class.

Both sides have obtained copies of an autopsy report prepared by Dr. Himes. Relevant portions of that report are set forth below.

AUSTIN GENERAL HOSPITAL

1217 Mount Auburn Boulevard

Austin, Ames 00327

Department of Pathology
Edgar H. Mullane, M.D.,
Chief Pathologist
Cameron Himes, M.D.,
Assistant Pathologist

Name: Geraldine Jelks
Address: Factory Ave., E. Austin, Ames
Receiving #: 238
Date of Death: 10/17
[ ]Male [X]Female Age: 42

FINAL ANATOMIC DIAGNOSES

1. Puncture wound -- (1) laceration of abdom. aorta (2) laceration of liver (3) laceration of stomach
2. Exogenous obesity
3. Hepatic cirrhosis

EXTERNAL EXAMINATION: Height 65 inches. Estimated weight 165 pounds. Race: Caucasian. Sex: Female. The apparent age is consistent with the stated age. The body is obese. There are small superficial lacerations on the face. The pupils are normal. The mouth is normal. Examination of the extremities reveals small superficial lacerations on both arms. Gross examination of the abdomen reveals a 2.5 cm X 0.6 cm puncture wound transversally oriented in the midline 10.0 cm above the center of the umbilicus. A probe placed through the patent wound orifice moved easily to a depth of 10.0 cm nearly perpendicular to the surface of the abdomen.

INTERNAL EXAMINATION: The abdominal cavity was opened by means of the customary Y-shaped incision revealing a marked increase in subcutaneous fat. The contents of the peritoneal cavity were then inspected. The peritoneum contains free blood, much of it clotted. A total of 2350 cc of blood was aspirated. The abdominal organs have the usual relationship to each other. . . . The wound in the abdominal wall was seen to continue through the mid-transverse colon and through the mid portion of the fundus of the stomach. The through and through perforations of these organs measured 2.0 cm X 0.75 cm and 1.8 cm X 0.8 cm respectively. The parietal peritoneum immediately adjacent to the wounds was stained with liquid stool and bile. There is a laceration on the anterior aspect of the liver measuring 2.0 cm X 0.8 cm. The liver is enlarged. It extends 8.0 cm below the costal margin in the mid clavicular line. There is a 1.5 cm X 0.5 cm laceration in the anterior aspect of the abdominal aorta, 5.0 cm cephalic to the base of the greater celiac artery. Clotted blood extruded through this laceration. The remainder of the abdominal aorta is not remarkable. No other lacerations were found in adjacent organs. The remainder of the gross examination of the abdomen revealed no further pathology.

MICROSCOPIC EXAMINATION

<u>Liver</u>: Microscopic examination reveals moderate change consistent with alcoholic cirrhosis. There is moderate fatty infiltration and enlargement.
<u>Aorta</u>: Laceration of abdominal aorta. No evidence of organization of the wound was found.

TOXICOLOGY REPORT

Analysis of blood sample revealed an alcohol content of 0.26 per cent.

(signed) Cameron Himes, M.D.
Date: 10/17

Assignments in Trial Practice

ASSIGNMENT 9B

Study §§3-29 through 3-31 and 9-8 of the Text.

The special assignment is the direct and cross-examination of the witness Sergeant Winters in the case of <u>Lois E. Sommers, Administratrix of the Estate of Stanley O. Sommers, Deceased v. Ames Transfer Co.</u>, for which the basic materials are set forth in Assignment 8B.

<u>Firm A</u> (Counsel for plaintiff): Conduct the direct examination of the witness, putting in evidence, insofar as you consider desirable, Winters' opinions set forth in paragraph B of his statement and any other useful opinion he may be willing to express. <u>Do not</u> go into the opinion expressed in paragraph A of his statement and the foundation for it, since that has been covered in Assignment 8B.

To the extent you deem necessary or advisable, you may employ hypothetical questions to achieve your objectives. Some attorneys make a practice of typing out any lengthy hypothetical question in advance since it aids them in putting the question precisely as intended. As a courtesy, a copy may sometimes be given to opposing counsel, as the question is about to be asked. Others decline to do this for tactical reasons. For the purpose of this assignment, prepare copies in advance if you intend to use any lengthy hypothetical questions. Provide the instructor with a copy at least two days before the class session. If you deem it tactically advisable, you may supply a copy to opposing counsel as well.

<u>Firm B</u> (Counsel for defendant):

1. Attempt to keep out any opinion evidence offered during the direct examination unless you think it tactically preferable to allow it to be received (see Ground Rule 16).

2. Cross-examine Winters, observing the same limitations as to subject matter as set forth above for plaintiff.

3. Within these subject matter limitations, offer any opinions of Winters you consider useful. Consider the advisability of using hypothetical questions. If you do use them, follow the instructions to plaintiff concerning the advance preparation and distribution of such questions.

Counsel are to assume that Sergeant Winters' experiment and observations, upon which he based the opinion expressed in paragraph A of his statement, have just previously been received in evidence and that the direct examination is proceeding from that point.

Assignments in Trial Practice

Statement of Sergeant George Winters Taken by Defendant's Counsel on November 19, 19Y1

(Sergeant Winters was given a copy of this statement. Upon request by plaintiff's counsel, he allowed them to make a copy of it for their files.)

I am a sergeant with the state highway patrol. I have been with the force for eight years and have investigated several hundred accidents during that time.

In addition, I took an eight-week course at Ames University Law School Traffic Institute (a well-known and respected institution) this past summer in which we heard numerous lectures and studied slides and various books and articles dealing with automobile accidents, their causes, and the relationship between speed and the extent of damage to vehicles. Of course, the extent of damage is a function of a number of factors in addition to speed: a relatively "slow" accident can result in major damage, while a "fast" accident can occasionally result in only minor damage.

It's my opinion, however, that the Ford was probably going faster than 55 m.p.h. at the time of the accident. I base this opinion on the very extensive damage to the vehicles and based on my experience and studies on the subject.

It is obvious to me, however, that even if the Ford was going no faster than the speed limit, if the driver first saw the trailer blocking his path when he was 101 feet away from the point of impact, it would be impossible for him to have stopped in time. I don't have at my fingertips figures as to the reaction distance or the braking distance for that speed, but I have checked authoritative charts prepared by the Motor Vehicle Department of the State of Ames. I don't need them to know it couldn't be done in time. It is, in fact, my opinion that even if the car had been going as slowly as 45 m.p.h., there probably would not have been sufficient time to avert the accident.

There is a rule of thumb for translating miles-per-hour roughly to feet-per-second. You multiply the miles-per-hour by one and one-half. That gives you the approximate number of feet traveled per second. At 55 m.p.h., a car would thus travel about 82 feet per second.

The average reaction time for a person who recognizes a danger is about one second.

Assignments in Trial Practice

ASSIGNMENT 9C

Study the following sections of the Text:

§§2-15, 2-22, 3-27, 3-29, 3-30 (expert witness);
§§2-19, 3-31 (hypothetical question);

This assignment involves the direct and cross-examination of Thomas DeGowin, M.D., an expert witness in the trial of State v. Devereaux. A memorandum of law concerning the case and a record of trial proceedings appears in Appendix B. Counsel should assume that the trial has proceeded as set forth in Appendix B up to the point at which Dr. DeGowin is called as a rebuttal witness. This exercise replaces Dr. DeGowin's summarized testimony. The record in Appendix B is to be supplemented by the materials in Assignment 11B (examination and cross-examination of Irene Gossage). If the Gossage assignment is scheduled for performance prior to this one, counsel should have taken careful notes of the witness's actual testimony so as to incorporate it into the materials here. If the Gossage assignment has not been performed prior to this summation, counsel should presume that the substance of Mrs. Gossage's statement of June 15 (to the prosecution) has been introduced testimonially, and that her statement of July 30 (to the defense) was introduced as a defense exhibit for impeachment purposes.

Firm A: You represent the state of Ames. Conduct the direct and any appropriate re-direct examination of Dr. DeGowin.

Firm B: You represent the defendant. Conduct appropriate cross-examination of the doctor.

Either side may deem it advisable to present evidence through the use of a hypothetical question. If you intend to use such a question, prepare it in writing and deliver a copy of it to the instructor two days before class.

Assignments in Trial Practice

ASSIGNMENT 10A

Study Chapter VIII of the Text.

This assignment involves trial of a case before a jury. From the point of view of attorneys for each side, consider whether you would have been willing to waive jury trial in this case, and what difference the absence of a jury might have made in the trial.

Firm A (Counsel for plaintiff).

Firm B (Counsel for defendant).

Make the following assumptions about the law of Ames:

(1) Ames has no dead man statute.

(2) A gift of a motor vehicle may be completed without endorsement or execution of any document.

As to potential witnesses, assume that leads have been checked and that the only witnesses known to plaintiff's counsel who might be available and useful to either party at the trial are

(1) Maude Oliver, plaintiff and executrix of the estate of the late Harrison C. Oliver;

(2) Cynthia Ballew, the defendant; and

(3) Reginald Royce, owner and manager of Royce's Garage, 478 Main Street, Langdell.

A fourth live witness, Ernest Pike, will be available if the instructor assigns Alternative Assignment 10A-1 set forth at the end of this assignment.

In addition, Dr. Charles Singleton, personal physician to the Oliver family, has testified by deposition, and his deposition may be used at trial since he will be out of the state at that time.

Counsel for plaintiff are junior partners in the firm of Austin and Blackstone of Langdell. Counsel for defendant occupy a similar position with the firm of Mansfield and Kenyon of Gray. In each instance, they have been put in charge of the litigation. Pleadings have already been filed, and certain other preliminary steps have been taken, up to and including the selection of the jury. The time and place of trial will be announced by the instructor. Following the trial, a critique of the trial will be conducted at a time to be announced by the instructor. Students will be expected to attend the trial and the critique.

Assignments in Trial Practice

Supplementary Ground Rules

1. Each witness will be examined by only one attorney for each side. The examining attorney may, of course, receive suggestions from his associates.

2. Only one attorney for each side will participate in the summation. Each side will be allowed 20 minutes. The party not having the burden of proof will speak first and the party with the burden will close.

3. Each side shall file requests for instructions with the instructor, after first serving a copy upon opposing counsel, and in no event later than five days before trial.

4. Pre-trial motions, if at all possible, should not be presented to the judge until immediately preceding the commencement of trial. If counsel consider it indispensable to have a ruling on a motion earlier than that in order to prepare properly for trial, they will serve a copy of such motion upon opposing counsel and then file it with the instructor. The instructor will then decide whether or not to hear the motion before trial.

5. The procedure of bench conferences at the practice trial will depart from that followed in the weekly exercises. Counsel will literally approach the bench and conduct the bench conference in the manner of an actual trial situation. If the conference is an extended one, the court may excuse the jury and have counsel present their argument from counsel table so the class may hear the proceedings.

Assignments in Trial Practice

IN THE SUPERIOR COURT FOR THE COMMONWEALTH OF AMES

COUNTY OF THAYER

MAUDE OLIVER, Executrix of the Estate)
        of Harrison C. Oliver) Civil Action
        Deceased, Plaintiff   ) File No. 9569
)
   v.   )
)
CYNTHIA BALLEW, Defendant   )

COMPLAINT

1. The plaintiff and the defendant are residents of Langdell, County of Thayer, Commonwealth of Ames.

2. At the time of his death, plaintiff's decedent, Harrison C. Oliver, was the owner of a 19Y3 Mercedes-Benz sedan. At that time, the fair market value of the said automobile was $39,000.

3. The said Harrison C. Oliver died on November 10, 19Y1. On or about November 14, 19Y1, the defendant, one Cynthia Ballew, did wrongfully take from the premises of the deceased the said automobile. The plaintiff had demanded return of the said automobile; but the defendant has refused and continues to refuse to return the automobile.

Wherefore, the plaintiff prays judgment for the sum of $39,000, the fair market value of the said automobile, together with interest and costs.

                                                 /s/ <u>Henry B. Austin</u>
                                                    Attorney for Plaintiff
                                                    58 Williston Place
                                                    Langdell, Ames

Plaintiff demands a trial by jury of the above cause.
                                          /s/ <u>Henry B. Austin</u>
                                                Attorney for Plaintiff

IN THE SUPERIOR COURT FOR THE COMMONWEALTH OF AMES

COUNTY OF THAYER

MAUDE OLIVER, Executrix of the Estate)
       of Harrison C. Oliver) Civil Action
       Deceased, Plaintiff   ) File No. 9569
)
)
   v.   )
)
CYNTHIA BALLEW, Defendant   )

DEFENDANT'S ANSWER

    1. The defendant admits the allegations of paragraph 1 of the complaint.

    2. The defendant admits that the fair market value of the car was $39,000 but denies all other allegations contained in paragraph 2 of the complaint.

    3. The defendant admits that Harrison C. Oliver died on November 10, 19Y1. The defendant further admits that on or about November 14, 19Y1, she did take a 19Y3 Mercedes-Benz sedan from the premises of the deceased, but denies that the taking was in any way wrongful. The defendant admits that the plaintiff has demanded return of the automobile, but that the defendant refuses to return it.

    Wherefore the defendant prays judgment dismissing the complaint.

                                            /s/ <u>Charles Kenyon</u>
                                               Attorney for Defendant
                                               165 Beale Avenue
                                               Gray, Ames

Defendant demands a trial by jury.

                                            /s/ <u>Charles Kenyon</u>
                                             Attorney for Defendant

Assignments in Trial Practice

Plaintiff's File Materials
Memorandum to File

November 23, 19Y1

Miss Maude Oliver, 1 River Oaks Boulevard, Langdell, Ames, has retained us to recover for her a 19Y3 Mercedes-Benz sedan which was the property of her late brother, Harrison C. Oliver. Miss Oliver is the executrix of her brother's estate, and, excepting certain charitable bequests, the sole beneficiary under his will. She says, in summary, that the car is now in possession of one Cynthia Ballew, her brother's private nurse from September until his death in mid-November, just a few days past. Her statement to me is attached.

H. B. Austin

Statement of Maude Oliver

My name is Maude Oliver. I lived with my brother, Harrison C. Oliver, at 1 River Oaks Boulevard, until his death on November 10, 19Y1. I have known Cynthia Ballew since she took the position as my brother's nurse last September. He had decided to hire a private nurse while in Thayer Memorial Hospital due to a broken hip, and retained Miss Ballew just a few days before he came home in mid-September. She was a pleasant young woman and an efficient nurse. It was plain that my brother liked her, but I never heard a word from either of them about being engaged, nor did I see any sign of a romantic attachment. I never heard my brother or Miss Ballew say anything about his giving her his Mercedes-Benz.

On October 27, my brother refractured his hip in a fall and had to return to the hospital. Miss Ballew continued to occupy a room in our home and served as one of his private nurses at the hospital.

On Friday, November 6, my car was laid up for repairs, and I asked my brother if he would lend me his car for the weekend. He said: "Of course, you know you are welcome to use my car any time, Maude." He told me to get the keys from Miss Ballew, saying he had given them to her in order that she might have the semi-annual inspection made. When I got the keys from her, she told me that she had to go back to the garage again because she hadn't taken along the registration papers when she went in the preceding Tuesday to get the car inspected. I used the car until November 8.

When Miss Ballew returned home that night, she said: "May I have the keys to Harrison's car? He wants me to get the inspection certificate for him tomorrow." Naturally, I gave her the keys.

On the morning of November 9, Dr. Charles Singleton, an old family friend, as well as my brother's doctor, called at the house as Miss

Ballew and I were finishing breakfast. He told the two of us that he was the bearer of bad news; that Harrison had developed virus pneumonia during the night and was in critical condition. In fact, he said that Harrison might not live out the day.

Miss Ballew was very sweet and comforting to me that morning before she left for the hospital. She drove the Mercedes when she left. But she said nothing about the supposed gift then, or at any other time before she took the car away on the 14th.

I would want her to have the car if I thought it was Harrison's wish, but I am convinced that her story is made up out of whole cloth.

/s/ Maude Oliver

November 23, 19Y1

Memorandum to File

Charles Kenyon, counsel for the defendant in this case, called me with a view to the taking of Miss Oliver's deposition. I told him that Miss Oliver was, on her doctor's advice, on a trip to Europe and would not return until shortly before the date of trial. Mr. Kenyon said that he would have to insist upon a postponement of the trial in order to permit him to take this deposition. We finally reached an understanding that I would give him a copy of the statement of Miss Oliver in our file and that he would not press his request for a deposition.

H.B.A.

Deposition of Cynthia Ballew Taken at the Instance of Plaintiff's Counsel on December 28, 19Y1

DIRECT EXAMINATION BY PLAINTIFF'S COUNSEL

Q. 1. State your name, age, address, and marital status, please. A. I am Cynthia Ballew; age 24; single. My address is 412 Locust Avenue, Apt. 3, Langdell, Ames.

Q. 2. Thank you, Miss Ballew.

Q. (3-29 Summarized.) I am employed at Thayer Memorial Hospital. I am a registered nurse. I started in nursing school when I was eighteen. After graduation from the nursing school in Gray, Ames, I worked in the Gray City Hospital until May of 19Y1, when I decided to move to Langdell. I placed my name with the personnel office at the Thayer Memorial Hospital, and through them got several placements as a private nurse. In early September, 19Y1, I was invited to see Mr. Harrison C. Oliver, a patient at the hospital, about possible employment. Mr. Oliver was fifty-five years of age. He had sustained a broken hip and leg a few weeks previously, and wanted to employ a private nurse who would continue to serve him at his home, as he was expecting to leave the hospital in a few days but would be unable to get about except by wheelchair. I took the job, served as his private nurse at the hospital for about a week, and continued in that position after he was released from the hospital about mid-September. On October 27, 19Y1, Harry fell out of his bed during the night and refractured his hip. He was returned to the Thayer Hospital for treatment, and, of course, I served one of the three eight hour shifts as private nurse, as well as being with him at other times. He appeared to be well on the way to recovery by November 8, but in the early morning hours of the ninth, the night nurse discovered that he had developed a virus pneumonia condition. Somehow he did not respond to treatment. His condition got steadily worse, and he died on November 10.

Q. 30. Miss Ballew, did you take Mr. Oliver's Mercedes-Benz and drive it away on the morning of November 14, 19Y1, the day after Mr. Oliver's funeral? A. Yes, I did.

Q. 31. Did you give Miss Maude Oliver, or anyone else in the household, any notice or hint that you were going to take the car? A. No, I did not.

Q. 32. So you took Mr. Oliver's car and left rather quietly at an early morning hour on the fourteenth? A. I don't like your insinuation. I wasn't trying to hide anything.

Q. 33. Can you explain your rather furtive behavior? A. Of course. I was shocked and grieved by Harry's death, and the situation was even harder on me because his sister seemed to blame me for Harry's death. She never had a kind word for me, and she insinuated that my grief was a synthetic and transparent attempt to play on her sympathies. Consequently, I did not try to talk with her when I left. I decided there was nothing more I could do, in view of her attitude, so I took my car, which Harry had given me, and left.

Q. (34-37 Summarized.) When I left on the morning of November 14, I drove over to the city of Gray, which is about sixty miles from Langdell, and later in the day I was stopped by the police and told that I had been charged with theft of the car. I told them the car was mine; that Harry had given it to me, and I would not permit them to take it back.

Q. 38. Did you consult with counsel as to whether you should surrender the car. A. Yes, I did.

Q. 39. Will you please tell us the substance of your talk with your counsel at that time?

    DEFENDANT'S COUNSEL: I advise the witness not to answer.

    PLAINTIFF'S COUNSEL: All right. Now will you answer the question, Miss Ballew?

A. I refuse to answer the question on advice of my lawyer.

Q. 40. You still have the car, do you? A. Yes, I do.

Q. 41. Would you tell us under what circumstances you claim Mr. Oliver gave you the car? A. It was at the hospital on the afternoon of November 3, 19Y1. He was much improved that day, and I took him out onto the sunporch at the hospital in a wheelchair.

Q. 42. Who else was present on the sunporch? A. No one. We were alone.

Q. 43. Please tell us what happened. A. He was excited about the expectation of being out of the hospital again, and he was very sweet to me. He had told me earlier that day that he was in love with me, and we had become engaged. Then he told me he was giving me the car.

Q. 44. Would you please tell us in substance what each of you said on the sunporch relating to the car? A. He told me he was giving me his Mercedes-Benz as an engagement gift. I was thrilled, and I accepted the gift. Of course, I thanked him. Then he gave me the keys.

Q. 45. What, if anything, did he say to you when he gave you the keys? A. He said, "Here are the keys." Then he said, "By the way, when you get a chance, you may want to take the car into my garage for a check-up. It's about due for one."

Q. 46. Did he say anything else? A. Not that I can remember.

Q. 47. Did Mr. Oliver ever in your presence tell anyone else about his giving the car to you? A. No, he didn't. In fact, he asked me not to mention the gift to his sister until he had had a chance to tell her in his own way about our engagement, which he said he would do at the first good opportunity.

Q. 48. When was the next time you went to the sunporch with him? A. As a matter of fact, that was the only time I ever took him on the sunporch.

Q. 49. You never went to the sunporch with him after that? A. Never.

Q. 50. Or before that occasion? A. No.

Q. 51. Did Mr. Oliver ever sign over title to the car to you? A. No. He died before he had the chance to.

PLAINTIFF'S COUNSEL: No further questions.

CROSS-EXAMINATION BY DEFENDANT'S COUNSEL

(Summarized.) Miss Maude Oliver was Harry's sister and I tried to be nice to her on that account. From the very first, Harry was wonderful to me, and I fell in love with him. We soon grew very close. His sister meant a lot to him too. She had never been married, and she was his only living relative. They had lived together for some years in the old family homestead, which is a kind of landmark in the River Oaks section of the city. His sister obviously did not like me, and she tried to turn Harry against me. In her presence he pretended a very formal relationship with me and spoke to me rather formally as Cynthia, but when she was not around he would be very sweet and close. He was always a perfect gentleman.

Assignments in Trial Practice

Deposition of Dr. Charles Singleton Taken at the Instance
of Plaintiff's Counsel on December 28, 19Y1

DIRECT EXAMINATION BY PLAINTIFF'S COUNSEL

Q. 1. State your name, age, address, and occupation, please. A. My name is Charles Singleton. I am a physician. I reside at 44 Bancroft Way, Langdell, Ames. I am 47 years old.

Q. 2. Were you acquainted with Harrison C. Oliver? A. Yes, I was his personal physician for better than 15 years.

Q. 3. Were you acquainted with Miss Maude Oliver? A. Yes, I think I could properly say that I became a good friend of the Oliver family, after being their doctor for some time.

Q. 4. Did you attend Mr. Oliver during his last illness? A. Yes.

Q. 5. Did you have occasion to call at the Oliver home on the morning of November 9, 19Y1? A. Yes, I did, on a very sad errand.

Q. 6. What was the nature of that errand? A. Well, as you know Harrison Oliver unexpectedly became critically ill that morning, and died the next day. When I reached the hospital early on the morning of the 9th, I learned of his condition. As soon after that as I could, I went to see Miss Oliver, thinking it best that I tell her myself.

Q. 7. Who was at the Oliver house when you arrived? A. Miss Oliver was there, and Miss Ballew, Harrison's nurse. They were in the dining room, just finishing breakfast. As I said, it was quite early in the morning.

Q. 8. What did you tell them? A. Well, I don't remember the precise words I used. But, as I recall, I told them that when I reached the hospital that morning, very early, I discovered that Harrison had developed pneumonia during the night, that he was not responding as we had hoped to treatment, and that his condition was very serious. Trying not to be too blunt, I believe I conveyed to Miss Oliver that Harrison might not live.

Q. 9. Doctor, could you describe Miss Oliver's reaction? A. It was quite as you'd expect; shocked and a bit unwilling to believe, and then, well, trying quite hard not to cry.

Q. 10. Did you note any reaction on the part of Miss Ballew? A. I wasn't really watching her as much, and of course she is a professional nurse, more accustomed to these things; but she seemed concerned, as anyone would be. However, I'd say she was pretty calm.

Q. 11. Then you'd say she reacted like a conscientious nurse, but nothing more?

DEFENDANT'S COUNSEL: Just a moment, Doctor. Let the record show we object. The question is leading, and the answer would be irrelevant in any event.

PLAINTIFF'S COUNSEL: All right. I'll rephrase it.

Q. 12. Doctor, did you notice anything about Miss Ballew's reaction at that time? A. Yes, she seemed a bit surprised and concerned, as I said. But more professionally so than anything else. She didn't react the way Maude did at all.

PLAINTIFF'S COUNSEL: Thank you Doctor. No further questions.

CROSS-EXAMINATION BY DEFENDANT'S COUNSEL

X. 1. Doctor, am I right in assuming you were more than the Oliver's physician? That you were a good friend of Harrison Oliver? A. Yes, I became a good friend, you might say, out of the doctor-patient relationship.
X. 2. Mr. Oliver was some years your senior, was he not? A. Yes, he was about eight years older than I.
X. 3. Were you also a good friend of Miss Oliver? A. I was a good friend of both.
X. 4. About how often did you see them socially? A. Over the past five years or so, about once a month, on the average.
X. 5. Do you still see Miss Oliver socially? A. I have called on her at her home, naturally, as have other friends since Harrison died. However, she has not entertained. It has been hardly two months you know.
X. 6. I understand, of course. Now, Doctor, if you please; could you tell us if you knew Miss Ballew? A. Yes, of course. She had been Harrison's nurse since September.
X. 7. As his physician, did you have any reservations about her performance as a nurse? A. No, she seemed quite competent for his needs.
X. 8. Did you have any other acquaintance with her? A. None whatsoever.
X. 9. One last question, please. Are you married? A. I am a widower, since 1979.

DEFENDANT'S COUNSEL: That's all, thank you.

PLAINTIFF'S COUNSEL: Thank you, Doctor. I have no further questions.

<u>Statement of Reginald Royce Taken
by Plaintiff's Counsel on December 2, 19Y1</u>

(Mr. Royce insisted on being left a copy of his statement. Upon defendant's counsel's subsequent effort to interview him, he informed them he had said all he had to say in his statement to plaintiff's counsel. He permitted them to make a copy of his copy for their file but refused to discuss the matter with them further.)

I am Reginald Royce, owner and manager of Royce's Garage, 478 Main Street, Langdell. Servicing of foreign cars is our specialty.

Harrison C. Oliver was one of our customers. According to our records, his 19Y3 Mercedes-Benz, 19Y1 Ames Registration 123-456, was in our shop for routine, semi-annual inspections on April 10, 19Y1, and on November 9, 19Y1. Mr. Oliver brought the car himself on April 10. For the November inspection his nurse, Cynthia Ballew, first brought the car in about ten days before November 9, 19Y1.

I said to her, "Well, this is the first time I've even seen anyone other than Mr. Oliver driving this car that he treats like a baby. He must really trust you." She replied that he couldn't very well bring it in himself since he was in the hospital. After I expressed regret and inquired about how he was getting along, she said Mr. Oliver wanted her to be sure the car was inspected on time, before the November 15 deadline. I asked her if she had the registration certificate with her, and when she said no, I told her I would have to have it before I could prepare the inspection certificate.

The next time I saw her driving the car was on the afternoon of November 8. She was coming out of Pirate's Cove Road toward the main highway just as I was turning off the highway to go down to the beach. It was about 2 p.m. I honked my horn and waved to her, and she waved back as we passed. I saw her only momentarily, but I am sure in my own mind it was she and that she was driving Mr. Oliver's car.

The only other time I have ever seen her driving this car was when she came back to the garage on November 9, 19Y1. On the 9th, she was bubbling over with conversation about the car being hers now because "Harry had given it to me." I took her seriously at first, but when she handed me the registration certificate, I saw that it had not been endorsed over to her, and I said, "You'll have a hard time proving it's yours as long as the registration certificate is not endorsed." She seemed crestfallen and asked if I couldn't make out the inspection certificate and report in her name, since "Harry wants it that way." She offered no explanation for such a valuable gift, and I assumed she was joking. I replied to the effect that I'd better make out the certificate in Harry's name if Harry didn't want her put in jail. I completed the inspection and the certificate in the routine way.

Defendant's File Materials

Assume that you have in your files all the materials in the plaintiff's file except Mr. Austin's Memoranda to File.

Assignments in Trial Practice

ALTERNATIVE ASSIGNMENT 10A-1

The instructor may change this assignment by adding an additional witness, Ernest Pike, who is described in the following letter from Cynthia Ballew to her attorney.

Letter from Cynthia Ballew to Her Attorney

It seems to me that if there's any justice, I should win this case. I'm confident I will, too, except for one thing which troubles me. I heard from some of my friends at the hospital that Ernest Pike plans to testify against me. I don't have any idea what he can testify about, since he had nothing at all to do with me or Mr. Oliver during the period I knew Mr. Oliver. But I don't know what kind of lies he may cook up. I met Ernest in May of 19Y1, when I first moved to Langdell. He was and is a technician at Thayer Memorial Hospital, where I met him. We started to go together, first casually, but more seriously after a few months. He, however, became a good deal more serious about our relationship than I wanted. He was very demanding and possessive and we began to quarrel a lot. By the end of August, I had decided the best thing would be if we broke off and didn't see each other any more. He argued with me and said I was making a very big mistake -- that I was hurting him and in the long run would be hurting myself too.

I insisted, however, that we end our relationship, and we did. The last time I saw him, except casually in the hospital corridors, was at the end of August.

He is very bitter and vindictive, and I don't known how far he'd go in this trial to hurt me.

Assignments in Trial Practice

ASSIGNMENT 10B

Study Chapter VIII of the Text.

The special case for this week's assignment will be tried before a jury. From the point of view of attorneys for each party, consider whether you would have been willing to waive jury trial in this case, and what difference the absence of a jury might have made in the trial.

Firm A (Counsel for plaintiff.)

Firm B (Counsel for defendant.)

Attached you will find file materials concerning the case of Lynch v. Ames Insurance Co. As to potential witnesses, assume that all leads have been checked and that the only available witnesses who might be useful in the trial are:

(1) the plaintiff, Marie V. Lynch,
(2) Lieutenant John A. O'Malley of the Langdell police force,
(3) Roger P. Johnson, driver for Langdell Bus Company,
(4) Dr. Bertram A. Fieldstone, medical examiner for Thayer County, and
(5) Amanda Rogers, resident at 120 Intervale Street.

Dr. Ahearn, who had treated the decedent in years past, died in November, 19Y1, and his records have been destroyed.

The time and place of trial will be announced by the instructor. Following the trial, a critique will be conducted at a time also to be announced. Students will be expected to attend the trial and the critique.

Supplementary Ground Rules

1. Each witness will be examined by only one attorney for each side. The examining attorney may, of course, receive suggestions from his associates.

2. Only one attorney for each side will participate in the summation. Each side will be allowed 20 minutes. The party not having the burden of proof will speak first and the party with the burden will close.

3. Each side shall file requests for instructions with the instructor, after first serving a copy upon opposing counsel, and in no event later than five days before trial.

4. Pre-trial motions, if at all possible, should not be presented to the judge until immediately preceding the commencement of trial. If

counsel consider it indispensable to have a ruling on a motion earlier than that in order to prepare properly for trial, they will serve a copy of such motion upon opposing counsel and then file it with the instructor. The instructor will then decide whether or not to hear the motion before trial.

5. The procedure of bench conferences at the practice trial will depart from that followed in the weekly exercises. Counsel will literally approach the bench and conduct the bench conference in the manner of an actual trial situation. If the conference is an extended one, the court may excuse the jury and have counsel present their argument from counsel table so the class may hear the proceedings.

Ames Statute

Ames Stat. §46-19 provides:

The record of the city registrar relative to a birth, marriage, or death shall be prima facie evidence of the facts recorded, but nothing contained in the record of a death which has reference to the question of liability for causing the death shall be admissible in evidence. A certificate of such a record signed by the city registrar or a certificate of the copy of the record thereof, required to be kept in the state secretary's office, signed by said state secretary or one of his deputies, shall be admissible as evidence of such record.

Excerpts from Memorandum of First Interview of Plaintiff by Plaintiff's Counsel

(Defendant's attorneys have the same information in the form of a memorandum of information given to them orally by Lieutenant O'Malley, the statements attributed to Mrs. Lynch having been made orally to O'Malley.)

Marie V. Lynch, 75 Pound Avenue, Langdell, widow of Timothy Lynch, deceased October 25, 19Y1. Mrs. Lynch is the beneficiary of life insurance policy issued by The Ames Insurance Company (No. 24759) on the life of her husband. She says the insurance company representative told her that the company would not pay her the amount of the policy because her husband had committed suicide. He did offer to return the first year's premium to her. The policy has the standard contestable clause for suicide.

Mrs. Lynch says her husband had just resigned from the police force in July, 19Y1, to go into business with another man, a Mr. Palmer, operating a bar known as Lynch's Cafe. They opened up in August and business at first was not too good. Mr. Lynch seemed to worry a lot about the business. One day Palmer came to her and asked her to have Lynch see a doctor; he was worrying too much and Palmer was afraid he might have a breakdown. At Mrs. Lynch's request Lynch went to see Dr. Ahearn, at 118 Intervale Street, whom he had known for many years and in whom he had great confidence. Dr. Ahearn lived in the third-floor apartment and Lynch on occasion would see him there. Dr. Ahearn died on November 12, 19Y1.

Lynch apparently had a partial disability from the Veterans's Administration for a condition called "anxiety." Dr. Ahearn gave Lynch some pills which Mrs. Lynch believed were tranquilizers.

On the morning of October 25, Lynch left the house early and took the car, which was registered in his wife's name. Mrs. Lynch did not know where he was going, but she presumed he was going to clean up the bar. There had been a fight there the night before and there was quite a bit of damage. Shortly after 8:00 a.m., she received a call from a Dr. Ingersoll at City Hospital, who said her husband had been found on Intervale Street and brought to the hospital. She went to the hospital and was told her husband was dead, and she was directed to Southern Mortuary where she identified the body. He was 38 years old, about 5 feet, 10 inches, dark complexion, 165 pounds. He was dressed in black pants and a brown leather jacket.

The medical examiner's report shows the cause of death was suicide. Mrs. Lynch doesn't believe that her husband would have committed suicide and left her with three small children to take care of.

Mrs. Lynch says that police believe that her husband had tried to jump in front of a Langdell Bus Company bus, about a half an hour before he was found on Intervale Street.

Police Journal Report -- Division 4   October 25, 19Y1

   7:15 a.m. Received a call from starter at Langdell Bus Company car barn that one of his drivers had just reported a man who tried to jump in front of his bus. Driver avoided man, who escaped. Did not get complete description. Man drove a blue 19Y3 Ford. Driver's name, Roger P. Johnson.
                                        /s/ Sgt. Lamson

   7:45 a.m. Received call from woman at 120 Intervale Street reporting a hit-and-run accident. Proceeded with Patrolman O'Brien to scene. Found body of man later identified as Timothy Lynch lying in middle of street 14 feet from curb. Ordered ambulance and upon arrival dispatched to Ames City Hospital. Lynch pronounced dead on arrival 8:00 a.m. (Dr. Ingersoll.) Body removed to Southern Mortuary, medical examiner notified. Widow notified.

   Conducted investigation with Patrolman O'Brien and found blue 19Y3 Ford sedan model parked on Corbin Street registered in name of deceased's wife. Woman who placed call was identified as Amanda Rogers. She is married and lives with her husband. She said she was leaving her residence at about 7:45 a.m. While locking her door she was aware of the sound of a truck passing and then she heard a thump; turned around and saw man lying in street, and dark color truck, stake body, moving away from scene going downhill on Intervale towards Warren. She did not hear any screech of brakes. Did not know deceased. She did not get a very good look at the truck because her view was obscured by two or three cars on the right side (even-numbered side of Intervale). She thinks the truck was about 50 feet beyond the body, which was in front of No. 118, but this is a rather hazy impression. She does not drive a car herself and is not very good at estimating speeds, but she would say the truck was going "pretty fast." She assumed that this was a hit-and-run accident and immediately went back into the house and telephoned a report to Division 4 to report hit-and-run accident.

   She did not go out again or even look out the window until after the body was removed because she wished to escape any further view of this unpleasant sight. Actually, she felt a bit ill. Her impression of where the body was when she saw it was that it was pretty close to the curb on her side of the street, no more than three or four feet, she thought.

   Investigated premises at 118 Intervale and found stairway to roof open and hatch cover pushed back. Deceased, a former Langdell policeman, is part owner of Lynch's Cafe, having acquired the same in July of this year. Partner reports that Lynch had been worried about business.
                                        /s/ Lt. O'Malley

Assignments in Trial Practice

Accident Report -- Roger P. Johnson, Driver (Ames Avenue Route)

Langdell Bus Company
October 25, 19Y1

About 7:05 a.m., while proceeding in trackless trolley toward car barn on Ames Avenue, I observed man crouching between parked cars. As I approached he suddenly dived head first in front of bus. I swerved and stopped suddenly. I got out of bus, the man got up and started to run away. I grabbed for him, but he wrenched away and knocked me down.

He got in blue 19Y3 Ford and drove off. I didn't get too good a look at him, but he was dark and I think he had on a jacket of some kind.

Three passengers claimed injury from sudden stop. Names attached.

Reported to starter, who called police.

/s/ R.P. Johnson

Assignments in Trial Practice

IN THE SUPERIOR COURT FOR THE COMMONWEALTH OF AMES,

COUNTY OF THAYER

<u>Marie V. Lynch</u>,)
       Plaintiff)
)
) Civil Action No. 6548
)
v.)
)
<u>The Ames Insurance Company</u>,)
       Defendant)

<u>COMPLAINT</u>

1. The plaintiff is a resident of Langdell, County of Thayer, Commonwealth of Ames, and the defendant is an insurance corporation duly organized and existing under the laws of Ames and having its principal place of business in the said Langdell.

2. The plaintiff's husband, Timothy Lynch, entered into a contract of life insurance with the defendant, as evidenced by Policy No. 24759, in which the plaintiff was named beneficiary, wherein the defendant agreed to pay the said beneficiary the amount of $50,000.00 in the event of the death of Timothy Lynch.

3. The said Timothy Lynch died on October 25, 19Y1, at which time the said policy was in full force and effect. Due proof of loss was submitted to the defendant and all other requirements contained in the policy have been complied with by the plaintiff. Plaintiff has demanded and defendant has refused payment of said amount, and there is now due and owing from defendant to plaintiff the sum of $50,000.00 plus interest thereon.

Wherefore, the plaintiff prays judgment for the sum of $50,000.00, the face amount of said policy, together with interest and costs.

                                    /s/ <u>Joseph P. Langdon</u>
                                        Attorney for Plaintiff
                                        58 Williston Place
                                        Langdell, Ames

Plaintiff demands a trial by jury.

                                    /s/ <u>Joseph P. Langdon</u>

IN THE SUPERIOR COURT FOR THE COMMONWEALTH OF AMES,

COUNTY OF THAYER

Marie V. Lynch,
       Plaintiff

v.

The Ames Insurance Company,
       Defendant

Civil Action No. 6548

DEFENDANT'S ANSWER

Now comes the defendant in the above-entitled action and answers the plaintiff's complaint as follows:

First Defense

1. The defendant admits the allegations of paragraphs 1 and 2 of the complaint, except the defendant denies that the policy provided for payment "in the event of the death of Timothy Lynch," and says that there were further qualifications of such promise, the policy itself being the best evidence thereof.

2. Defendant admits that Timothy Lynch died on October 25, 19Y1; that the policy was in force; and that due notice and proof of loss was filed, but defendant denies all other allegations of paragraph 3 of the complaint.

Second Defense

Further answering, the defendant says that the policy date of the policy declared upon the plaintiff is October 3, 19Y1; that Timothy Lynch committed suicide on or about October 25, 19Y1; that under the terms of the policy declared upon by the plaintiff, death from suicide within two years from the policy date, whether the insured is sane or insane, shall limit the company's liability to the return of the amount of premiums paid; and that the defendant has tendered to the plaintiff the amount of premiums paid on said policy, but that plaintiff has refused said tender.

Wherefore, the defendant prays judgment that plaintiff take nothing.

                /s/ Thomas P. Wilson
                    Attorney for Defendant
                    164 Williston Plaza
                    Langdell, Ames

Assignments in Trial Practice

IN THE SUPERIOR COURT FOR THE COMMONWEALTH OF AMES,

COUNTY OF THAYER

<u>Marie V. Lynch</u>,)
        Plaintiff)
)
) Civil Action No. 6548
v.)
)
<u>The Ames Insurance Company</u>,)
        Defendant)

<u>PRE-TRIAL STIPULATION</u>

1. Plaintiff is the widow of Timothy Lynch, late of Langdell, Ames, who died on October 25, 19Y1.

2. On October 3, 19Y1, the defendant issued a policy of life insurance, No. 24759, to Timothy Lynch on his life in the amount of $50,000.00. The said policy was in full force and effect at the time of Timothy Lynch's death. The plaintiff was named as beneficiary of said policy.

3. Timothy Lynch was pronounced dead on arrival at Ames City Hospital on October 25, 19Y1, at 8:00 a.m., and the body was then taken to the Southern Mortuary, where it was identified by the plaintiff.

4. At the time of his death, Timothy Lynch was 38 years of age and was part owner of Lynch's Cafe, a bar located at the intersection of Peters Avenue and Story Road in Langdell.

5. After the death of Timothy Lynch, defendant tendered to plaintiff an amount equal to the first year's premium on Policy No. 24759, and plaintiff declined to accept.

6. Due notice and proof of loss, as required by the policy, have been filed.

7. The following exhibits are true copies of the documents they purport to represent, and no further authentication will be required. Objections on grounds other than authentication are reserved:

    Exhibit A. Excerpt from Policy No. 24759, issued by the defendant on the life of Timothy Lynch.

    Exhibit B. Death certificate issued by Dr. Bertram A. Fieldstone, medical examiner of Thayer County, on the death of Timothy Lynch.

Exhibit C. Autopsy findings, medical examiner, County of Thayer, concerning Timothy Lynch, deceased.

Exhibit D. Plan of certain streets in Langdell, Ames. North is towards the top of this diagram.

8. The following exhibits are true and accurate representations of the scenes shown, and no further authentication will be required. Objections on grounds other than authentication are reserved:

Exhibit No. 1. Photograph of residential block on Intervale Street, taken from opposite side of street, the camera pointing in a southwesterly direction. The entrance to No. 118 Intervale Street is the third door from the left of the picture, and No. 120 Intervale Street is the fourth door from the left of the picture.

Exhibit No. 2. Photograph taken from roof of No. 118 Intervale Street, Langdell, with the camera pointing downward and across the street in a northwesterly direction.

EXHIBIT A

Policy No. 24759, dated October 3, 19Y1, was issued by The Ames Insurance Company to Timothy Lynch, designating Marie V. Lynch as beneficiary. This was a five-year term policy, renewable to age 65, obtained at age 38. The premium was $446.50 annually. The first annual premium was paid in cash in advance. The policy contained the following provisions:

> The Ames Insurance Company . . . will pay the face amount of the policy, $50,000.00, to the beneficiary immediately upon receipt at the Home Office of due proof of the insured's death, subject to the provisions of this policy.
>
> Death from suicide within two years from the policy date, whether the insured is sane or insane, shall limit the company's liability to the return of the amount of premiums paid.

EXHIBIT B

HEALTH DEPARTMENT -- REGISTRY DIVISION, CITY OF LANGDELL
County of Thayer, Commonwealth of Ames, United States of America
Certified Copy of Record of DEATH in Office of the City Registrar
Certificate No. 588032

I, the undersigned, hereby certify that I hold the office of City Registrar of the City of Langdell and I certify the following facts appear on the records of Births, Marriages, and Deaths kept in said City as required by law.

No. 59882   Date of Death October 25, 19Y1

Name and surname of Deceased (If Married, Widowed, or Divorced, Maiden Name)

Timothy Lynch

Sex and Color	Condition (Single, Married, Widowed, Divorced)	Supposed Age Yrs. Mo. Days	Name & Surname of Husband or Maiden Name of Wife of Deceased	Residence
M	Married	38 -- --	Marie V. Lund	73 Pound Avenue
W				

Occupation and Place of Business	Place of Death	Place of Birth	Names & Birthplaces of Parents (Maiden Name of Mother)
Tavern Owner; Peters Avenue & Story Road, Langdell	120 Intervale Street Langdell	Langdell Ames	Daniel J. Lynch, Langdell Annie Hobart, Langdell

Medical Examiner	Disease or Cause of Death (Primary or Secondary)	Place of Burial (Name of Cemetery)
Dr. Bertram A. Fieldstone	Fracture of skull. Jumped from roof. Suicide during profound depression	Mt. Benedict Cemetery, Langdell

Date of Record: Oct. 29, 19Y1   Name of Undertaker: Frederick Horn
                                                     438 Seavey Avenue, Langdell

WITNESS my hand and the SEAL of the CITY REGISTRAR   (SEAL)
on this 18th Day of Dec., A.D. 19Y1

/s/ Charles C. Landers City Registrar

EXHIBIT C
AUTOPSY FINDINGS

OFFICE OF MEDICAL EXAMINER
County of Thayer

Deceased: Timothy Lynch   Age: 38   Date: October 25, 19Y1

The body is that of a white male; height 5 feet, 10 inches; weight 165 pounds.

Admitted to mortuary from Accident Ward at City Hospital.

Data from Dr. Ingersoll, City Hospital: "Subject admitted to City Hospital at 7:55 a.m. by police ambulance. Dead on arrival. Body found in street. Referred to medical examiner."

Body clothed in brown leather jacket, black cotton pants, black leather shoes, white shirt with open collar, T-shirt of white cotton, jockey shorts of white cotton, and colored rayon socks. Slight blood staining on anterior chest area of T-shirt.

Autopsy begun at 11:23 a.m., concluded at 12:45 p.m., then discharged to undertaker at 4:40 p.m.

Description of Findings:

Contusion, forehead bilaterally with ecchymosis.

Fracture, nose with displacement to right.

Laceration 1 inch long, left eyebrow.

Fracture, left supra-orbital region.

Fracture and depression, right zygoma with overlying contusion.

Skull: Stellate fracture, left parietal; bilateral fracture basilar

with extension on right to tempero-parietal suture.

Contusion of lips and chin.

Fracture of upper incisor teeth.

Fracture, rami of both mandibles.

Spine: Fracture of odontoid process of the axis, with posterior displacement of atlas.

Contusion of cervical spinal cord at first cervical level.

Brain: Contusion with ecchymosis, bilateral frontal cortex. Contusion and laceration, left parietal cortex.

Chest: Contusion and ecchymosis anterior chest wall, bilateral with fractures right 3, 4, 5, ribs anterior; and left 2, 3, 4 ribs anterior.

Heart: Ecchymosis anterior pericardium.

Abdomen: Contusion over anterior aspect liver; vertical anterior rupture of liver with bile leakage.

Pelvis: Fracture through left pubic ramus with posterior depression and dislocation.

One inch (1") rupture of bladder.

Extremities: Spiral fracture, right femur with fracture of socket.

Bilateral fracture, left lower leg (tibia and fibula).

Fracture, right patella with overlying contusion of skin.

Fracture, right clavicle.

Abrasions and contusions of volar surface, both forearms.

Fracture, right wrist with silver fork deformity.

Fracture, left humerus.

<u>Primary cause of death</u>: Fracture of skull.

<u>Secondary cause of death</u>: Suicide, profound depression. (Police Lt. O'Malley said deceased had been nervous and worried.)

/s/ <u>Bertram A. Fieldstone</u>
Medical Examiner for Thayer County

EXHIBIT D
DIAGRAM

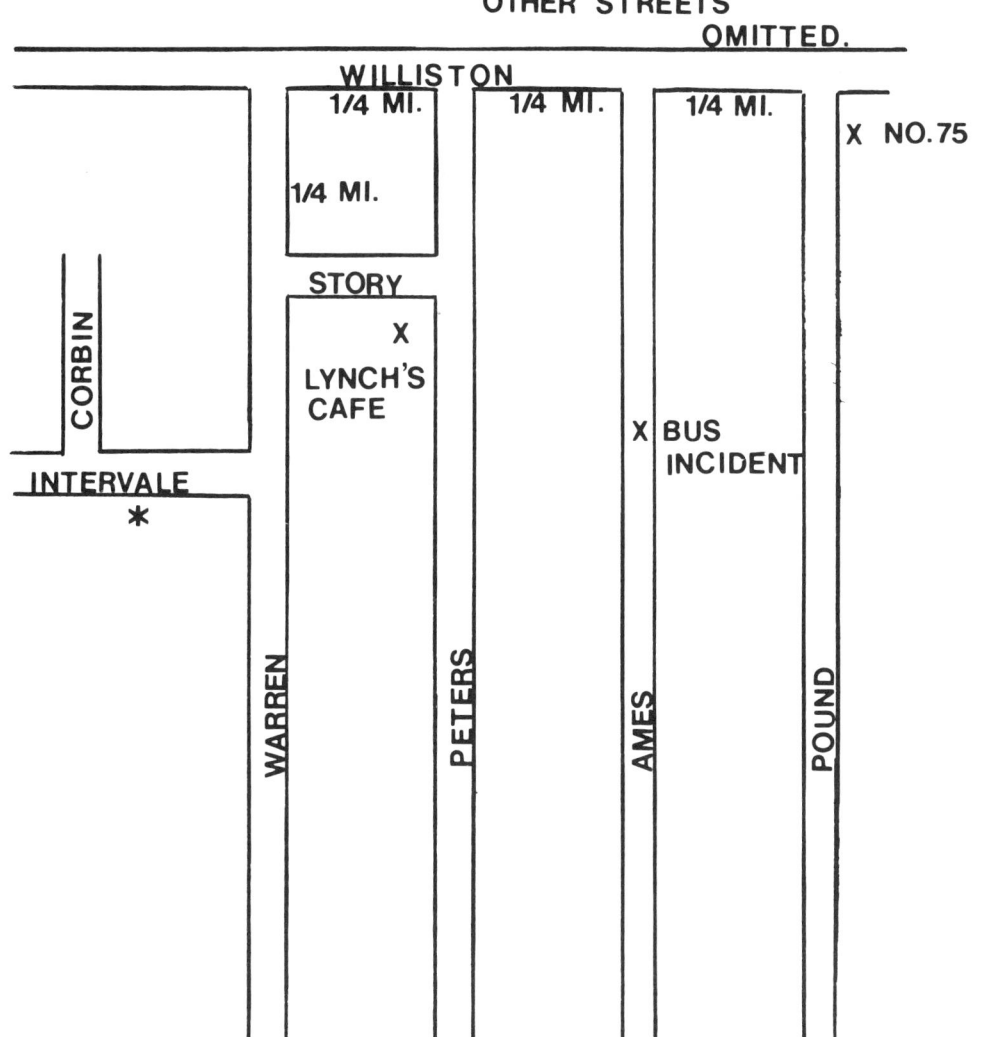

*NUMBER 120 INTERVALE; LOCATED 100 FEET FROM CORNER OF INTERVALE AND CORBIN.

WIDTH OF STREETS NOT DRAWN TO SCALE.

EXHIBIT NO. 1

EXHIBIT NO. 2

ASSIGNMENT 10C

Study Chapter VIII of the <u>Text</u>.

This problem involves the full trial of a medical malpractice case in which the plaintiff, Alan Myers, claims liability on the part of the defendant anesthesiologist, Dr. Henry Davis, for professional negligence and battery in the administration of anesthesia. The action will be assumed to have been commenced in the appropriate Ames Federal District Court, and further assumed that it will be tried to a jury on the liability issue alone. If the verdict is for plaintiff, damages, if not agreed upon by the parties, will be determined at a later separate trial.

<u>Firm A</u> (Counsel for plaintiff).

<u>Firm B</u> (Counsel for defendant).

The time and place of trial will be announced by the instructor. Following the trial, a critique of the trial will be conducted at a time to be announced by the instructor. Students will be expected to attend the trial and the critique.

Supplementary Ground Rules

1. Only three witnesses will testify: the plaintiff; Dr. Robert Kent (plaintiff's medical expert); and the defendant. Only one attorney may examine or cross-examine any particular witness, and only one attorney may make the opening and only one attorney the summation for each side. Despite the fact that damages are not in issue, plaintiff and Dr. Kent will be permitted to give otherwise admissible testimony concerning the symptoms, nature, and extent of Myer's injury, but without going into details relating to lost earnings, projected loss of future earning capacity, medical expenses, or the like.

2. Each side will be allowed 20 minutes for summation. The party not having the burden of proof will speak first, and the party with the burden will close.

3. Each side shall file requests for instructions with the instructor, after first serving a copy upon opposing counsel, and in no event later than five days before trial.

4. If at all possible, pre-trial motions should not be presented to the judge until immediately preceding the commencement of trial. If counsel consider it indispensable to have a ruling on a motion earlier than that in order to prepare properly for trial, they will serve a copy of such motion upon opposing counsel and then file it with the instructor. The instructor will then decide whether or not to hear the motion before trial.

Assignments in Trial Practice

5. The procedure of bench conferences at the practice trial will depart from that followed in the weekly exercises. Counsel will literally approach the bench and conduct the bench conference in the manner of an actual trial situation. If the conference is an extended one, the court may excuse the jury and have counsel present their argument from counsel table so the class may hear the proceedings.

Summary of Pleadings: Count I of the complaint alleged that in his intravenous administration of liquid anesthesia upon plaintiff on January 6, 19Y1, the defendant was professionally negligent, in that the defendant negligently injected the anesthesia into the tissues of plaintiff's left arm rather than into the vein, thereby causing resulting injury to the median and ulnar nerves, and flexion deformity to the 3rd and 4th digits of plaintiff's left hand.

Count II alleged that the defendant committed a battery upon the plaintiff on January 6, 19Y1, in that despite plaintiff's express request that defendant not employ anesthetic gas during the operation, defendant nonetheless did administer such gas, and in that defendant, together with the oral surgeon, Dr. John Rogers, continued with the operation, including further administration of gas and liquid anesthesia by defendant, after plaintiff asked that the operation be stopped and that he be allowed to leave the clinic.

In his answer, defendant, with respect to Count I, admitted that he unintentionally injected a quantity of liquid anesthesia into the tissue of plaintiff's left arm, but denied that this was itself negligence or the result of any negligence or the result of any negligence on his part. As to Count II, defendant answered that plaintiff consented in writing to all proper medical procedures, including anesthesia, that might become necessary or appropriate during the course of the operation, and that defendant did nothing that was not necessary or appropriate under the circumstances and in accordance with sound medical practice. The answer admitted that while the operation was in progress, plaintiff orally requested that it be stopped, but stated that such request was legally without effect as a withdrawal of the general consent previously given.

Deposition Testimony: The following are excerpts from the transcripts of depositions of Alan Myers, Dr. Kent, and Dr. Davis on April 2, 19Y1. It shall be taken as stipulated that each deposition was duly signed by the deponent, certified, sealed, endorsed, and filed by the reporter, and that all objections are preserved until trial except as to matters that are obviable within the meaning of Fed. R. Civ. P. 33(d)(3)(B).

Deposition of Alan Myers Taken by Defendant's Attorney

Q. (1-20 Summarized.) My name is Alan Myers. I live at 810 First Street in Field. Until the trouble with my hand, I worked as a clerk-typist, but am no longer able to type well enough for that job, and now drive a cab. I served in the United States Army. I am single.

Q. 21. When did you first go to the Dental Clinic at Field Memorial Hospital? A. I'd been to that hospital several times, but first went to the Dental Clinic on January 4, 19Y1. I went there because I was having terrible pain in my mouth and gums, and I wanted treatment.

Q. 22. What happened on that date at the Dental Clinic? A. A dentist named Dr. Rogers examined my mouth and scheduled an operation at the Clinic the following Saturday morning at 10:00 a.m. He told me there was serious infection in my gums, and that they would have to be opened up and cleaned out, and that I might lose some teeth.

Q. 23. And did you return for the operation as scheduled: A. Yes, I went to the Clinic on January 6 about 9:30 a.m. I talked to Dr. Rogers, who explained the operation and that it would be performed while I was seated in a dental chair. Of course, I was kind of jumpy and nervous, and I told the doctor I didn't want any gas used, because I'd had that once before, and had choked on it. He said not to worry, that this kind of operation required only liquid anesthesia shot into my arm.

Q. 24. Was anyone else present during this conversation with Dr. Rogers? A. Yes, there was a nurse, whose name I don't know, and also Dr. Davis, who was looking over some charts and preparing the equipment.

Q. 25. Did Dr. Davis give any indication that he heard you request that no gas be used?

PLAINTIFF'S COUNSEL: Objection. Go ahead and answer, Mr. Myers.

A. I was talking to Dr. Rogers, but it was a small operating room and Dr. Davis was standing right there, so he must have heard me. I said "no gas" two or three times, and Dr. Rogers kept saying "don't worry."

Q. 26. I show you a document marked Deposition Exhibit A, and ask you if you recognize it. A. Yes, that's the form the nurse gave me to sign just before they started the operation. She said it was a consent to be operated on and that I would have to sign it before they could do anything, so I did.

Q. 27. Did you sign Exhibit A before or after you told Dr. Rogers you didn't want any gas used? A. Just afterwards, I think. This was all going on just as they were getting ready to operate. I was in great pain and very nervous.

Q. 28. Now, will you tell us exactly what happened, starting from the point you signed the consent form? A. I was told to relax in the chair. Dr. Davis put a sort of band around my left arm above the elbow, and put a needle in my arm where they usually put injections into veins. He asked me to hold the tube with the fluid in it, injected some of the fluid and told me to relax for a minute. For a minute, I thought I was going to sleep, but I didn't. Then he shot more fluid into my arm. Right after that, I felt a sharp burning pain in my left arm, and I screamed out that the injection was killing me. Dr. Davis hesitated a few seconds and said the pain would go away in a few minutes. Then I think he shot me with another dose. This made the pain all the more excruciating, and I began to feel my left hand close up. In fact, my whole left arm closed up and I couldn't control it. By that time I was yelling for them to stop the operation and let me go. I was scared to death and in great pain. Dr. Rogers held me in the chair, and Dr. Davis said he would inject something to stop the pain. He took the needle out of my arm, and injected something else. This helped the pain, but I still could not move my fingers, which were clamped in a closed position. Dr. Rogers was still holding me down, and before I knew it, they put a gas mask over my face and I passed out. I woke up later on a cot, and someone told me I was out for about a half hour. A nurse told me the operation had been successfully completed. I complained of pain in my left arm, and still couldn't open the fingers in my left hand. She said this would go away in an hour or so. After a few minutes, I left the hospital. Just before I left, a resident told me to come to the outpatient clinic in a few days if the problems with my left arm didn't clear up. He said that there was always the possibility of nerve damage in these cases.

Q. 29. Did you, in fact, return to the hospital? A. Yes, a week later I went to the outpatient section and told the resident what happened and showed him I still couldn't open the fingers on my left hand. He sent me to the nerve clinic, where another doctor performed some tests.

Q. 30. And what did those tests show?

PLAINTIFF'S COUNSEL: Objection -- no foundation.

A. The doctor told me that there appeared to have been some irritation from the anesthesia not going into the vein, but said that these tests indicated there was no permanent damage, and that it would clear up in a few days. If it didn't, he told me to come back and they would take another look.

Q. 31. Did the situation subsequently get better or worse? A. The pain went away, but I was never able to open the third and fourth fingers of my left hand.

Q. 32. Did you ever return to Field Memorial, as the doctor instructed you? A. No, I got the impression they would not take it very seriously, because one of their own doctors had fouled up.

DEFENDANT'S COUNSEL: Move to strike all after "No" as nonresponsive.

Q. 33. What did you do about this so-called condition? A. In February, I went to see Dr. Kent, a neurologist who was recommended by a friend. He asked me some questions, and examined my arm. He told me that the fluid injected by Dr. Davis had caused permanent damage to a nerve in my left arm, and that I would probably never have normal use of my left hand.
Q. 34. Were you still suffering pain? A. No, not much.
Q. 35. Did you ever discuss bringing a lawsuit against Dr. Davis with Dr. Kent?

   PLAINTIFF'S COUNSEL: Objection -- go ahead and answer.

A. Dr. Kent told me he thought I had been the victim of medical malpractice, and said I should see a lawyer.
Q. 36. Did you, your lawyer, and Dr. Kent ever meet together to discuss your testimony or his at this deposition? A. Yes, we met a few days ago at my lawyer's office to go over --

   PLAINTIFF'S COUNSEL: Objection, and I instruct Mr. Myers not to answer further.

CONSENT FOR OPERATIVE PROCEDURE

Date *January 6, 1971*

I, the undersigned, hereby grant permission for the administration of my anesthetic to, and for the performance of any operation upon, *Alan Myers* as may be deemed advisable by the Surgeons in attendance at *Field Memorial Hospital*.

Signature:

Alan Myers

Relationship:

Witness:

Jane Ray, R.N.

Deposition Exhibit A

Deposition of Dr. Robert Kent Taken by Defendant's Attorney

Q. (1-10 Summarized.) My name is Robert Kent. I live at 322 King Street, Field, Ames, where I also have an office. I am on the staff of Mercy Hospital in Field, and am an adjunct professor of neurology at the University of Ames School of Medicine. I received my M.D. from Harvard Medical School and was an intern at Massachusetts General Hospital. I was a resident in neurology at the Beth Israel Hospital in Boston, Massachusetts. Since 19Y9, I have been in practice in Field, confining my practice to the specialty of neurology, in which I am board-certified by the American College of Neurologists.

Q. 11. When did you first see Alan Myers? A. He came to my office, by appointment, on February 5. He was complaining that he was unable to open the third and fourth fingers on his left hand.

Q. 12. Did you conduct an examination of Mr. Myers? A. Yes, I first had my nurse get a history from Mr. Myers, and then examined the arm myself.

Q. 13. What were your findings? A. I found sensory and motor deprivation in Mr. Myers' left arm centering in the region of the third and fourth digits of his hand. He was unable to extend fully his third and fourth fingers to an open position, and there was some loss of sensation.

Q. 14. Could you explain a bit more simply the nature of this injury? A. Motor and sensory deprivation does not refer to an injury, but are symptoms of an underlying trauma or nerve degeneration that can be produced by a number of factors. It means that, in the regions affected, Mr. Myers showed a deprivation of sensation and motor control functions caused by peripheral neuropathy -- damages to nerves, in other words. In Mr. Myers' case, the damage was to the ulnar and median nerves of the left arm.

Q. 15. Was that your diagnosis, doctor; damage to the ulnar and median nerves? A. Yes.

Q. 16. On what did you base your diagnosis? A. On a clinical examination of the arm, plus Mr. Myers' history. I conducted sensation tests -- pin pricks, in other words, to disclose the pattern and distribution of the sensory deprivation. That, combined with what I observed about the flexion deformity -- his inability to extend his third and fourth digits in a normal, open-hand manner -- led me to conclude that Mr. Myers had suffered peripheral nerve damage, and this was accounted for by his history with respect to the Brevitol injections on January 6.

Q. 17. What treatment did you prescribe for Mr. Myers' condition? A. Unfortunately, there is no treatment capable of restoring the nerve damage, although there is always the possibility the nerves will regenerate themselves in the future. Mr. Myers might also get some improved use of his fingers from physiotherapy. But barring spontaneous regeneration, I'm afraid Mr. Myers' impairment is likely to be permanent, and that he will never have normal use of his left hand.

Assignments in Trial Practice

Q. 18. Doctor, do you know of any tests for determining the existence and extent of nerve damage, other than the symptomatic techniques you used? A. Yes, there is the electromyogram test, the nerve conduction test, the so-called Tinel sign -- one or more of these are sometimes used when nerve impairment is suspected.

Q. 19. Did you perform any of the tests you have just mentioned? A. No, they were not called for, because the symptoms apparent from my clinical examination left no room for doubt that Mr. Myers had suffered a degree of peripheral nerve impairment.

Q. 20. What led you to advise Mr. Myers to bring suit against Dr. Davis?

    PLAINTIFF'S COUNSEL: Objection -- you can answer, Dr. Kent.

A. I did not advise Mr. Myers to sue Dr. Davis or anyone else. I did mention that I thought he had been the victim of some careless practices in connection with the anesthesia used in his operation, and also that I had known anesthesiologists to make some terrible mistakes.

Q. 21. Did you tell Mr. Myers he should consult a lawyer? A. Of course not -- that would be unethical. I don't think much better of lawyers than I do of anesthesiologists, as a matter of fact.

Q. 22. What made you conclude that Mr. Myers had been the victim of malpractice? A. Malpractice is your term, and I never said anything about malpractice. I said it was darn fool carelessness, like I've seen a hundred times. Myers told me what happened to him at the clinic when they were trying to anesthetize him -- the sharp pain; the crawling sensation in his fingers; the fact that two shots didn't put him out -- and it was clear to me that the anesthesiologist had missed the vein and shot a batch of the stuff into the tissues of the arm, where it infiltrated to the nerves and impaired their function. That sort of thing happens often enough, but usually doesn't cause serious harm unless it gets into an artery.

    PLAINTIFF'S COUNSEL: I move to strike all after "impaired their function" as nonresponsive.

Q. 23. Doctor, do you have some sort of bias against anesthesiologists in general? A. No, just against doctors who are sloppy about details, and who don't follow up when complications develop from their mistakes.

    DEFENDANT'S COUNSEL: I move to strike all after "No."

Q. 24. What do you maintain Dr. Davis did that was sloppy or careless? A. Shooting that much caustic liquid into a patient's arm without taking pains to insure the needle remained seated in the vein.

Q. 25. That's a guess, isn't it, doctor? You weren't present, after all. A. No, I think that's what you lawyers would call an inference -- what I deduced from my examination, plus what Mr. Myers told me.

Q. 26. But you didn't see Dr. Davis do anything careless or sloppy, did you?

> PLAINTIFF'S COUNSEL: Objection, that's argumentative.
>
> DEFENDANT'S COUNSEL: All right, I'll withdraw the question.

Q. 27. Doctor, have you ever injected Brevitol yourself? A. No, that is an anesthetic, and I have had no occasion to administer anesthesia. But, of course, I have made hundreds of intravenous injections -- every doctor has, and the techniques of making a proper injection are all the same, regardless of what you're injecting.

> DEFENDANT'S COUNSEL: I move to strike all after "No."

Q. 28. Are you aware that a few days after the operation, Mr. Myers was given an electromyogram test at the Field Memorial Nerve Clinic, and the results were negative, indicating no nerve damage? A. Yes, I am aware of that, but even if that test was properly performed, the nerve damage can still take some interval of time before it shows up, and that is what happened here, assuming there was in fact no damage at the time of the test.

Q. 29. Do you have any reason to believe the electromyogram was not properly done? A. No.

Q. 30. Dr. Kent, when you examined Mr. Myers, were you aware that he was a heroin user? A. No, I know that now, but I didn't then.

Q. 31. Did you know he was an alcoholic? A. No, not then.

Q. 32. Didn't Mr. Myers say anything about alcoholism or drug use in the history he gave you or your nurse? A. I don't think he did.

Q. 33. Are you familiar with the properties of Brevitol? A. Yes, I am.

Q. 34. Since you've never used it in your practice, how do you come to be familiar with it? A. A couple of weeks after I examined Mr. Myers, I got a call from the lawyer he had retained, who told me he'd learned that Dr. Davis used Brevitol. I then looked it up in the <u>Physician's Desk Reference</u>, which gave its chemical composition, recommended dosage, contraindications, and so forth.

Q. 35. But you had formed your opinion about the cause of Mr. Myers' nerve impairment before you learned that it was Brevitol that was injected, isn't that correct? A. Yes -- I knew that any liquid anesthetic would have an alkaline base, and could have about the same damaging effect on nerve tissue.

> DEFENDANT'S COUNSEL: No further questions; you may inquire, counsel.

Assignments in Trial Practice

PLAINTIFF'S COUNSEL: No questions of this witness.

Deposition of Dr. Henry Davis Taken by Plaintiff's Counsel

Q. (1-15 Summarized.) My name is Henry Davis and I live at 3010 Mountain Vista Road, Field, Ames. I received my M.D. from the University of Colorado School of Medicine. After interning at Denver General Hospital, I completed a residency in anesthesiology at Roosevelt Hospital in New York City. I moved to Field in 19Y8, and since then have practiced the specialty of anesthesiology, in which I am board-certified. In addition to my staff appointment at Field Memorial Hospital, I spend a good deal of my time on a consultation basis at other hospitals, especially in connection with the anesthesiological aspects of open-heart surgery, a subject on which I have published a number of articles in various professional journals.

Q. 16. Doctor, would you tell us under what circumstances you first treated Alan Myers? A. Yes, last January 6, I was called to the Dental Clinic to administer anesthesia to Mr. Myers in connection with some oral surgery he was to undergo for gingivitis.

Q. 17. Was there anything unusual about this case which would require a doctor of your eminence to administer anesthesia? A. Well, any surgery involving anesthesia requires a competent, qualified anesthesiologist. My work is certainly not restricted to such advanced and complicated matters as open-heart surgery. In this case, there were complications of a sort, stemming from Mr. Myers' past history of alcoholism, drug use, and also the highly anxious and nervous state he was in.

Q. 18. Were you aware, prior to the operation, that Mr. Myers had insisted that no gas be used? A. Yes, I heard him say this to Dr. Rogers and to the nurse while I was preparing my equipment.

Q. 19. But you subsequently administered gas anyhow? A. Yes, it became necessary when the Brevitol initially failed to take effect. Mr. Myers had become terribly excited, was hyperventilating, and was trying to leap out of the operating chair. I felt at that point gas was called for to put him out right away.

Q. 20. At the point you used gas, had the surgery itself actually started? A. No, but some Brevitol had already been administered, and it would have been impossible to simply let Mr. Myers get up and walk out at that point, as he wanted to.

Q. 21. If you heard Mr. Myers say he didn't want gas, why didn't you explain to him that gas might become necessary at some point? A. Mr. Myers was talking to Dr. Rogers, and I considered that anesthesia was my responsibility. If he'd asked me directly, I don't think I would have told him I would guarantee not to use gas under any circumstances. On the other hand, he was so excited and seemed so terrified of gas, I was just as glad he didn't put the matter to me directly. Sometimes, it's unwise to tell a patient facing surgery everything that might happen in every contingency. As a doctor, I would have to use my best judgment as the situation developed. I would always have gas standing by and available.

Q. 22. Even if it meant doing something a patient has expressly asked not to be done? A. Sometimes, yes; particularly when you're confronted with irrational phobias of a highly agitated patient with Mr. Myers' medical background.

Q. 23. What do you mean by his "medical background"? A. His history of alcoholism and heroin addiction, plus his tendency towards extreme nervous agitation and hyperventilation. All of that made anesthetizing Mr. Myers more difficult than the average patient.

Q. 24. Now, doctor, would you describe just what you did in administering the Brevitol? A. I first inserted the needle of my syringe into the vein in his left arm, drew a small amount of blood back into the syringe to insure the needle was in the vein, and then injected a test dose of 2cc. I waited a minute or so to observe Mr. Myers' reaction, and saw that he became slightly drowsy. I had, of course, first placed a tourniquet around his arm above the point where the needle was inserted. After waiting for the test dose to take effect, I injected 10cc. more of Brevitol from the tube attached to the syringe. Instead of going to sleep, Mr. Myers started to complain of pain and began hyperventilating quite markedly. I concluded a second 10cc. dose would be needed, and I then injected the second dose. When that failed to render him unconscious, and when the pain seemed to become more intense, I concluded that the needle must have slipped out of the vein. It was then that Mr. Myers began yelling about leaving, so while Dr. Rogers and the nurse held him in the chair, I placed a mask over his face, administered gas, and took the needle out. I then injected 10cc. of Brevitol into Mr. Myers' right arm, and that, together with the gas, put him out. The operation then proceeded without further difficulties.

Q. 25. Did you do anything about Mr. Myers' pain in his left arm? A. Yes, using a separate syringe, I injected some xylocaine into the left arm, to neutralize the tissue irritation from the Brevitol.

Q. 26. Did you ever see Mr. Myers following the operation? A. No. Postoperative care is usually handled by staff personnel -- residents, interns, and so forth, unless unusual complications arise.

Q. 27. Didn't you consider that some unusual complications had arisen in this case? A. No. Mr. Myers, I expected, might have some pain in his left arm from the caustic effect of the Brevitol, but this was not serious and would pass away.

Q. 28. Did you observe any crawling or other unusual effects in Mr. Myers' lefthand fingers? A. No. The crawling effect that Mr. Myers complained of is a symptom of hyperventilation, and is purely subjective.

Q. 29. Didn't you consider the possibility of nerve damage from infiltration of the Brevitol? A. No. In my opinion, Brevitol could not cause any damage to nerves, unless perhaps it were injected directly into a nerve, and that didn't happen here.

Q. 30. At what point did the needle slip out of Mr. Myers' vein? A. I can't be sure, but probably before I injected the first 10cc. dose, because that produced no effect of drowsiness.

Q. 31. Why did you not check to be sure the needle was properly seated before injecting the second 10cc. dose? A. I thought it was most urgent to render him unconscious as soon as possible. I was also afraid that if he saw some blood in the syringe, he would become totally uncontrollable.

Q. 32. Did it occur to you, before you injected the second 10cc. dose, that the needle might have slipped out of the vein? A. Of course. I know, generally, it can always occur, but I honestly don't recall thinking about it at that instant. It wasn't my major concern at that moment.

Q. 33. Doctor, have you ever been sued for malpractice before?

DEFENDANT'S COUNSEL: Objection, that's immaterial, but you may answer, doctor.

A. No, I have not.

Q. 34. And is it your opinion that the Brevitol could not have caused Mr. Myers' nerve damage? A. Yes.

PLAINTIFF'S COUNSEL: That's all. You may inquire.

DEFENDANT'S COUNSEL: No questions of this deponent.

Stipulations

1. It is stipulated by and between the parties to this action that Dr. John Rogers, the oral surgeon who performed the surgery on Alan Myers on January 6, 19Y1, died on January 10, 19Y1.

2. It is stipulated by and between the parties to this action that the following are true and accurate excerpts from the hospital record of Alan Myers, the plaintiff herein, which is maintained at Field Memorial Hospital, and that any or all of said excerpts may be offered in evidence by either party to this action on the same basis, and subject to the same objections, as the entire original of said record might be offered in evidence after being duly authenticated by the official custodian thereof:

1/15/Y2	Drug Clinic -- admitted for drug counseling and treatment for heroin withdrawal symptoms. Recommended that patient seek meth. treatment at V.A. hospital.
2/22/Y2	Drug Clinic -- adm't for drug counseling and detox. Patient has not sought meth. treatment.

3/14/Y2	Outpatient Clinic -- patient treated for multiple subcutaneous abscesses, apparently caused by hypodermic needles.
5/12/Y2	Outpatient Clinic -- set fracture of rt. arm suffered while patient acutely intoxicated.
6/9/Y2	Psychiatric Clinic -- patient received psychiatric counseling. Recommended that he seek continuing therapy from V.A. or other facility. Suffers from acute hyperanxiety, depression, and hypertension. Extended treatment may be required.
8/9/Y2	Alcoholism Clinic -- patient adm't suffering acute intoxication. Given detoxifier and prescribed detoxificant pills. Repeat recommendation of psychiatric therapy.
10/10/Y2	Drug Clinic -- patient treated for heroin withdrawal.
11/5/Y2	Drug Clinic -- patient treated for heroin withdrawal.
1/4/Y1	Dental Clinic -- patient adm't complaining of severe pain in gums. Dr. Rogers diagnosed condition as advanced gingivitis. Surgery scheduled for 1/6/Y1.
1/6/Y1	Dental Clinic -- Oral surgery performed by Dr. Rogers. Gums lacerated and abscesses removed. Patient made satisfactory recovery from surgery.
1/13/Y1	Nerve Clinic -- patient complains of pain in left arm, loss of motor control, sensation in fingers of left hand. Electromyogram performed: results negative. Symptoms believed related to patient's drug abuse, or possibly psychosomatic. Told to return if condition persists.

Assignments in Trial Practice

ASSIGNMENT 11A

Study §§3-6 through 3-28 and review §§2-2 through 2-8 of the <u>Text</u>.

The special assignment is based on <u>Felicia Fortune v. Barton Bilder, doing business as Happy Haven Motel</u>.

<u>Firm A</u> (Counsel for plaintiff):

1. Conduct the examination (or cross-examination) of the witness Hope Hollow, in accordance with directions set forth below. Pick up special materials from the instructor.

2. Assume that the only available witnesses whose testimony might be of any value are those about whom information appears below. In a memorandum of not more than three pages, submitted in satisfaction of the outline requirement indicate your trial plan, specifying what witnesses or other evidence you would offer, and in what order, and at what point you would rest. Indicate how major choices of opposing counsel would alter your plans or cause you to introduce evidence in rebuttal. Except as to Hope Hollow, concerning whom directions are given in paragraph 5 below, whenever you indicate that you would call a witness, state whether you would choose to omit from your direct examination any part of his available testimony and, if so, what part. Indicate what you would attempt to exclude from your opponent's case and your grounds of objection. Indicate what motions you would make.

3. The instructor may use the memoranda from counsel on both sides as a basis for briefly describing their trial plans at the beginning of the class session. Be prepared to defend at that time your positions on any matters that should be resolved before Hope Hollow is called. Also be prepared to explain other choices during the critique.

4. Hope Hollow is the only witness whose live testimony will be presented in the performance of this assignment. At whatever point she is called to the stand as indicated in the memoranda of counsel, either by you or by defense counsel, conduct the interrogation for the plaintiff.

5. If neither Firm A nor Firm B chooses to call the witness, then the judge may call the witness and determine the order of interrogation, or the instructor may direct counsel on either side to proceed on the assumption that they have elected to call the witness.

<u>Firm B</u> (Counsel for defendant): Follow the instructions to counsel for plaintiff, except that you are to act for the defendant. Pick up special materials from the instructor.

Plaintiff sues for $50,000 on account of personal injuries alleged to have been sustained as a result of the negligence of the defendant

Bilder. Her complaint asserts that on July 17, 19Y2, she was a paying guest of the Happy Haven Motel, owned and controlled by him; that his agents or servants were negligent in the installation, operation, maintenance, and equipment of the bathroom of the unit occupied by the plaintiff; that as a result of said negligence plaintiff on that date she was caused to fall and suffered serious and incapacitating injuries, severe pain of body and mind, and great expense for medical care and nursing.

The defendant denied negligence and pleaded contributory negligence and voluntary assumption of the risk by plaintiff. The defendant admitted that he constructed the Happy Haven Motel in the spring of 19Y2 and that he owned and controlled it on the date of the accident.

<u>Testimony of Felicia Fortune on Deposition</u>
<u>Taken at the Instance of Defense Counsel on January 8, 19Y1</u>
<u>Interrogation by Defense Counsel</u>

(Summarized.) I am 28 years old, unmarried, and was employed before the accident as a physiotherapist at the Ames General Hospital, Amesville, Ames. In the late afternoon of July 17, 19Y2, I drove 75 miles to Langdell and engaged for the weekend a unit at Happy Haven Motel. The purpose of the trip was to see my fiance, Dr. Abel M. Dee, a house physician at the Langdell Medical Center. Dr. Dee was coming to take me to dinner. I decided to take a shower before dinner. When I entered the bathroom, I noticed that there was no bath mat. There were two knobs on the wall at the end of the tub, the left one for hot water and the right one for cold. The shower was over these fixtures. I stepped into the tub and had a lot of difficulty making the knobs move, but finally I got a mixture of hot and cold water, sort of lukewarm. Suddenly the water became hot and I tried to turn the hot water off, first with one hand and then with both. I could not budge it. By this time the water was really getting hot and I tried to get out of the tub. As I tried to get out, I slipped on the wet tile floor and landed very hard. There was nothing to stop my fall, and I slid across the bathroom to the opposite wall. I sustained a fracture of the left wrist. Attracted by my screams, a Miss Hollow came in and helped me to the bed.

Dr. Dee arrived very soon thereafter and administered first aid. He then took me to the hospital in his car. Before we left, he succeeded in turning off the hot water. (The plaintiff's testimony as to disability, loss of earnings, pain and suffering, and medical expenses is here omitted.)

<u>Interrogation by Plaintiff's Counsel</u>

Q. 1. You have told us that a Miss Hollow came in and assisted you. Can you tell us who she was? A. She worked for the motel.
Q. 2. Had you seen this Miss Hollow before? A. Yes.

Assignments in Trial Practice

- Q. 3. When and under what circumstances? A. When I checked in, she was just finishing tidying up the room. She told me she was the housekeeper and to be sure to call the desk if there was anything I wanted.
- Q. 4. Returning to the time of the accident, did she have any conversation with you? A. Yes.
- Q. 5. What did she say? A. She said (1) that they had been having a lot of trouble with sticking faucets, including the one in the unit I was in, (2) that she had asked Mr. Bilder that very morning to get the plumber to come over and make things right, (3) that she thought it was a shame for a brand new motel not to have proper water faucets, and (4) that she was very sorry to see a nice young girl hurt because Mr. Bilder had put these cheap fixtures in to save a little money.

Re-Interrogation by Defense Counsel

- X. 1. Isn't it true that both of your feet were outside the tub when you slipped? A. Yes.
- X. 2. As a matter of fact, weren't you leaning back into the tub to turn the water off when you slipped and fell? A. That certainly is not the fact.
- X. 3. Didn't you tell Miss Hollow right afterward that was what happened? A. I never did.
- X. 4. The tile floor was wet, I believe you said? A. Yes. There was no bath mat there.
- X. 5. Wasn't the shower equipped with a regular shower curtain? A. Yes, it was.
- X. 6. Did you close it during your shower? A. No, I don't believe I did.
- X. 7. How long was the bathtub? A. Six feet or so.
- X. 8. Why didn't you simply step back from under the shower and climb out at your leisure? A. I don't know. I guess I was so surprised by the hot water I thought was scalding me that I didn't think of anything like that. I just tried to get out in a hurry.
- X. 9. But you weren't scalded, were you? A. No.
- X. 10. You said on direct examination that you engaged the motel room. Isn't it so that it was Dr. Dee who engaged it? A. Well, he made the reservation for me.
- X. 11. It was a double room, wasn't it? A. I don't see what difference it makes.
- X. 12. May I have your answer, please? A. Yes, it was, but I resent your insinuation.
- X. 13. How did Miss Hollow get into your room after the accident? A. She unlocked the door with a pass key.
- X. 14. What did you say when she entered? A. I thought the person entering was Dr. Dee, and I said, "Darling, I'm so glad you're early. I've had a terrible accident."
- X. 15. Then when you called out "darling" as someone entered, you

understood that Dr. Dee had a key, didn't you? A. Well, I don't remember and I still resent your insinuations.

Summary of Deposition of Barton Bilder
Taken at the Instance of Plaintiff's Counsel on January 8, 19Y1

I am the owner of the Happy Haven Motel, which was built under my direction in the spring of 19Y2. I think that Miss Fortune's story is complete fabrication and that she probably slipped on the wet tile floor after forgetting to close the shower curtain. This is because as soon as I heard of the plaintiff's claim I personally tried the handles in question and they worked to perfection.

In the late fall of 19Y2, I ordered Peter Plummer, my employee, to remove all the old fittings from the motel and replace them with a mixing valve with a single handle to control the mixture. I made this change because most luxury motels use this type of installation. The chief virtue is that it is easier for the guest to regulate the temperature. The change was not made because of Miss Fortune's accident or any trouble with sticking handles.

Summarized Excerpts from
Written Statement of Dr. Abel M. Dee, August 1, 19Y2

(This statement was obtained by plaintiff's counsel. Dr. Dee refused to talk to defense counsel, but a copy of this statement was delivered to defense counsel by plaintiff's counsel during pre-trial negotiations.)

When I got to the motel unit in which Miss Fortune had fallen, the shower was running and the bathroom was full of hot steam. After splinting Miss Fortune's wrist, I tried to shut off the hot water and was unable to do so until I put a towel around it and pressed with all my might.

I continued to treat Miss Fortune's wrist until it was healed, even though we had decided before that time to break our engagement. Of course I never made any charge. I would estimate that $500.00 would be reasonable charge for the medical attention I gave her, including a charge for an emergency call outside the office.

Miss Fortune and I continue to be good friends despite our broken engagement.

Frederick Fawcett

Plaintiff's counsel consulted with Fawcett, a master plumber, in January, 19Y1. Defense counsel learned about this through Peter Plummer and Barton Bilder, as indicated below.

Mr. Fawcett is a master plumber duly licensed in Ames for forty years. He had installed hundreds of showers and is familiar with the operation of hot and cold water valves in all types of shower installations.

At the request of plaintiff's counsel he tried to talk with Peter Plummer, who he learned made the original installations at the Happy Haven Motel. Plummer refused to talk on instructions from defense counsel. Fawcett went to see the installations at the motel, but Mr. Bilder told him that he had taken out all the installations of this type because he had so much trouble with them.

As an expert, Fawcett is ready to testify that if a person is unable to turn off the hot water under the circumstances described by Miss Fortune and if a man of Dr. Abel Dee's strength has difficulty doing so, the valve is undoubtedly defective, most likely due to faulty installation in failing to pack the fixture properly.

Peter Plummer

(When plaintiff's attorneys attempted to interview Plummer in November, 19Y2, he declined to sign a statement but told them that so far as he knew all the plumbing fixtures at the Happy Haven had always been in good order except for routine needs for occasional repairs).

Defense counsel first interviewed Plummer in January, 19Y1. They have obtained the following information not known to plaintiff's counsel.

He has been a full-time employee of Bilder for three years. He is a licensed plumber and has done the heating and plumbing work in various Bilder projects, including the Happy Haven Motel. He installed the plumbing fixtures in the Happy Haven Motel. He used Elijah plumbing fittings in the showers, a standard and commonly used type. After the installation, he checked all of the fittings and all of them were operating without difficulty.

At the request of junior counsel for the defendant, Plummer brought into counsel's office for demonstration purposes an Elijah fitting which he said was a duplicate of the ones installed in the bathroom occupied by the plaintiff. He had never installed Elijah fittings himself before. In demonstrating it to counsel, Plummer found the hot water handle tight and hard to close. He explained that this was doubtless because some solder had got in the packing value, which would cause the handle to turn hard or freeze. Counsel said it would be embarrassing if an improperly functioning handle were brought into court and asked Plummer if he could be sure this would not happen. Plummer said he could inspect and clean the packing valve and pull out the seat of the fixture to see if any solder had been left there. Counsel asked Plummer if he had made this kind of test at the time of the installation. Plummer said he had not, that he had turned both the hot and cold water faucets on and that the water had run freely, and that this was a proper and sufficient test.

Asked where the demonstration fitting had come from, Plummer said that it had originally been in one of the other units of the Happy Haven Motel, and that all of these fittings had been removed in the late fall of 19Y2 because Mr. Bilder had decided that a mixing valve with a single handle to control the mixture would be more popular with the guests and had directed Plummer to make the change.

Assignments in Trial Practice

ASSIGNMENT 11B

Study §§ 2.6, 2.9, 2.14, 2.24, 2.25, 3.3, 3.4, 3.5, 3.6 through 3.28, 3.30, and 3.35 of the Text.

This assignment is based upon the case of State v. Devereaux. The special assignment of counsel will consist of the direct and cross-examination at trial of Mrs. Irene Gossage as a witness called during the state's direct case.

Firm A (Counsel for the state): Announce the order in which you would call your witnesses, including Irene Gossage, and be prepared to defend this order of witnesses during critique. Then conduct the direct examination of Irene Gossage.

Firm B (Counsel for defendant): Conduct the cross-examination of Irene Gossage.

The state is prosecuting David Louis Devereaux, M.D., for murder. It is the state's contention that Dr. Devereaux, while a resident surgeon at Austin County Medical Center, Austin, Ames, deliberately killed Edward Pfizer, a patient at the medical center. The state contends that while Pfizer lay comatose and in the final stages of terminal cancer, Dr. Devereaux injected potassium chloride (KC) into Pfizer, causing death; and that Deveraux did this anticipating Pfizer's death later the same day but desiring to avoid the necessity of returning at the later time to pronounce death.

Testimony of the other witnesses is set forth in Appendix B and should be referred to for additional context in preparation of this assignment. Exhibits found there may be used here. Other materials available to counsel prior to trial are set forth below. (All dates are "last year.")

Prosecutor's File: Statement of Mrs. Irene Gossage

My name is Irene Gossage. I live at 456 Maple Street, Austin, Ames. I am a licensed practical nurse (LPN) employed by the Austin County Medical Center in Austin, Ames. I received my LPN training at Kirkland Community College in Blakesburg, Ames, in 1969; I have been employed at Austin Medical Center ever since.

I was on duty at the Medical Center the evening of January 23 and was conducting my routine check of the patients in the surgical ward. At a few minutes before 9:00 p.m., I checked Mr. Edward Pfizer. I found no vital signs of life. Mr. Pfizer was in the hospital as a terminal cancer patient and he appeared to have lapsed into a coma. I then called Dr. Devereaux, and he came and looked at Mr. Pfizer. Dr. Devereaux asked me for some potassium. I asked him why. And then I said, "Never mind, I don't want to know." Anyway, I went down to the floor pharmacy and filled a 5cc. syringe with KC -- that's potassium chloride -- and I went back to Mr. Pfizer's room and gave Dr. Devereaux the syringe, and I started to leave the room. I wasn't going to watch what the doctor did with the syringe, but my curiosity got the better of me -- so I went back into Mr. Pfizer's room, and I saw Dr. Devereaux give the injection to Mr. Pfizer. And then Mr. Pfizer did sort of like some convulsing movements. I asked him what the patient was doing, and he said it was a reaction to the potassium. He said it had something to do with the heart. And then Mr. Pfizer breathed easily and he was gone, and Dr. Devereaux said he was dead.

Then Dr. Devereaux said something like "Now I won't have to be bothered later on." I knew that some of the interns were having a going-away party for one of the doctors in the doctor's commons across the street from the hospital. Dr. Deveraux said earlier in the day that he was looking forward to going to the party and would want me to be extra careful about things while he was gone, and he would let me know when he left, because he would still be on call.

Dated: June 15 /s/ Irene Gossage
Witnessed: Alan Ruger

Defense File: Statement of Irene Gossage

(not available to prosecution)

Under questioning by the Austin County Assistant District Attorney Lois Cavender about Mr. Pfizer's death, I told her I had no memory of any event at all. Miss Cavender then told me that Dr. Devereaux had made a statement that he had had me prepare some KC and that he then injected it into Mr. Pfizer. I did not recall preparing any KC for Dr. Devereaux or knowing anything about his injecting it into anybody, but at the time I talked to Miss Cavendar I assumed that if Dr. Devereaux said it, it must have been true. I therefore agreed that it probably did occur as Dr. Devereaux said in the statement although I did not personally remember the incident at all.

Dated: July 30 /s/ Irene Gossage

ASSIGNMENT 12A

Study §§9-18, 9-21, and 9-22; Chapter X; and §§11-13 through 11-23 of the Text.

The special assignment concerns aspects of pre-trial practice in the case of Peter Pyle v. Ace Storage Corp. and Kwik Construction Corp., based on injuries sustained by plaintiff while working as an employee of Steele Reconstruction Co. (not involved in this litigation) in the renovation of warehouses for defendant Ace. Ace and Kwik are Wisconsin and New York corporations, respectively. Plaintiff is a resident of Ames.

Firm A (Counsel for plaintiff):

1. Prepare the complaint against Ace and Kwik corporations, either in one suit or separately and in either the state or federal court sitting in Ames, as you choose. The original is to be filed with the instructor and a copy served by you upon opposing counsel at least 4 class meetings before the class session for this assignment.

2. Prepare requests for admissions or interrogatories, or both, to each defendant. Limit the subject matter of your requests or interrogatories to information about the screws, the handle, and the door from which the handle came loose in plaintiff's hand. You are further limited to a maximum of two pages (for requests and interrogatories combined) of single-spaced typewriting (in addition to the caption and other formal parts of the document or documents). Your judgment in utilizing the limited opportunity thus afforded will be considered during the critique. The original is to be filed with the instructor and a copy served by you upon opposing counsel after you have received their responsive pleading to your complaint but at least 2 class meetings before the class session.

Firm B (Counsel for defendant Ace Storage Corp.):

1. Prepare appropriate responsive pleading to the complaint served upon you. The original is to be filed with the instructor and a copy served by you upon opposing counsel at least 3 class meetings before the class session for this assignment.

2. Respond to the requests for admissions and interrogatories served upon you by plaintiff. If you are confronted with a question to which you think you would know the answer if your file were complete, but don't, and which you would answer if you did, insert a line of dashes by way of answer to that interrogatory or request. The original of your response is to be filed with the instructor and a copy served by you upon opposing counsel at least 12 days before the class session.

Firm C (Counsel for defendant Kwik Construction Corp.): The above instructions to Firm B apply to you as well.

Assignments in Trial Practice

Supplementary Ground Rules

1. It will be assumed that proper venue and jurisdiction attaches to the federal district court in Ames and that the state court of Ames also has jurisdiction. The action (or actions) may be brought in either of these courts but in no other.

2. It will be further assumed that the defendants are amenable to both federal and state process in Ames and that they have been properly served.

In sum, there is no question as to jurisdiction of the courts mentioned either as to subject matter or as to the person of the defendants.

3. Assume a six-year statute of limitations as to any relevant cause of action.

4. Firms B and C are not required to prepare responsive cross pleadings.

5. Note that all papers called for must be filed with the instructor and served by counsel upon opposing counsel by the deadlines indicated. The papers should be neatly typewritten. All papers should name all students responsible for them and the sections in which they are submitted. This information should be typed in the upper right hand corner of the first page of each document.

6. Copies of all documents required to be prepared by counsel will be reproduced and distributed to the students one week before the class session.

7. Note that various items of information set forth hereafter are assumed not to be known to counsel for one or another party.

Procedure During the Session

Each firm will be prepared to state:

1. Their reasons for pleading as they did.

2. What, if any, discovery procedures under Rules 26-37 they would have used before trial and when. The instructor may call for this information chronologically, by asking what is the soonest after the date of filing suit that any of counsel would have used any step of discovery, calling upon counsel who would have acted the soonest to explain his step. In this way allowance may be made for the effect of early steps on counsel's decision concerning later discovery. An opportunity to explain use or nonuse of various possible procedures will be available during the critique.

Assignments in Trial Practice

3. Their reasons for handling the interrogatories and requests for admission as they did.

4. What pre-trial motions they would present. The instructor may choose to hear some or all of such motions during the class period.

5. What stipulations or agreements, if any, they would seek at a pre-trial conference under Federal Rule 16.

Background of the Case

While standing on the bed of a truck that was backed up to the loading platform of Ace Warehouse 29 in Warren, Ames, on Friday, April 17, 19Y1, Pyle grasped the metal handle of the sliding door on the warehouse and pulled for the purpose of opening the door. The handle came loose from the door and Pyle fell off the bed of the truck. Pyle believes that the handle was attached with screws of 3/4 inch length, and that much longer screws should have been used. He had no information as to whether the handle was attached in this way by an employee of Kwik Construction Corporation, the contractor who originally built the warehouse, or by a maintenance employee of Ace Storage Corporation.

Memorandum of Law

In Price v. Cornwall Construction Co., 267 Ames 431 (1928), the Ames Supreme Court held that the negligence of Cornwall in constructing the Flicker Theatre in Langdell "could not render it liable to a third person injured in consequence thereof after the work had been completed and accepted by the owner of the building." The plaintiff and others had been injured when the ceiling of the theater collapsed, and the Ames Supreme Court cited and followed Ford v. Sturgis, 14 F.2d 253 (D.C. Cir. 1926), a case very closely analogous on the facts. In Hanna v. Fletcher, 231 F.2d 469 (D.C. Cir. 1956), involving a claim against a contractor who was allegedly negligent in repairing an iron stair railing that subsequently gave way and caused injuries to plaintiff, a tenant in the apartment building where the railing was located, the court reviewed developments in the law concerning liability of manufacturers, suppliers, and contractors following MacPherson v. Buick Motor Co., and declared:

> in view of these developments in the law, so widely approved and so sound, we reject Ford v. Sturgis insofar as it stands for the general rule that a person injured by reason of a contractor's negligence cannot recover from the contractor if the injury occurred after the product of his defective work was accepted by the party who engaged him.

No case involving this question of law has been before the Ames Supreme Court since Price v. Cornwall Construction Co.

Assignments in Trial Practice

Excerpts from Statement of Peter Pyle Taken by Plaintiff's Counsel in August, 19Y1

I am 54 years old and have been an iron worker for over 30 years. On April 17, 19Y1, I was employed by Steele Reconstruction Company. My crew was moving machinery from one warehouse to another in a flatbed truck. I was sitting on the back of the truck as it was backed up to the Ace Warehouse door. I caught hold of the warehouse door handle with my right hand and pulled to open the door. When I did, the handle came off and I fell off backwards to the ground, a distance of 4 to 5 feet. I was taken to the first-aid station and then to the hospital. I was released April 19. I went back to work April 27, but they put me on light work. I continued this work until I was laid off, along with others, on May 12. On that day, I went with Bill Weld to the truck and got a handle and screws from under the seat, which Weld told me he had picked up and put there after the accident. Of course, I didn't actually see him do it. I sealed them in an envelope and later gave them to my attorney along with two other screws Weld had left for me at the union hall.

A few days after the accident, I went to Dr. Gray, my family doctor. I told Dr. Gray about my suffering, and he took X-rays and made various tests, which I understood did not show anything wrong. I have continued to see Dr. Gray off and on right up to now. I am still having trouble, having pain this minute. About 2 weeks ago, I was hired by the Robertson Construction Company to do the same kind of work I was doing for Steele just before I was laid off. It is true that I am now earning more money than I did before, but that is due to economic conditions. I'm not the worker I used to be. Dr. Gray says he thinks I will be 10 percent permanently disabled.

/s/ Peter Pyle

Plaintiff's Worker's Compensation Recovery

Plaintiff's worker's compensation claim was settled by Steele's insurer for a lump sum payment of $4,000. Under Ames Law, the acceptance of compensation does not bar a claim against a negligent third person.

Medical Data in Plaintiff's File

Dr. A. A. Stakely, who is in the general practice of medicine and customarily treats employees of Steele Reconstruction Company, reported as follows to the worker's compensation carrier on September 15, 19Y1. (History of accident omitted.)

> I examined the patient at the hospital on the day of the accident, and the following day, and again on April 18,

June 2, August 15, and September 1, 19Y1. The patient
has continued to complain of shooting pains through his
head, back, and shoulders and of numbness and loss of all
his strength in his hands and arms at times. X-rays
disclosed no evidence of injury. The patient's condition
was diagnosed as muscular strain in the back of the neck
and between the shoulders. The patient was discharged as
fully recovered on August 15, 19Y1. He was again seen on
September 1, 19Y1, at which time he continued to complain
of intermittent "headaches all the way down my back" and
occasional numbness of the extremities and loss of strength.
He reported that he got along fairly well as long as he did
only light work and followed Dr. Gray's instructions of
applying traction to his neck by weights rigged up on his
bed. Repeat X-rays were negative. I can find no objective
explanation for his subjective complaints of pain, and in
my opinion he will be able to return to full duties
promptly after settlement of his compensation claim. I
have examined the report of Dr. M. D. Gray, and I do not
believe Dr. Gray will disagree with me on the proposition
that his estimate of 10 per cent permanent disability is
necessarily based on purely subjective rather than
objective complaints.

Statements of William Weld Taken by Plaintiff's Counsel

My name is William Weld. I live at 417 Maple Lane in Warren, Ames. I am a steelworker. I went to work for Steele Reconstruction Company in May, 19Y2. My work as a steelworker has taken me to jobs in various parts of the country. Steele Reconstruction Company is a large firm which specializes in refurbishing warehouses and large manufacturing buildings, usually by replacing the interior bracing with steel girders and then covering the exterior with corrugated steel sheeting.

Since I have been with the company my job has been working on a crew which applies steel sheeting. I have had considerable experience working with various sizes of screws and nails and have developed considerable knowledge about the appropriate size nail or screw required by various stress situations. Principally my work has been that of hanging corrugated sheets, but I have had some experience in replacing handles, hinges, and other types of hardware. I have seen and worked with doors comparable in size and weight to those used on the Ace Warehouse. I am convinced that it would be careless to attach a handle to such a door with anything less than 1½ inch screws.

My relationship with Peter Pyle was one of casual acquaintance with a co-worker. I had seen Pyle off and on in the year I worked with the company, but had never been on the same crew until the Ace Warehouse job. I only worked with Pyle about a week before the accident on April

17, 19Y1. As I remember, the day of the accident Pyle and I were assigned to unload some materials at the warehouse. As I backed the truck up to the door, Pyle was standing on the truck-bed and was directing me. The truck was a 19Y2 model, 2-ton Chevrolet flatbed. I stopped the truck and got out. Then I noticed Pyle trying to open the door from the rear of the truck. The door was about 14 feet long and 13 feet high. The handle was in the lower left hand corner. The door was mounted on the outside of the warehouse on a track so it would slide to the right.

Pyle gave a hard pull on the handle and the handle came off in his hand. Pyle fell backward off the truck, landing on the upper part of his back. I don't think he was knocked unconscious, but the fall knocked the wind out of him, and he was unable to talk for a brief period. Immediately after that I saw the handle and screws on the ground. I picked up the handle. It had four screw holes. I saw three screws. Some were still stuck in the handle. I can't say for sure how many, but at least one. I laid the handle and screws under the seat of the truck, then took Pyle off to first aid, maybe five to six minutes after the accident. We all commented about the screws. They seemed short for the type of door -- only 3/4 inch long.

Several weeks after the accident, Pyle came to me, told me he was being laid off, expressed concern that he would not be able to get other work because of his back and asked me what had become of the handle and screws which he had pulled out of the door. I took Pyle to the truck and I got the handle and three screws out from under the seat. One or two were stuck in the handle and others were loose. I gave them to him. Other than this, I've not seen Pyle since the accident. The above one-page statement is true and correct.

July 9, 19Y1   /s/ William Weld

P.S. At the request of Mr. Pyle's lawyer, I got some other screws out of other door handles on the Ace premises in August, 19Y1. I got two more screws. They were short ones just like the ones on the handle I picked up the day of the accident.

September 5, 19Y1

/s/ William Weld

Construction Contract Between Ace and Kwik

Through negotiations with attorneys for Kwik and Ace, plaintiff's attorney has obtained a copy of the contract entered into between Kwik and Ace for the construction of the warehouse where the accident occurred. The contract provided that Kwik was to construct for Ace a warehouse with an estimated life of five years to be located at Warren,

Ames (a small town about 100 miles from Langdell). Construction was completed in August, 19Y9. The warehouse was to be used for storage of military supplies under government contract. Plaintiff has also learned that defendants have an expert who is prepared to testify among other things that 3/4 inch screws such as those in the possession of plaintiff are adequate to hold such a door handle in place subject to normal use for a period of five years.

Plaintiff's Experts

North Arkwright, 45 years old, has been a carpenter for 20 years in Langdell, working mostly on houses. He had known Pyle for several years, and at times they have worked on the same jobs. Arkwright is willing to testify that he is familiar with the various kinds of screws used in building construction and that in his opinion it was not proper or customary to use screws as short as 3/4 inch in attaching to a 250-pound warehouse sliding door, 2½ inches thick, a handle like the one Pyle brought to his attorney.

Benjamin Bolt, 30 years old, is in charge of the Nationwide Hardware Store in Langdell. In that position he advises builders and architects as to proper hardware, including size of screws, for use in construction. He had examined the Ace warehouses in Warren. He is willing to testify that in his opinion, screws of at least 1½ inch length should have been used to attach the handles to the warehouse doors. Screws of 3/4 inch length, in his opinion, might hold the handle and might not; they are too risky, especially after a period of use.

Statement of William Weld Taken by Defense Investigator

on September 15, 19Y1

(This information is shared by defendants.)

My name is William Weld. My home is at 417 Maple Lane, Warren Ames.

On April 17, 19Y1, I was working for Steele Reconstruction Co. I am a steelworker. We were repairing and remodeling warehouses of Ace Storage Company in Warren. Peter Pyle was on the job with me. He grabbed a door handle of a sliding door on Warehouse 29 to open it, as he stood on the rear of our flat-bed truck. He gave a quick, hard pull on the handle -- more of a jerk than a steady pressure -- and it yanked loose from the door. He fell off the truck, still holding the handle. I picked up the handle and some screws a few minutes after the accident and put them under the seat of the flatbed truck. I found the screws on the ground close to the handle scattered over a two-foot area. They were short screws -- about 3/4 inch long. When Pyle was laid off several weeks later, I took him to the flatbed truck. I got the handle out from under the seat and gave it to him. I also picked up the screws from under the seat and gave them to him.

Assignments in Trial Practice

I have read the above one-page statement and it is true and correct.

/s/ William Weld

Spectroscopic Examination

(Before suit was commenced, counsel for Ace obtained from plaintiff's attorney the handle and screws represented to be those referred to by the plaintiff, for spectroscopic examination. Plaintiff's attorneys do not know the results of the examination nor were they at any time promised a copy of the findings. The screws have been returned to plaintiff's counsel.)

Special Materials for Counsel for Ace

Counsel for Ace should obtain special materials from the instructor.

ALTERNATIVE ASSIGMENT 12A-1

The instructor may assign everyone in the class to perform the out-of-class pleading and discovery portions of this assignment by dividing the class into several groups, each consisting of a Firm A, B, and C. Each group will serve pleadings and discovery papers within the group in accordance with the instructions in Assignment 12A. These papers must also be filed with the instructor. The instructor will either distribute the documents prepared by one group and assign that group to act as principal counsel during the class session, or will devote the class session to a discussion of common problems faced by all groups. If the last procedure is used, all students should be prepared not only to discuss the documents they prepared but to answer questions 2, 4, and 5 set forth under "Procedure During the Session."

Assignments in Trial Practice

ASSIGNMENT 12B

Study §§ 9-18, 9-21, and 9-22; Chapter X; and §§ 11-13 through 11-23 of the Text.

This assignment concerns aspects of pre-trial practice in the case of Albert A. Birch v. Asher Associates, Inc. and Mammoth Industries, Inc.

Firm A (Counsel for plaintiff):

1. Prepare the complaint against Asher Associates, Inc. and Mammoth Industries, Inc. either in one suit or separately, and in either the state or federal court sitting in Ames, as you choose. The original is to be filed with the instructor and a copy served by you upon opposing counsel at least 4 class meetings before the class session for this assignment.

2. Prepare requests for admissions or interrogatories, or both, to each defendant. Keep in mind the possibility of additional actions or of additional defendants. The original is to be filed with the instructor and a copy served by you upon opposing counsel after you have received their responsive pleading to your complaint, but at least 2 class meetings before the class session. You are limited to a maximum of two pages (for requests and interrogatories combined) of single-spaced typewriting (in addition to the caption and other formal parts of the document or documents). Your judgment in utilizing the limited opportunity thus afforded will be considered during the critique.

3. Respond to the requests for admissions and interrogatories served upon you by the defendants. If you are confronted by a question to which you think you would have the answer if your file were complete, but don't, and which you would answer if you did, answer that interrogatory or request with a line of dashes. The original of your response is to be filed with the instructor and a copy served by you upon opposing counsel at least 12 days before the class discussion.

Firm B (Counsel for defendant Asher Associates, Inc.):

1. Prepare appropriate responsive pleadings to the complaint served upon you. The original is to be filed with the instructor and a copy served by you upon both other firms of counsel at least 3 class meetings before the class session for this assignment.

2. Prepare requests for admissions or interrogatories to the plaintiff. The original is to be filed with the instructor and a copy served by you upon both other firms of counsel at least 2 class meetings before the class session. You are limited to a maximum of two pages (for requests and interrogatories combined) of single-spaced typewriting (in

Assignments in Trial Practice

addition to the caption and other formal parts of the document or documents). Your judgment in utilizing the limited opportunity thus afforded will be considered during the critique.

3. Respond to the requests for admissions and interrogatories served upon you by plaintiff. If you are confronted by a question to which you think you would have the answer if your file were complete, but don't, and which you would answer if you did, answer that interrogatory or request with a line of dashes. The original of your response is to be filed with the instructor <u>and</u> a copy served <u>by you</u> upon both other firms of counsel <u>at least</u> 12 days before the class session.

<u>Firm C</u> (Counsel for defendant Mammoth Industries, Inc.): Your instructions are the same as the instructions to Firm B above.

Supplementary Ground Rules

1. It will be assumed that proper venue and jurisdiction as to the two corporate defendants attaches to the federal district court in Ames and that a state court of Ames also has jurisdiction. The action (or actions) may be brought in either of these courts but in no other.

2. It will be further assumed that the named corporate defendants are amenable to both federal and state process in Ames and that they have been properly served.

3. Firms B and C are not required to prepare responsive cross-pleadings.

4. Note that all papers called for must be filed with the instructor <u>and</u> served by counsel upon all other counsel by the deadlines indicated. The papers should be neatly typewritten. All papers should name all students responsible for them and the sections in which they are submitted. This information should be typed in the upper right hand corner of the first page of each document.

5. Copies of all documents required to be prepared by counsel will be reproduced and distributed to the students one week before the class session.

Procedure During the Session

Each firm will be prepared to state:

1. Their reasons for pleading as they did.

2. What, if any, discovery procedures under Rules 26-37 they would have used before trial and when. The instructor may call for this

information chronologically, by asking what is the soonest after the date of filing suit that any of counsel would have used any step of discovery, calling upon counsel who would have acted the soonest to explain his step. In this way allowance may be made for the effect of early steps on counsel's decision concerning later discovery. An opportunity to explain use or nonuse of various possible procedures will be available during the critique.

3. Their reasons for handling the interrogatories and requests for admission as they did.

4. What pre-trial motions they would present. The instructor may choose to hear some or all of such motions during the class period.

5. What stipulations or agreements, if any, they would seek at a pre-trial conference under Federal Rule 16.

Plaintiff's File Materials

Memorandum to File

Albert A. Birch was in today with a claim he wants asserted against any and all responsible parties.

Birch is a part-time real estate broker and a full time officer or administrator of a right-wing group called the Sons of White America. Most of his real estate income goes to finance this group.

He is suing for a real estate commission on the basis that he has procured a customer ready, willing, and able to purchase certain industrial real estate. He had done this by doing very little. First, on June 23, 19Y1, he saw a "For Sale" sign on the property in the Sturdy Oaks Industrial Park. He called the office of a real estate company called Asher Associates, Inc., said he was calling about the property of sale in the Industrial Park, and was referred to someone else whose name he did not get. Birch said he was a broker and asked for and received the figures on the property, including area, assessment and an asking price of $300,000, and a statement of willingness to sell for $275,000. He then wrote a letter to Asher Associates, Inc., confirming the figures and saying he was listing the property at $300,000. (Exhibit 1.) About a week later he was told by Vera Luce, a soon-to-be-divorced secretary whom he was dating, that Mammoth Industries (where she was employed) might be looking for a new location for manufacturing and warehousing. The next day he called Mammoth and asked for its real estate division. Someone came to the phone whose name he was given but does not remember. Birch told the person of the availability of the Sturdy Oaks Industrial Park property. The person said he had not heard of this property before and that the price and other figures were in the right ballpark. Birch told the person he spoke to that he (Birch) was the broker and that Asher would pay the commission.

Birch then wrote Asher the letter marked Exhibit 2, which confirmed he had brought the property to Mammoth's attention. A copy was sent to Mammoth. Some weeks later, Mammoth wrote to Asher and made an offer of $250,000 and sent a copy to Birch (Exhibit 3). The letter was signed by Brian Mergewell, Assistant to the Vice President.

Birch heard no more for several months. He then called Mammoth and asked for Mergewell. Birch says he recognized Mergewell's voice as that of the person with whom he had first talked at Mammoth. Mergewell told him that in October, 19Y1, Mammoth had made a deal with Asher at Asher's price of $275,000, that a purchase and sale agreement had been executed and a closing date set, but that the deal had never been closed because Asher said it was unable to get a zoning variance. Mergewell said that Asher later found Mammoth another parcel of land elsewhere, which was entirely satisfactory at a lower price.

Birch did nothing to earn his commission, apart from the phone calls and letters. He never showed the property to anyone, never advertised it, and only saw it once himself when he passed by in the car.

On these facts he has asked us to sue for a commission. He gave me carbon copies of three letters, none of which bears any signature. He wants the secretary's name kept out of the case if possible.

Birch says that he does not remember the conversation with Asher's office when he first called but thinks it is likely he would have said, "My commission is at the usual rate," and probably the other person said "O.K." Birch knows it would be of some help to his case if this were the testimony and has volunteered to so testify at trial, if we think it is proper. I told him he must have mentioned commission and asked him whether he usually did so. He said he did, and that I was right in suggesting that he must have mentioned it.

Birch also thinks the zoning was an excuse and that Asher did not want to see his commission paid because of Birch's connections with the Sons of White America and the fact that Birch was a contributor. Leonard B. Asher, the President of Asher Associates, was quoted in the paper as being critical of Birch's activities, and Birch thinks Asher and Mammoth conspired to do him out of a commission by calling off the original deal and entering into a new one. The property is highly desirable, but Asher has not yet sold it to anyone else.

Birch also gave me a newspaper clipping from the Ames Argus for November 1, 19Y1, reporting a speech of Leonard B. Asher at the Ames Boosters Club, a civic organization. Asher is quoted as having said: "Albert Birch has a constitutional right to speak out on any public issue. Preservation of that right is indispensable, however repugnant to us his views are. Moreover, he has every right to put his money where his mouth is. But we too have some rights, including the right of any of us who think as I do not to enter into business dealings with him so as to increase the funds available to him to promote his insidious views."

Mammoth is a Delware corporation. Asher Associates is a New York corporation and does most of its business there although Leonard B. Asher, its founder, continues to live in Ames.

I have asked one of our associates to research the law, and his memorandum is attached.

Memorandum Re: Payment of Broker's Commission

The law on payment of real estate commission has been clearly spelled out in a series of Ames decisions, which are consistent with the law in other jurisdictions. Under the customary arrangement, to be entitled to a commissions a broker must show that (1) he was engaged by the owner of the property as broker and (2) that there was an agreement, express or implied, that he would be paid a commission if he produced a customer ready, willing, and able to buy on the seller's terms. See Swartz v. Sanders, 302 Ames 61.

If the broker proves that he has been engaged and that he has produced a customer acceptable to the seller, he is entitled to a commission whether the transaction is consummated or not. See Fastbuck Realty v. Nosale, 281 Ames 37. (The theory is that the broker's job is finding customers, not putting through completed sales.) If a broker solicits a "listing" of property from an owner and the owner permits the property to be listed with the broker, the jury may infer that the broker has been engaged to find a customer ready, willing, and able. The existence of a purchase and sale agreement between the buyer and seller is evidence that the customer has been accepted by the seller. Heartfelt Ltd. v. Cooley, 120 Ames 10.

Broker's commission cases of course depend on the agreement of the parties, and if the parties agree that a commission will be payable only if, as, and when a sale is actually consummated and title passes, then no commission is payable merely for producing a customer. See Able v. Cove City Properties, 260 Ames 111.

Assignments in Trial Practice

EXHIBIT 1

June 24, 19Y1

Asher Associates, Inc.
47 Portnoy Boulevard
Ames, Ames

Gentlemen:

I am the real estate agent who called your office yesterday about the parcel of property for sale in Sturdy Oaks Industrial Park.

As I understand it, you are asking $300,000 for 10.4 acres fronted on Little Acorn Drive. I will list the property accordingly.

Thank you for the opportunity to serve you.

Very truly yours,

Albert Birch, Realtor

EXHIBIT 2

July 2, 19Y1

Asher Associates, Inc.
47 Portnoy Boulevard
Ames, Ames

Gentlemen:

I have brought your 10.4 acres of property to the attention of Mammoth Industries Inc. who seem interested in purchasing. I shall keep you advised in this matter.

                              Very truly yours,

                              Albert Birch, Realtor

cc: Mammoth Industries

EXHIBIT 3

August 5, 19Y1

Asher Associates, Inc.
47 Portnoy Boulevard
Ames, Ames

Gentlemen:

    For your 10.4 acres in Sturdy Oaks Industrial Park, we hereby offer $250,000.

                                              Very truly yours,

                                              MAMMOTH INDUSTRIES, INC.

                                              Brian Mergewell

                                              Assistant to the Vice President

cc: Albert A. Birch

Assignments in Trial Practice

Defendant's File Materials

Defendant's counsel should obtain their file materials from the instructor.

ALTERNATIVE ASSIGNMENT 12B-1

The instructor may assign everyone in the class to perform the out-of-class pleading and discovery portions of this assignment by dividing the class into several groups, each consisting of a Firm A, B, and C. Each group will serve pleadings and discovery papers within the group in accordance with the instructions in Assignment 12B. These papers must also be filed with the instructor. The instructor will either distribute the documents prepared by one group and assign that group to act as principal counsel during the class session, or will devote the class session to a discussion of common problems faced by all groups. If the last procedure is used, all students should be prepared not only to discuss the documents they prepared but to answer questions 2, 4, and 5 set forth under "Procedure During the Session."

ASSIGNMENT 12C

Study §§ 9-18, 9-21, and 9-22; Chapter X; and §§ 11-13 through 11-23 of the Text.

This special assignment concerns aspects of pre-trial practice in an action or actions for the wrongful death of Jane Day, brought by James Day as administrator of the estate of his wife, Jane Day, against Dawson Cleaners, an Ohio corporation, and Key Equipment, Inc., a Missouri corporation. Plaintiff James Day is a resident of Ames.

Firm A (Counsel for plaintiff):

1. Prepare the complaint against the defendant corporations, either in one suit or separately, and in either the state or federal court sitting in Ames, as you choose. The original is to be filed with the instructor and a copy served by you upon opposing counsel at least 4 class meetings before the class session for this assignment.

2. Prepare requests for admissions or interrogatories, or both, to each defendant. You are limited to a maximum of two pages (for requests and interrogatories combined) of single-spaced typewriting (in addition to the caption and other formal parts of the document or documents). Your judgment in utilizing the limited opportunity thus afforded will be considered during the critique. The original is to be filed with the instructor and a copy served by you upon opposing counsel after you have received their responsive pleading to your complaint but at least 2 class meetings before the class session.

Firm B (Counsel for defendant Dawson Cleaners):

1. Prepare appropriate responsive pleading to the complaint served upon you. The original is to be filed with the instructor and a copy served by you upon opposing counsel at least 3 class meetings before the class session for this assignment.

2. Respond to the requests for admissions and interrogatories served upon you by plaintiff. If you are confronted with a question to which you think you would know the answer if your file were complete, but don't, and which you would answer if you did, insert a line of dashes by way of answer to that interrogatory or request. The original of your response is to be filed with the instructor and a copy served by you upon opposing counsel at least 12 days before the class session.

Firm C (Counsel for defendant Key Equipment, Inc.): The above instructions to Firm B apply to you as well.

Assignments in Trial Practice

Supplementary Ground Rules

1. It will be assumed that proper venue and jurisdiction attaches to the federal district court in Ames and that the state court of Ames also has jurisdiction. The action (or actions) may be brought in either of these courts but in no other.

2. It will be further assumed that the defendants are amenable to both federal and state process in Ames and that they have been properly served.

In sum, there is no question as to jurisdiction of the courts mentioned either as to subject matter or as to the person of the defendants.

3. Firms B and C are not required to prepare responsive cross-pleadings.

4. Note that all papers called for must be filed with the instructor <u>and</u> served by counsel upon opposing counsel by the deadlines indicated. The papers should be neatly typewritten. All papers should name all students responsible for them and the sections in which they are submitted. This information should be typed in the upper right hand corner of the first page of each document.

5. Copies of all documents required to be prepared by counsel will be reproduced and distributed to the students one week before the class session.

6. Firms B and C should obtain special materials from the instructor.

Procedure During the Session

Each firm will be prepared to state:

1. Their reasons for pleading as they did.

2. What, if any, discovery procedures under Rules 26-37 they would have used before trial and when. The instructor may call for this information chronologically, by asking what is the soonest after the date of filing suit that any of counsel would have used any step of discovery, calling upon counsel who would have acted the soonest to explain his step. In this way allowance may be made for the effect of early steps on counsel's decision concerning later discovery. An opportunity to explain use or nonuse of various possible procedures will be available during the critique.

3. Their reasons for handling the interrogatories and requests for admissions as they did.

4. What pre-trial motions they would present. The instructor may choose to hear some or all of such motions during the class period.

5. What stipulations or agreements, if any, they would seek at a pre-trial conference under Federal Rule 16.

Background of the Case

On July 30, 19Y1, plaintiff James Day and his wife Jane Day took all of their household drapes to an automatic laundry and drycleaning business in Austin, Ames, operated by Dawson Cleaners. They cleaned all of the drapes in two automatic coin-operated drycleaning machines which they found there, and returned to their home. James Day left his wife at home while he made a short shopping trip. On his return he found Jane Day dead in their bedroom as a result of fumes from drycleaning solvent which had not been removed from the drapes by the automatic drycleaning machines. James Day was appointed administrator of his wife's estate on August 15, 19Y1. Under Ames law the administrator of an estate is authorized to bring a wrongful death action based upon either tort or contract. The two drycleaning machines which Day and his wife used were manufactured and installed by Key Equipment, Inc. Day told both Dawson and Key of the facts of this wife's death shortly after her death. Day wants his counsel to bring whatever actions they can.

Jane Day was 28 years old when she died. She is survived by her husband, James Day, her 3-year-old daughter, Susan Day, and her father, George Thomas. Jane Day worked as a time clerk for Ames Manufacturing and earned $10,500 a year. She also performed all the usual roles and tasks of a wife and mother of a young child. George Thomas is 66 and retired, but he has never needed any assistance from the Days.

Ames Statute

<u>Ames Stat. Ann. tit. 21</u> (Courts), § 2125.02 provides:

> An action for wrongful death must be brought in the name of the personal representative of the deceased person, but shall be for the exclusive benefit of the surviving spouse, the children, and other next of kin of the decedent. The jury may give such damages as it thinks proportioned to the pecuniary injury resulting from such death to the persons, respectively, for whose benefit the action was brought. Except as otherwise provided by law, every such action must be commenced within two years after the death of such deceased person. Such personal representative, if he was appointed in this state, with the consent of the court making such appointment may, at any time before or after the commencement of the suit, settle with the defendant the amount to be paid.

Ames Commercial Code

Ames has adopted the Uniform Commercial Code as the Ames Commercial Code. It is cited as "ACC § ___." Ames adopted the 1972 Official Text of the Uniform Code, but all sections involved in this assignment are the same in both the 1972 and 1962 Official Texts. Ames adopted Option A for ACC § 2-318.

Ames Case Law

In Edwards v. Polk, 174 Ames 602 (1958), the Ames Supreme Court held that an employee could not sue the dealer who had sold a tractor to his employer for breach of warranty.

> A warranty, express or implied, is contractual in nature. Whether considered collateral thereto or an integral part thereof, a warranty is an element of a contract of sale. Subject to some exceptions and qualifications, it is a general rule that only a person in privity with a warrantor may recover on the warranty. Our decisions are in accord. [Citations omitted.] Absent privity of contract, there can be no recovery for breach of warranty except in those cases where the warranty is addressed to an ultimate consumer or user.

That case was decided before Ames adopted the Uniform Commercial Code, and the Ames Supreme Court has not considered this question since. In a 1972 case the intermediate Ames Appellate Court suggested that the time had come for a reexamination of that rule. In L'Enfant v. Maraist, 17 Ames App. 106 (1980), the Ames Court of Appeals stated:

> We find persuasive plaintiff's arguments in favor of abandoning the privity doctrine in warranty actions. However, the authority to reexamine the rule belongs to the Supreme Court and not to us. We therefore affirm the judgment of the District Court.

Appeals to the Ames Supreme Court in such cases is by permission of the Supreme Court; permission is granted in approximately a third of the cases in which it is requested. It was refused in L'Enfant.

ALTERNATIVE ASSIGNMENT 12C-1

The instructor may assign everyone in the class to perform the out-of-class pleading and discovery portions of this assignment by dividing the class into several groups, each consisting of a Firm A, B, and C. Each group will serve pleadings and discovery papers within the group in accordance with the instructions in Assignment 12C. These papers must also be filed with the instructor. The instructor will either distribute the documents prepared by one group and assign that group to act as principal counsel during the class session, or will devote the class session to a discussion of common problems faced by all groups. If the last procedure is used, all students should be prepared not only to discuss the documents they prepared but to answer questions 2, 4, and 5 and set forth under "Procedure During the Session."

Assignments in Trial Practice

NEGOTIATION ASSIGNMENT

For this special assignment, counsel will attempt to settle the case involved in whichever one of the following assignments the instructor indicates: 12A, 12B, 12C, 6A, or 6B.

This negotiation assignment may be made in combination with the regular performance of the special assignment being negotiated or as an independent assignment. If it is performed as an independent assignment, the first hour of the class session will be available for the negotiations. If it is performed as a combination assignment, the instructor will direct whether or not negotiations should be conducted prior to the class session and indicate how much class time, if any, will be available for negotiations.

Negotiation

Negotiation is a form of advocacy; and in order to be effective advocates during negotiation, counsel must prepare their case just as carefully as they would for trial. Negotiation is also, however, a process of seeking to discover how favorable a settlement can be obtained. Counsel have undoubtedly been carrying on such settlement explorations throughout their lives, but they should carefully observe the tactics which both they and other teams use to advocate and to explore. There is a good introduction to negotiation tactics in pages 219-260 of Peck, Cases and Materials on Negotiation, Second Edition, (Unit Five of Labor Law Group, Labor Relations and Social Problems, BNA 1980).

ALTERATIVE-ASSIGNMENT N-1

The instructor may assign the entire class to carry on negotiations. If this is done, the class will be divided into groups of two or three firms (depending upon the problem) who will negotiate prior to the class session. The instructor will also assign two or three firms who did not negotiate with each other prior to class to conduct an in-class negotiation. They will have up to one hour for this.

ALTERNATIVE ASSIGNMENT N-2

The instructor may assign any other of the assignments in this book for negotiation.

ALTERNATIVE ASSIGNMENT N-3

The instructor may require each firm to turn in a typewritten 5-page report on their negotiations. The negotiation report is intended to be a device which will permit and require you to analyze the tactics used by the other teams in your group and by yourselves. You should summarize the history of the negotiations in your group, state what tactics you tried and what tactics you believe the other teams tried, explain how well you believe the tactics worked, and draw such conclusions as you can as to how you would conduct similar negotiations in the future. Of course, one negotiation is not a fair test of any tactic, but if you carefully observe what you are doing and what is being done to you, you should have no trouble in filling a 5-page report with your tentative conclusions.

Assignments in Trial Practice

ASSIGNMENT 13A

Study §§11-1 through 11-12 of the Text.

The special assignment consists of taking the deposition of William Weld in the case of Pyle v. Ace Storage Corp. The materials in this case are set forth in Assignment 12A.

Firm A (Counsel for plaintiff).

Firm B (Counsel for defendant Ace).

Firm C (Counsel for defendant Kwik).

Weld's deposition is being taken by plaintiff's attorneys because Weld has moved to Florida and it is feared that he will not be available at trial, though he had indicated that he may be willing to come to Ames for the trial. Plaintiff's attorneys have arranged for Weld to come from Florida to their office in Ames to have the deposition taken at an hour agreed upon between counsel. Defense counsel will have no opportunity to talk with Weld prior to the deposition.

While plaintiff might wish testimony from Weld as to other matters, the examination is to be limited to:

(a) the general subject matter of the screws, the handle, and the door from which the handle came loose in plaintiff's hand -- in short, those facts relating to the basic liability of the defendants rather than to the extent of injury suffered by plaintiff, and

(b) such general introductory material as counsel considers necessary to make effective use of Weld's deposition testimony.

It is assumed that all parties, through the proper use of discovery procedures, have acquired all the information set forth in the Assignment 12 materials, including Weld's several statements.

Counsel should consider the implications of Federal Rule 32, as amended, upon their tactics during the deposition.

ASSIGNMENT 13B

Study §§ 11-1 through 11-12 of the Text.

The special assignment consists of taking the deposition of Albert A. Birch in the case of Albert A. Birch v. Asher Associates, Inc., and Mammouth Industries, Inc. The materials in this case are set forth in Assignment 12B.

Firm A (Counsel for plaintiff).

Firm B (Counsel for defendant Asher Associates, Inc.).

Firm C (Counsel for defendant Mammouth Industries, Inc.).

Defendants have obtained the general outlines of Birch's statement to his attorney from discussion of the case, and have copies of the three letters set forth in Assignment 12B.

Counsel should consider the implications of Federal Rule 32, as amended, upon their tactics during the deposition.

ALTERNATIVE ASSIGNMENT 13B-1

If Assignment 12B has been performed, the instructor may instruct defense counsel that their only knowledge of Asher's story prior to the deposition consists of the information actually revealed by the pleadings and discovery in Assignment 12B and of the defendant's files in Assignment 12B.

Assignments in Trial Practice

ASSIGNMENT 13C

HEARSAY REVIEW PROBLEMS

This special assignment consists of a series of short items of testimony involving hearsay problems. It is designed for universal preparation. Anyone who is not at that moment being called upon to act as examing counsel may be called upon to act as a witness, opposing counsel, or the judge.

ABC CORP. v. XYZ INC.

You represent ABC Corp., a beer distributing company, in a lawsuit to recover the value of 200 cases of beer that were stolen from a disabled truck belonging to ABC on April 2, 19Y2, by three employees of XYZ, Inc., a supermarket chain. The three employees were convicted of the theft in Ames Superior Court and ordered to make restitution but that case is on appeal. Meanwhile this civil action against their employer for the value of the beer has come on for trial.

Among the witnesses who are available to be called are the following:

> (A) William Davis was the driver of the truck from which the beer was stolen. He can remember the robbery but not what was the matter with his truck that forced him to park it beside the road or what he was carrying besides the 200 cases of Heavy Beer that were missing when he returned to the truck. He does remember that a woman who lived in a neighboring house, Mrs. Jones, told him that she had seen three men from a truck marked XYZ Inc. take something from his truck ten minutes before. He made a full written statement of all these matters to a company vice president, John Olds, three hours after the robbery. ABC computer records show that 200 cases of Heavy Beer were put on the truck and there is no record that these cases were delivered to any customers.
>
> (B) Emily Everhart, who is a vice president of ABC, can testify that the computer printouts of ABC records are computer printouts of ABC records and that the driver's statement is kept in a company file on the matter and that this is what the company would normally do with such statements. She has worked for ABC Corp. since April 15, 19Y1.
>
> (C) One of the three men who stole the beer, Jerry Padgett, testified for the state at the criminal trial and stated that the three men took the beer from the disabled

truck and distributed it to XYZ supermarkets where XYZ Inc. sold it. You will be able to produce him as a witness at trial but he is refusing to talk to you and you fear he will lie or refuse to testify.

(D) Another one of the three men, Glenn Weis, died in a trucking accident this winter. An available eyewitness to his death reports that his last words were "the only thing I regret about my life is stealing that beer from ABC for XYZ."

(E) Officer Gary Steffan who investigated the robbery turned in a report in which he stated: (1) the truck driver told him that 200 boxes of heavy beer had been stolen from his truck and that a women who lived in the neighborhood had told the truckdriver that she had just seen three men from a truck marked XYZ Inc. taking something from the truck, (2) that Officer Steffan went to XYZ supermarket and found three men unloading Heavy Beer from an XYZ truck, (3) that the truck contained nothing else, (4) that the men could not show him any documents for the beer (5) that one of the men, Scott Ayers said "you can't prove we stole this beer from ABC" before Officer Steffan had said anything about ABC, (6) that Ayers also said that the three men had been distributing Heavy Beer to several other XYZ supermarkets, and (7) that when he talked to Mrs. Jones (the women who lived in the neighborhood) nine hours after the robbery she also told the him that she had seen three men from a truck marked XYZ taking something from the ABC truck. The report ends with officer Steffan's conclusion that the three men stole 200 cases of Heavy Beer for XYZ and put it in XYZ Inc. supermarkets for XYZ Inc. to sell. The officer is available to be called.

Assignments in Trial Practice

ASSIGNMENT 14A

Study §§ 9-19 and 9-20 of the Text. (Also study §§ 11-1 through 11-12 if these sections have not been previously assigned.)

The oral deposition of Harry L. Timmons, in the case of Elizabeth Carroll Parry v. Ames & Western R.R. and Harry L. Timmons will be taken during the class period. It will be assumed that it is being taken under stipulation in the office of one of the attorneys.

Firm A (Counsel for plaintiff): Take the deposition for discovery purposes.

Firm B (Counsel for defendants): One of you will represent Timmons and the other will represent Ames & Western Railroad. It will be assumed that you are practicing independently, not as members of the same firm. You will cooperate or not, as you see fit.

Make the following background assumptions:

1. Everett C. Parry, husband of the plaintiff, died in May, 19Y1, as a result of drinking sulphuric acid from a beer bottle in the Ames & Western Railroad shop where fire extinguishers were serviced. At the time of the incident, Parry was on sick leave, and it is clear that he was not on duty as an employee. Plaintiff's attorneys conclude that they should claim that the employee in charge of the shop was negligent in placing an unlabeled bottle of acid where it might reasonably be mistaken for beer. Unless the Ames courts adopt the doctrine of Rowland v. Christian, 69 Cal. 2d 108, 443 P.2d 561, 70 Cal. Rptr. 97 (1968), plaintiff's rights may depend upon whether the deceased is held to have been a business invitee or a licensee.

2. The defendant Timmons was the foreman in charge of the railroad shop when deceased drank the sulphuric acid. He has since acquired a gasoline station and left the railroad's employment. He has a farm in Ames, not exempt from execution, with a value of $200,000.

3. Elizabeth Carroll Parry is her husband's only survivor within any of the groups named in the Ames Death Act.

Plaintiff's counsel's file consists of the statements taken by members of their firm or by investigators in their behalf, summarized below; a memorandum that an attempt to interview defendant Harry L. Timmons, the witness in this deposition, was unsuccessful; negative statements (i.e., indicating want of knowledge of any material facts) from other potential witnesses who were seen during investigation by plaintiff's counsel; and a legal memorandum.

Plaintiff's Counsel's Preliminary Analysis of Case

(a) <u>As against the defendant railroad</u>. To prevail, plaintiff must establish that the railroad violated some legal duty owed the decedent. Unless Ames adopts <u>Rowland v. Christian</u>, the nature and extent of the railroad's duty varies depending on whether decedent was a trespasser, a gratuitous licensee, or a business invitee. (See generally Prosser, <u>Torts</u> §§ 57-62 (1971).)

At common law, as in Ames, the occupier of land is not generally liable to trespassers for the manner in which he carries on his activities or maintains his land. He is liable only for "willful and wanton" misconduct. Plaintiff can thus recover on a trespasser theory only if she either establishes that defendant's conduct was of such a character or can convince the court to move to a more "modern" position by imposing a duty of reasonable care upon the possessor of land toward known trespassers for "active operations" conducted thereon. This latter tack, even if successful, might involve us in the largely unpredictable metaphysics of distinguishing "active operations" from "condition." Clearly, it is desirable that decedent be characterized a licensee or, better, an invitee.

If decedent is classified as a licensee under Ames law, defendant is subject to liability if, but only if, it "knows of the dangerous condition causing injury, realizes (not 'should realize' in the exercise of due care, but subjectively 'realizes') that it involves unreasonable risk to the licensee, and fails to exercise care to make the condition safe or to warn the licensee." (<u>Hander v. Mallett</u>, 142 Ames 562, 568 (1928).)

As to an invitee, defendant would be under a duty at least to warn or make the premises safe, both as to dangerous activities and conditions, of which he knew or <u>should have</u> known.

(b) <u>As against defendant Timmons</u>. It may, at first blush, appear strange to suggest that our theory of recovery against the railroad may differ from that against Timmons. There is, after all, not the slightest suggestion that Timmons' conduct was outside the scope of his authority. Nor would it be to plaintiff's interest to suggest that it was. We are delighted to have any negligence on Timmons' part fully attributable to the employer.

But there is a further problem. We have previously discussed the variations in degree of immunity from liability that may protect the railroad, depending on decedent's status. We should consider whether the same immunity enshrouds Timmons as an <u>employee</u> of the occupier. Yes, says the Restatement of Torts Second § 383:

One who does an act or carries on an activity upon land on

behalf of the possessor is subject to the same liability,
and enjoys the same freedom from liability, for physical
harm caused thereby to others upon . . . the land as though
he were the possessor of the land.

This appears to be the rule prevailing in the majority of jurisdictions. A minority, however, hold to the contrary. If Ames is such a jurisdiction, it means that Timmons, as himself a defendant, might be held to a higher duty than the railroad as possessor.

With respect to decedent's negligence, it is clear that we will have to proceed on one of two theories -- that he was not contributorily negligent or, if he was, that the doctrine of last-clear-chance applies.

Statement of Elizabeth Carroll Parry Taken on May 28, 19Y1

I am the widow of Everett C. Parry. We were living on Main Street in Gray, Ames, which is about a five-minute walk from the Ames & Western Railroad Station in Gray. Mr. Parry had been working for the railroad for 35 years. He had a heart attack in 19Y8 and was taking medication for it. He was under Dr. Singleton's care from that time till his death. In January, 19Y1, he had another heart attack and has been on sick leave since that time. He also had asthma and it was difficult for him to breathe during the night. I was up with him about every midnight on account of his asthma.

He left the house at 9:00 o'clock the morning of his accident (May 8). I learned of the accident when Dr. Singleton came and told me. I got into a taxi and went to the hospital. He was conscious and in very great pain. (Description of Mr. Parry's pain and suffering until his death early the next morning omitted.)

My husband drank beer and kept it in the house for his asthma. He had some beer for lunch and sometimes some in the evening. In recent years he had beer and coffee for breakfast. On the night before the accident, I gave him a small glass of beer at midnight, and another at 3:00 a.m. He also had some pills to take around midnight. He didn't get to sleep until 4:00 o'clock and was up at 7:30 so that he had not more than three and a half hours' sleep. He had his usual breakfast of beer and coffee. He left the house around 9:00. His heart condition was such that I didn't like to leave him alone. He took pills and a small glass of beer to relieve the asthmatic condition. His having only three and a half hours' sleep was kind of unusual.

Statement of James L. Carroll Taken on May 28, 19Y1

I am 28 years old. I live in Gray, Ames. I am a son of Mrs. Parry. The first time I saw my stepfather, Mr. Parry, on the day of the accident was in the hospital. I arrived a little before two, and was there most of the time until he died. He was in great pain.

While I was at the hospital I had a chance to talk to my stepfather and I definitely did not think he was under the influence of liquor. Before the accident I had a conversation with my stepfather about Mr. Timmons' drinking in the shop. I cannot pinpoint the date of this conversation but it was about five or six weeks before the accident. Mr. Parry told me that Mr. Timmons was in the habit of drinking at the shop on the railroad premises.

Mr. Parry was in the habit of drinking beer, but he was not an extensive beer drinker. He did have his bottle of beer every night.

<u>Letter to Plaintiff's Counsel from
Dr. Marvin F. Singleton</u>

June 11, 19Y1

Dear Sir:

Everett C. Parry was first seen by me professionally in 19Y8, when I was called by him to treat a condition which I diagnosed as coronary heart disease. Throughout the time he has been my patient he has suffered from asthma.

In January, 19Y1, Mr. Parry had a second heart attack and was under my care continuously until his death. He was hospitalized for 10 days but had not yet returned to work.

On May 8, 19Y1, an employee of the railroad called me and I went to the scene of an accident involving Mr. Parry. My first impression was that he was having a cardiac attack, but very quickly I noticed otherwise because he was in some agony abdominally and in his throat and chest. I asked what had happened and was told in rather garbled tones by Mr. Parry and by the two other men present that Mr. Parry had taken something out of a bottle. I found the bottle in the building around the corner from the doorway where Mr. Parry was sitting. I smelled the bottle, and it smelled like sulphuric acid. We took Mr. Parry to the hospital and arrived in the emergency room at 11:00 a.m. I began treatment to relieve the pain and reduce tissue damage. (Details omitted.) There was no evidence of his being under the influence of intoxicants. He told me that he took only one mouthful and then tried to get rid of the acid.

Sulphuric acid is very corrosive to human tissue. It cauterizes or burns human tissue and the action of the acid is very penetrating; it continues for some period of time. It caused him to slough off the mucous membrane of his mouth and as far back in his throat as we dared to inspect. His tongue was swollen and there were patches of red and patches of white where some of it had sloughed off and some had not.

I continued to give opiates as late as 1:00 a.m. on the 9th and he died at 3:00 a.m. The cause of the death was accidental poisoning, sulphuric acid. Coronary heart disease was a secondary cause. The immediate cause of the death was the extreme edema of the lungs due to the caustic effect of the sulphuric acid.

> Yours very truly,
>
> /s/ Marvin F. Singleton, M.D.

Memorandum of Interview of Dr. Singleton Taken on June 25, 19Y1

Dr. Singleton advises that he did not pay close attention to the beer bottle, because he was primarily concerned about emergency treatment of the patient. He does not recall whether it was dirty, but only that it was a green bottle with a Ballantine label on it. He does not recall anything else distinctive about the bottle. He does not remember how full it was, except for the fact it did not have to be tipped much to get liquid to the edge of the bottle. Arno Anderson and Harry Timmons were the two men with Mr. Parry. Dr. Singleton did not advise Mr. Parry's drinking beer for asthma, but neither did he advise against it.

Statement of Arno Anderson Taken on July 7, 19Y1

My name is Arno Anderson. My home is in Gray, Ames. I am employed by the Ames and Western Railroad, and have been for 13 years. I am an assistant foreman in the motive power department. I have seen sulphuric acid used once or twice over a period of ten years. The acid was kept in a glass beer bottle. I don't recall seeing any label on it. I have also seen beer bottles occasionally on the premises.

I am familiar with General Rule G of the Railroad, which reads: "The use of intoxicants or narcotics by employees subject to duty, or their possession or use while on duty, is prohibited." That general rule has been in existence in my department as long as I have worked on the railroad. I have no knowledge of rules relating to the handling of sulphuric acid in my department or in general. My attention has never been called to any rules relating to the use of sulphuric acid. I have been given other books of rules but they did not contain rules about sulphuric acid. I have never seen a rule relating to the handling of sulphuric acid.

(Anderson refused to sign this statement. A.N.G.)

ASSIGNMENT 14B

Study §§ 9-19 and 9-20 of the Text. (Also study §§ 11-1 through 11-12 if these sections have not been previously assigned).

The oral deposition of James McGuire, the defendant in Beatty v. McGuire, will be taken during the class period. It will be assumed that it is being taken under stipulation in the office of one of the attorneys. The materials in this case are set forth in Assignment 1B.

Firm A (Counsel for plaintiff).

Firm B (Counsel for defendant).

For purposes of this assignment assume that no deposition of James McGuire has yet been taken, and therefore ignore the excerpt that appears in Assignment 1B.

Counsel must consider the full range of attacks which the plaintiff is making upon defendant James McGuire's claim to be a holder in due course of the plaintiff's note. Plaintiff contends first, of course, that defendant James McGuire is the "David Hill" to whom the promissory note was written and if this is proven McGuire cannot be a holder in due course. But the plaintiff also contends that even if it cannot be proven that James McGuire is "David Hill," nevertheless James McGuire is too closely connected with the business activities of "David Hill" to qualify as a holder in due course.

Ames has adopted the Uniform Commercial Code as the Ames Commercial Code (ACC) (Ames adopted the 1972 Official Text, but all sections involved in this assignment were the same in the 1962 Official Text.) Under the ACC a "holder in due course" of a promissory note may enforce it even though the person who signed the note was defrauded in the transaction that led him or her to sign the note, but a person who is not a holder in due course cannot enforce such a note (§§ 3-305 and 3-306 of the ACC). Section 3-302 of the ACC provides that, in addition to other requirements, in order to be a holder in due course a person who takes an instrument must take it:

"(b) in good faith; and

(c) without notice . . . of any defense against or claim to it on the part of any person."

No Ames court has construed these provisions with respect to arguments such as those made by plaintiff.

Assignments in Trial Practice

Alternative Assignment 14B-1

The instructor may direct defense counsel not to interview their client before class. They will be given the first 20 minutes of the class period to conduct an interview with their client. COUNSEL FOR PLAINTIFF WILL LEAVE THE ROOM DURING THIS INTERVIEW.

Assignments in Trial Practice

ASSIGNMENT 15A

The assignment is based upon the case of <u>Gloria Gates v. Williston Hotel Corp.</u> The special assignment of counsel will consist of the direct and cross-examination at trial of Harold Frank as a rebuttal witness for plaintiff.

<u>Firm A</u> (Counsel for plaintiff): Direct examination.

<u>Firm B</u> (Counsel for defendant): Cross-examination.

Plaintiff's case-in-chief consisted of the testimony of Gloria Gates, reproduced below, and an expert witness as to the value of the missing jewelry. Defendant, after having presented a motion for directed verdict that was overruled, called three witnesses, whose testimony appears below, and then rested. Plaintiff now decides to call Frank in rebuttal.

Before Frank's testimony is presented, counsel for plaintiff will state whether, if the decision had been left to them, they would have called Frank as a witness at trial and if so, at what stage. During the critique they will be called upon to explain their decision.

Suggestion to counsel: Ordinarily the plaintiff has the burden of proving negligence and causation by a preponderance of evidence. Thus, a trial judge might exclude evidence of intoxication offered in support of a claim of negligence unless the proponent of the evidence was prepared to offer evidence also that the intoxication was causally connected with the loss claimed; he might be concerned that the jury would be influenced by such evidence, even though instructed in the charge that this theory of negligence was not in the case in view of the want of evidence of causal connection.

Consider now the statutory inference of negligence created by the last sentence of the Ames Hotelkeeper's Liability Statute. In view of this statute, consider the argument that, contrary to the suggestion above, plaintiff might here be permitted to offer evidence of particular negligent acts and omissions even though she is unprepared to prove that any of them is a probable cause of the loss. Could she, in short, suggest such possibilities to buttress the statutory inference, even though her evidence would be insufficient to make a case for the jury absent the statutory inference? Why might she want to?

Pleadings

Plaintiff sues for $50,000 on account of the loss of jewelry belonging to her, deposited by her with defendant for safekeeping, and not returned upon demand. Plaintiff alleges that the loss resulted from defendant's negligence, and alternatively from defendant's gross

Assignments in Trial Practice

negligence. Defendant denies that it was negligent; denies that the jewelry was deposited with it on the occasion in question, contending that the jewelry case was empty when deposited; and alleges that the loss resulted from plaintiff's own negligence. Defendant also alleges that its maximum liability is $250 under the Ames Hotelkeeper's Liability Statute.

Ames Hotelkeeper's Liability Statute

"As to property deposited by a guest for safekeeping, a hotelkeeper shall not be liable for an amount in excess of $250 unless the value in excess of that amount is stated upon delivery of the property for safekeeping and a written receipt stating such value is obtained, and in no event shall he be liable for any sum unless it shall appear that such loss occurred through his negligence and without contributory negligence of the guest, or that it occurred through his gross negligence or greater fault and without similar fault of the guest. Provided, however, that a hotelkeeper shall not be permitted to take advantage of the limitation of liability because of failure to state the value in excess of $250 unless he has posted in a conspicuous place in the room occupied by the guest a notice of such limitation. And provided further that proof of acceptance for deposit and failure to return property of a guest on demand shall support an inference of negligence of the hotelkeeper, regardless of whether or not further evidence is offered by either party."

Testimony at Trial by Gloria Gates, Called by Plaintiff

DIRECT EXAMINATION

Q. (1-17 Summarized.) I am Gloria Gates, wife of Gerald Gates. I am the plaintiff in this case. My husband is in the retail appliance business. He operates a chain of stores throughout Ames. We live in Austin, Ames. We registered at the Williston-Langdell Hotel on June 16, 19Y1, to attend a trade association convention, expecting to leave on June 21. We occupied room number 1406. When we registered, we made arrangements for my jewelry to be checked in the hotel safe. The registration clerk directed me to another clerk, Mr. Frank, and Mr. Frank took my case -- a locked jewelry case about 6" by 9" by 15". Then he went to a drawer underneath the counter and picked out a key. The drawer must not have been locked since he opened it so quickly. Then he disappeared behind the rack of boxes they have there for keys -- you know, for door keys and mail and messages -- and he was hidden from my view back there. In a moment he returned with a tin box large enough to hold my jewelry case, and we put the locked case inside the tin box. He took it behind the rack and in a moment returned and handed me the key. He did not give me a receipt. I asked for one and he said the key was my receipt. I signed on a page in a book he had there with blanks for signing things in and out. Our dinner-dance was held on the evening of June 19th, and I checked the case out before I dressed. I wore the most expensive pieces of jewelry and left the others in the locked case, placing it in a dresser drawer in the room.

Q. 18. What did you do with the jewelry when you returned to your room after the dance? A. I placed it inside the case, locked it, and put the case back in the dresser drawer.

Q. 19. When did you take the jewelry back to the hotel desk? A. About 10:45 the next morning, when I first left the room.

Q. 20. Did you check it in with the same person, Mr. Frank, and by the same procedure as before? A. Yes.

Q. 21. Either at that time or when you first checked in the jewelry, did Mr. Frank or anyone else ask you to state the value of the jewelry? A. No.

Q. 22. Mrs. Gates, was there any notice anywhere in your hotel room telling guests that the hotel would not be responsible for more than $250 of the value of articles checked with the hotel unless a higher value was stated? A. No.

Q. 23. Are you sure of that? A. Yes, because they claim the notice is on that little card in the slot on the door that also says what the rate for the room is. I know it wasn't there because a friend of mine was in the room with me one day and joked that we must be paying a pretty penny for the room since they wouldn't even post the rate on the door.

Q. (24-28 Summarized.) After checking the case on June 20, I next asked for it on June 21 as we were about to leave the hotel to return home. As I was about to walk away with my case, suddenly I had the feeling it was terribly light. I turned around to the counter, put it down, and said to my husband, "We'd better check this." We opened the case and discovered that the jewelry was gone. I reported the theft to the clerk, and he started an investigation. We decided to stay another day, but they never found the jewelry they had lost.

Q. 29. Did you demand that they return the jewelry that you had deposited with them? A. I did.

Q. 30. Did they return it? A. No.

Q. 31. Mrs. Gates, how much insurance coverage did you have on the jewelry? A. None.

PLAINTIFF'S COUNSEL: You may examine the witness.

CROSS-EXAMINATION BY DEFENDANT'S COUNSEL

X. 1. Mrs. Gates, was your husband with you when you went down to the hotel desk about 10:45 a.m., June 20? A. No, he had left the room earlier.

X. 2. Did you have any conversation with him before he left? A. No, I was rather exhausted from being out late the evening before, and I didn't wake up until after he had left.

Assignments in Trial Practice

X. 3. You were sleeping heavily then? A. I wasn't sleeping off a drunk if that's what you're trying to insinuate.

X. 4. Please, Mrs. Gates, just answer my question. Were you sleeping heavily? A. Well, let's say I was resting well.

X. 5. You did not hear your husband walking around the room as he got up and dressed, and you did not hear him open or close the door as he left? A. No, but if you're trying to insinuate that we left the door open that night, you're wrong.

X. 6. Now if you didn't hear your husband open and close the door, of course somebody else could have opened it, walked into the room for a time, and then walked out and closed it without your hearing.

PLAINTIFF'S COUNSEL: Is that a question or an argument?

DEFENDANT'S COUNSEL: It was a question, but if you don't want your witness to answer, I won't press the matter.

X. 7. Isn't it a fact, Mrs. Gates, that you never opened the jewelry case on June 20th to see what was inside it? A. I don't remember whether I did or not, but I know the jewelry was there because I put it there myself and locked the case before I went to bed.

DEFENDANT'S COUNSEL: Your Honor, I move to strike that part of the witness' answer after, "I don't remember whether I did or not," and also to strike her testimony on direct examination that she took the jewelry to the desk on June 20th, since it is now obvious that she has no personal knowledge as to whether the jewelry was in the case on June 20th when she took the case to the desk.

COURT: Sustained.

X. 8. Now, Mrs. Gates, since you don't remember whether you looked in the case or not that morning, it's also true, isn't it, that you don't remember checking the case to see whether it was locked? A. I didn't need to, I locked it the night before.

X. 9. What time was that? A. About 2:30

X. 10. You were, as you put it a moment ago, rather exhausted at that time, were you not? A. I was tired, but in full possession of my mental faculties.

X. 11. Wouldn't you concede that it is just possible that you did not lock the case when you put the jewelry in at 2:30? A. No.

X. 12. Was the case locked when you checked it out as you were about to leave the hotel? A. Yes.

X. 13. I remind you that you are under oath, Mrs. Gates. Isn't it a fact that if it had been locked then you would not have been able to open it because you had lost your key ring containing a hotel room key and the key to your jewelry case? A. My husband had a spare key to my case, and we used it.

X. 14. Precisely. And you admit then, first, that you had lost your

Assignments in Trial Practice

keys to the hotel room and to your jewelry case; second, that you were sleeping so soundly that you didn't hear your husband moving around the room and opening and closing the door; and third, that you don't remember looking in the case to see if the jewelry was there on June 20th? A. You're twisting things. I didn't lose the key ring until after I had returned the jewelry case to the hotel desk.

X. 15. Oh? You know just where and when you lost the keys? A. No, but I know it was later.

    DEFENDANT'S COUNSEL: Your witness.

RE-DIRECT EXAMINATION BY PLAINTIFF'S COUNSEL

R. 1. How do you know, Mrs. Gates, that you lost the keys after rather than before you returned the jewelry case to the hotel desk on the 20th? A. Because I remember having them after that. I first missed the keys when I tried to get into the hotel room late on the afternoon of the 20th, and I had entered the room alone, using my key, when I returned from brunch about 11:30 a.m. on the 20th.

R. 2. Mrs. Gates, will you describe the items of jewelry that were in the case? A. (Description given, but omitted from from this report.)

    PLAINTIFF'S COUNSEL: No further questions.

    DEFENDANT'S COUNSEL: No further questions.

    COURT: The witness is excused.

Testimony at Trial by Helen Howard, Called by Defendant

DIRECT EXAMINATION

Q. (1-5 Summarized.) I am Helen Howard. I worked for the Williston-Langdell Hotel for 35 years. For several years before I retired in September, 19Y1, I was the floor housekeeper for the 14th floor. I was responsible for inspection of the rooms after each guest checked out. It was my job to see that the room was in good order before the next guest came in and to make sure that no hotel property was missing. It was also my duty to check the posted notice and replace it if it had been removed or defaced.

Q. 6. Turning your attention to Room 1406 and the afternoon of June 16, 19Y1, did you make your usual inspection on that day? A. I did.

Q. 7. Can you tell us whether or not the posted notice was on the door at the time? A. Yes, it was.

Assignments in Trial Practice

Q. 8. Have you any particular reason for remembering? A. Yes, the occupants who had checked out were typical souvenir hunters. Two ash trays, a soap dish, and some towels were missing. Because of that I made an extra careful check of the room. Guests of this type occasionally like to have a souvenir showing, I suppose, what an expensive room they occupied. But this time the notice was right there where it belonged. I'm sure of that. In fact, it was still there when the hotel detective, Mr. Traill, came to investigate the loss of jewels two or three days later.

DEFENDANT'S COUNSEL: Thank you Mrs. Howard, that's all.

CROSS-EXAMINATION BY PLAINTIFF'S COUNSEL

X. 1. You know, don't you, Mrs. Howard, that you might be in trouble if the hotel lost a lot of money because you failed to keep the notice posted? A. It's nothing to me, one way or the other. I don't owe the hotel anything; I'm living on my social security. But anyway I didn't fail to keep the notice posted.

PLAINTIFF'S COUNSEL: May that last go out, your Honor?

COURT: She's already said the same thing before.

X. 2. Did it often happen that a souvenir hunter would take the notice out of a room you were responsible for? A. Well, it happened every now and then.
X. 3. Did you replace the notice without making any report whenever that happened and you noticed it, just as a routine? A. Yes. I made no reports.
X. 4. So this kind of thing didn't make any special impression on your mind? A. Well. I remember this case all right.
X. 5. All this was some while ago, Mrs. Howard. Isn't it pretty hard to remember these details? A. It might be, but Mr. Triall took down a statement from me just a couple of days later. He showed me the statement this morning and it brought it all back as clear as can be.
X. 6. Right! You admit then that you have no idependent memory of all these event? A. Yes, I suppose that is true.

PLAINTIFF'S COUNSEL: No further questions.

Testimony at Trial by Arnold Morgan, Called by Defendant

(Summarized.) I am and was in June, 19Y1, the assistant manager of the Williston-Langdell Hotel. Our procedure on guest lock boxes in June, 19Y1, was that the guest keys to the safe deposit boxes were kept in a locked drawer under the counter at the registration-information desk. A key to the drawer was given to each of the persons having a master key to the boxes and to no other person. One of three persons behind the registration-information desk on each shift had such a master key. Harold Frank was this person on his shift. I had nothing to do with the hiring or discharge of Mr. Frank. That was handled by the manager, Mr. Dwight Fallon.

Testimony at Trial by Kurt Smith, Called by Defendant

(Summarized.) On June 19, 19Y1, at about 10:00 p.m., while working as a bellboy, carrying ice to another room, I saw a key, attached to a key ring, in the door of the room occupied by Mr. and Mrs. Gates. I did not notify them or anyone else about what I had seen until I learned about the loss of the jewelry, at which time I told the hotel detective.

Deposition of Harold K. Frank Taken at the Instance of Plaintiff's Counsel on October 2, 19Y1

Q. 1. State your name, age, address and occupation, please. A. I am Harold K. Frank, 32 years old. I reside at 105 Everett Street, Langdell, Ames. At present I am employed as a salesman in a department store in Langdell.

Q. 2. Where were you employed between June 16 and June 21, 19Y1? A. At the Williston-Langdell Hotel, as a desk clerk.

Q. 3. Were you on duty on June 16 and June 20 and June 21, 19Y1? A. I was.

Q. 4. On the first date, June 16, did you have any occasion to serve Mrs. Gloria Gates? A. Yes. I was the clerk on duty at the desk that day, when Mrs. Gates checked a locked jewelry case at the desk.

Q. 5. On that occasion, what did you do with the case? A. I placed the case in one of our safe deposit boxes, and delivered the "guest" key to Mrs. Gates.

Q. 6. Did you wait on Mrs. Gates on June 20, 19Y1? A. Yes, I did.

Q. 7. What occurred on that date between you and Mrs. Gates? A. It was exactly the same thing; she brought a locked jewelry case to the desk, and I put it in a safe deposit box for her, and gave her the "guest" key to the box.

Q. 8. Did you have any conversation with her concerning the case? A. Well, yes.

Q. 9. Will you state the substance of that conversation? A. She said . . .

DEFENDANT'S COUNSEL: I object to the hearsay.

PLAINTIFF'S COUNSEL: You may answer, Mr. Frank.

A. She said, "This case contains a fortune in jewelry. I'm certainly happy you have these safe deposit facilities."

Q. 10. Is the "guest" key to the box the only one that will open it? A. No. The locking of the safe deposit boxes at the Williston-Langdell Hotel is like that in a bank. Two keys are required to get into any particular box. One is a master key without which none of the boxes can be opened and the second is a "guest" key without which the particular box for which it is made cannot be opened. Both keys have to be used to open a box.

Q. 11. Who on the hotel staff has custody of the master key? A. One of the three persons behind the registration-information desk on each shift had a master key issued to him. I was that person on my shift.

Q. 12. Where were the "guest" keys customarily kept? A. A complete set of "guest" keys was kept in a drawer under the counter.

Q. 13. How many "guest" keys were there for each box? A. One; never more than one.

Q. 14. What was your procedure when a guest asked for a safe deposit box? A. Well, when we assigned a box to a guest we were to take the "guest" key to that box from the drawer, use it in locking the box, and deliver it to the guest right then and there.

Q. 15. Was the drawer which contained the "guest" key kept locked? A. No, there was a lock on the drawer, but the lock was never used.

Q. 16. Then is it true that anybody who worked for the hotel could at any time have taken a key from the box? A. Well, not anybody; but any of the people who worked behind the desk regularly and a number of others who came behind the desk occasionally could have done so.

Q. 17. How many people worked behind the desk regularly. A. There were ten.

Q. 18. Were the keys in the "guest" key box counted and checked regularly? A. Not that I know of.

Q. 19. Could an employee have taken and kept one of the "guest" keys long enough to have a duplicate made? A. Yes.

Q. 20. Can you recall any occasion when you saw a master key in the "guest" key drawer? A. Well, yes I did, on one or two occasions. I can't remember any exact date but I know I did see one there a couple of times.

Q. 21. Do you know why a master key was left in the drawer? A. I believe that occurred when somebody was on duty who did not have a key issued to him permanently.

PLAINTIFF'S COUNSEL: Thank you, your witness.

CROSS-EXAMINATION BY DEFENDANT'S COUNSEL

X. 1. Mr. Frank, you testified that Mrs. Gates gave you a locked jewelry case on both occasions when she checked it at the desk, is that right? A. Yes, that's right.

X. 2. Did you see her lock the case at the desk? A. No I didn't.

X. 3. Then you don't really know whether it was locked, do you? A. Yes sir, I do. I handled the case both times and as I always did, I

tested the lid to make sure it was locked.
X. 4. You did that on both occasions? A. Yes.
X. 5. You never actually saw any jewelry of Mrs. Gates then, did you? A. No sir, all I saw was the case.
X. 6. It is possible, isn't it, that the jewelry case was absolutely empty when she gave it to you? A. I suppose it's possible. But I couldn't really say from the feel of the case one way or another.
X. 7. Did you yourself ever place a master key to the safe deposit boxes in the "guest" key drawer? A. No, certainly not. I always kept the one issued to me on my person.
X. 8. Was it ever brought to your attention during your employ with the hotel that any of the safe deposit box keys were missing? A. No sir.
X. 9. To your knowledge, was any employee ever discovered with a duplicate key to any of the boxes? A. No sir.
X. 10. Mr. Frank, you are no longer working for the hotel company, are you? A. No sir, as I told you I'm working in a department store in Langdell.
X. 11. Did you leave the hotel company of your own initiative, or were you discharged? A. The manager discharged me, sir.

DEFENDANT'S COUNSEL: Thank you, no further questions.

<u>Excerpts from Supplement Statement of Harold K. Frank
to Plaintiff's Attorney Taken on November 2, 19Y1</u>
(Defense counsel has substantially the same information,
but not in the form of a statement signed by Frank.)

About 19Y9 I was under financial pressure because I had made too many easy credit purchases. I was working for Rapid Sales, Inc., a discount house that handles all kinds of household goods and is located in the town of Warren, 40 miles southwest of Langdell. I made the mistake of taking some money from my employer by not ringing up sales and pocketing cash. When I was caught, I confessed the full extent of my takings -- roughly $2700 over a period of 18 months, and served one year in a state prison. I was then on parole for another two years until the end of my sentence. During the two years I was on parole I worked in a service station at Warren, and I continued on that job until about the middle of 19Y4. At that time I went to work as an assistant clerk at the Plaza Hotel in Langdell. In January, 19Y1, I was offered a promotion and was quite pleased about it until I learned that my new duties would require that I be bonded, and I was afraid my old records would have to be brought out in the open. Rather then just leaving without explanation, I decided to look for a job at a better hotel to which a move would seem very natural, and they accepted my application for employment at the Williston-Langdell Hotel. I went to work there on February 1, 19Y1, and remained there until I was discharged on June 23, 19Y1. The application form of the Williston-Langdell asked for the names of all my former employers, and I gave them accurately, except that I left out Rapid Sales, Inc., for obvious reasons. The service station operator for whom I worked in Warren is no longer living, and I reported that information. The application form did not ask about criminal convictions.

I had nothing to do with the disappearance of jewelry belonging to Mrs. Gates, but my criminal record was discovered during the investigation, and the hotel manager discharged me without any explanation. Since my discharge from the hotel I have been continuously employed in the men's ready-to-wear department of the Langdell Department Store.

I was born in Ames and went to high school there. I was married in 19Y10 and divorced in 19Y9. Until I was arrested in 19Y8, I worked at Rapid Sales. I was in the Ames state prison from February, 19Y8 to February, 19Y7.

/s/ Harold K. Frank

Deposition of Dwight Fallon Taken at the Instance of Plaintiff's Counsel on November 6, 19Y1

(Summarized.) I am and was in June, 19Y1, the manager of the Williston-Langdell Hotel. I am the person who employed Harold Frank. At the time of employing him I did not ask whether he had ever been convicted of a crime. No investigation was made as to his background other than a routine check with his previous employer, the Plaza Hotel. During the course of the investigation arising out of Mrs. Gates' claim, I discovered that Frank had served a year in the state prison for grand theft. I discharged Frank promptly after learning that fact. I found nothing during the investigation, however, to indicate that Frank or anyone else working for the Williston-Langdell Hotel was in any way responsible for Mrs. Gates' alleged loss.

ASSIGNMENT 15B

This special assignment involves the completion of the preliminary hearing in the case of State v. McGuire. This case is based upon the factual situation in Beatty v. McGuire as set forth in Assignment 1B, but this is a criminal prosecution of James McGuire for obtaining property by false pretenses. The official purpose for a preliminary hearing is to determine whether or not a defendant who is in custody (or released on bond) should be kept in custody (or on bond) until the grand jury has an opportunity to decide whether or not to indict him.

The magistrate or judge who presides at a preliminary hearing does not decide questions of fact. Instead he decides only whether or not the evidence against the defendant, if it were believed, would be adequate to support a conviction. If this is so, the magistrate or judge finds that there is "probable cause" to believe the defendant committed an offense. There is therefore no reason for a defendant to present evidence that merely contradicts the state's evidence. Defendants themselves therefore seldom testify at preliminary hearings, and they normally present no evidence at all.

Two unofficial uses which are often made of a preliminary hearing are actually more important than the question of whether or not probable cause exists. The first such unofficial use is a test of the adequacy of the state's case. The state could seek an indictment by the grand jury regardless of the result of the preliminary hearing, but in ordinary circumstances that state will not seek to continue a case that was apparently so weak as to be dismissed at a preliminary hearing. The second unofficial use is as a device to discover the state's case. (The kinds of discovery that are normally used in civil cases are frequently impossible or very difficult to obtain in criminal cases. Furthermore, when the defendant uses the preliminary hearing as a discovery device, he avoids any demands for discovery by the state in return.)

These two unofficial uses of a preliminary hearing complicate the goals of both prosecution and defense counsel during the hearing. Since a decision against the state will probably end the prosecution of the defendant, the prosecutor will want to introduce enough evidence to convince the magistrate or judge that "probable cause" exists, but will not want to expose all the state's case if that can be avoided. Defense counsel, on the other hand, would like to prevent the introduction of evidence of probable cause but would also like to find out all the state's evidence.

The evidence available for use by the prosecution at the preliminary hearing in State v. McGuire is the same as the evidence available to the plaintiff in Assignment 1B for the civil trial, with one exception -- instead of having a deposition of the defendant, the prosecution has a statement by the defendant to Officer Brandenburg which is described below.

Assignments in Trial Practice

The preliminary hearing has already proceeded as follows:

The prosecution and the defendant stipulated that some person posing as an official furnace inspector rendered John Beatty's furnace inoperative, persuaded Beatty that he would have to sign a note for $2,500 to pay for a replacement furnace, and obtained the note from Beatty by delivering a furnace worth no more than $100. Beatty then described the events of March 5 in accordance with his statement in Assignment 1B. He did not testify concerning his identification of McGuire on March 10. He did identify McGuire as the purported furnace inspector. On cross-examination, however, Beatty stated that he really didn't remember what the purported furnace inspector looked like and that James McGuire might be the purported inspector but that half a dozen other persons in the courtroom, including the judge, might also be the one. On re-direct Beatty stated that James McGuire must be the purported furnace inspector because he had wound up with the $2,500 note.

Firm A (Prosecutor): Conduct the rest of the preliminary hearing on behalf of the state, including arguments to the court in support of a finding of probable cause.

Firm B (Defense): Represent the defendant throughout the rest of the preliminary hearing and present arguments to the court opposing a finding of probable cause. You will waive your right to call any witnesses but you may, if you think it desirable to do so, introduce any of the pre-trial stipulations that the prosecution has not introduced.

There will be only one live witness, Frank Anthony, who will be called by the state.

Additional Pre-trial Stipulations Between Counsel

The investigating officer, Thomas Brandenburg, cannot be present at the preliminary hearing. In order to avoid postponing the hearing, counsel for the state and the defendant entered into the following pre-trial stipulations.

It is hereby stipulated between counsel for purposes of the preliminary hearing only that Officer Thomas Brandenburg would testify in accordance with the following statement:

1. On March 28, 19Y1, I questioned James McGuire at his store about his dealings with John Beatty. McGuire stated to me that he had never had any dealings with John Beatty except that David Hill had given McGuire a promissory note written by Beatty. McGuire also stated that he had not seen Hill for several weeks and guessed that Hill might have left town as a result of the fuss Beatty was making.

2. I showed James McGuire a photograph which Frank Anthony had told me he had obtained from the barbershop next to McGuire's business. I asked McGuire if it was a picture of his brother, George McGuire. McGuire stated that it was a picture of his brother.

3. McGuire went on to say, however, that you probably would not be able to recognize his brother from the picture, since his brother was now five years older than when the picture was taken. He had not seen his brother for several years and did not know where he was living, but he did know that Frank Anthony was wrong when he said that George had been driving Hill's truck. Hill's driver didn't look anything like George.

4. McGuire denied that he had ever seen Beatty except on Beatty's March 10 visit to McGuire's store.

Ames Statute

Ames Statutes Annotated, Title 3 (Crimes and Criminal Procedure), § 2911.01 provides:

> No person shall, by false pretense and with intent to defraud, obtain anything of value or procure the signature of another as maker, indorser, or guarantor to a bond, bill, receipt, promissory note, draft, check, or other evidence of indebtedness or sell, barter, or dispose of a bond, bill, receipt, promissory note, draft, or check or offer to do so, knowing the signature of the maker, indorser, or guarantor thereof to have been obtained by false pretense.

ASSIGNMENT 15C

Review §§ 9-13 through 9-17 of the Text.

One firm will be assigned to conduct an interview during the class period and to obtain a written statement from the person interviewed. It will be assumed that the interviewers have reached the witness by telephone and have arranged the hour and place of the interview, but they will not have met the witness before they enter the room for the interview. Counsel will be briefly informed, in advance of the session, as to how they learned of the witness and the general nature of the case to which the witness' statement relates.

Firm A: Conduct the interview.

The questions discussed during the critique will include the following: What further investigation would be advisable? Were leads for further investigation adequately developed during the interview? Did counsel pursue proper tactics during the interview to protect the interests of their client?

ALTERNATIVE ASSIGNMENT 15C-1

The instructor may assign an additional team, Firm B, to conduct the same interview. If this format is used, Firm B will leave the room for 20 minutes while Firm A conducts the interview. Firm B will then return and have 20 minutes to conduct its own interview.

Assignments in Trial Practice

APPENDIX A
Sanders v. Bennett
Plaintiff's Memorandum to File

1. Possible causes of action. This claim arises from the shooting of plaintiff's decedent on March 6, 19Y2, by an unidentified gunman at the scene of an attempted jewelry store burglary. The defendant was arrested at the scene under circumstances indicating that he may have been a conspirator in the attempted crime. His story indicates that he was not a conspirator, but rather was the victim of coercion and participated only because of fear for his own safety and the safety of his fiancée. The deceased died on May 30, 19Y2.

The unknown assailant who fired the gun clearly committed a battery on Mr. Rubin. Our theory will be that Bennett was a participant in a conspiracy to break into the store and steal the jewelry, and thus is liable as a joint tort-feasor for the intentional torts of his coconspirator committed in furtherance of the objects of the conspiracy. Bennett will surely claim that his participation in the burglary was involuntary, the result of coercion by Phil Ricker and his unnamed associate; this is a matter of defense, and will be considered below. In addition, Bennett can argue that whether his participation was voluntary or not, a shooting was outside the scope of any agreement to enter the store and take the jewelry. This will be a fact question for the jury to decide. We may contend that implicit in any planned crime of violence is an agreement that appropriate action will be taken to insure a getaway, not excluding the possibility of firing in the direction of a would-be captor.

2. Coercion as a defense to battery.

a. Is coercion a defense? As yet no authorities have been found which deal with this issue in tort law. Many decisions have held that coercion is a defense to criminal prosecution, e.g., Shannon v. United States, 76 F.2d 490 (10th Cir. 1935). It is at least arguable, however, that the criminal cases should not be controlling, since the problem in our case is not punishment, but the determination of the proper person to bear a loss which has already occurred. Nevertheless, it is probable that coercion which is sufficient to excuse from criminal liability will be a good defense in our case.

b. What constitutes coercion? Assuming now that coercion is a defense to Bennett's liability, what must he show in order to avail himself of this defense? Bennett will probably claim to have been coerced in two ways: first, by threats to his own life, if he should fail to cooperate; and second, by threats to his fiancée's life. Since there was a time when he was alone and could have called the police, we should contend that he must be taking the position that the threat of future harm to himself or to Miss Mather justified his continuation.

Again the precedents are to be found in the criminal cases. It has generally been held that in order to excuse an act which is otherwise criminal, coercion must be immediate, and must cause the coerced person to fear death or bodily injury. Shannon v. United States, supra. Usually the threat of future harm is not a good defense to criminal prosecution. E.g., Bain v. State, 67 Miss. 557, 7 So. 408 (1890). There may well be an issue of fact as to the immediacy of the threatened harm to Bennett, even assuming his story is true. Cf. Rhode Island Recreation Center v. Aetna Casualty & Security Co., 177 F.2d 603 (1st Cir. 1949).

Whether the harm threatened is immediate or future, it is not clear that a threat to the life of another can constitute coercion. However, such meager authorities as there are appear to be against us on the point. See, e.g., Rex v. Steane, (1947) 1 All E.R. 813.

The defense may argue that vicarious liability for the acts of the gunman should not be imposed on Bennett under these facts, since he never had any control over the gunman's acts, either during the planning stage of the burglary or during its execution. Thus the element of joint control -- which is the theory of liability for the acts of a coconspirator -- is absent. The criminal cases which hold that threats of non-immediate harm do not excuse conduct otherwise criminal are distinguishable, since they hold persons responsible only for their own wrongful acts. This argument, if made by the defense, will probably be successful, and therefore it will be necessary for us to convince the jury that Bennett is not telling the truth.

Extracts from Ames Civil Code

Sec. 3017(a). Whenever the death of a person shall be caused by the wrongful act, neglect, or default of another, and the act, neglect, or default is such as would, if death had not ensued, have entitled the party injured to maintain an action and recover damages in respect thereof, then, and in every such case, the person who or the corporation which would have been liable, if death had not ensued, shall be liable to an action for damages, notwithstanding the death of the person injured, and although the death shall have been caused under such circumstances as shall amount to a felony.

(b) Every such action shall be brought by and in the names of the personal representatives of such deceased person, and the amount recovered in every such action, except as hereinafter provided, shall be for the exclusive benefit of the surviving spouse, if no children, and of the children, if no surviving spouse, and if both, then for the exclusive benefit of the surviving spouse and the children equally, and if neither, of his or her heirs.

(c) In every such action, the jury may give such damages as they shall deem fair and just for the death and loss thus occasioned, not exceeding $20,000, with reference to the pecuniary injuries resulting from such death, and in addition thereto, shall give such damages as will compensate the estate of such deceased person for reasonable expenses of medical, surgical, and hospital care and treatment, and for reasonable funeral expenses.

(d) Every such action shall be commenced within one year after the death of the deceased person.

Assignments in Trial Practice

IN THE SUPERIOR COURT OF THE COMMONWEALTH OF AMES

COUNTY OF POUND

MYRA RUBIN SANDERS, Executrix of the will of Joseph A. Rubin, deceased, Plaintiff v. IRA M. BENNETT, Defendant	Civil Action File No. 1284 COMPLAINT

1. Plaintiff and defendant are residents of the city of Gray, in the Commonwealth of Ames. Plaintiff is the duly qualified, appointed, and acting executrix of the will of Joseph A. Rubin, deceased, having been duly appointed by order of the Probate Division of this court dated June 22, 19Y2. Myra Rubin Sanders is the surviving spouse of Joseph A. Rubin.

2. On March 6, 19Y2, on Third Avenue in Gray, Ames, Joseph A. Rubin, now deceased, then husband of the plaintiff, was willfully shot by a person whose identity is unknown to the plaintiff. This unknown person and the defendant were, at the time of the shooting, engaged in burglarizing Karron's Jewelry Shop, 613 Third Avenue, Gray, Ames. Defendant is, therefore, liable for the assault and battery committed upon the deceased.

3. As a result of being shot by the unknown person described in paragraph two, Joseph A. Rubin incurred medical, surgical, and hospital expenses in the sum of two thousand dollars.

4. On May 30, 19Y2, Joseph A. Rubin died as a result of the shooting described in paragraph two. Plaintiff incurred funeral expenses for the burial of Joseph A. Rubin in the sum of one thousand dollars. In addition, Myra Rubin Sanders suffered damages from the death and loss of Joseph A. Rubin in the sum of twenty thousand dollars.

Wherefore plaintiff demands judgment against defendant in the sum of twenty-three thousand dollars and costs.

/s/ <u>Richard H. Field</u>
Richard H. Field
2050 Seavey Street
Gray, Ames

Assignments in Trial Practice

IN THE SUPERIOR COURT OF THE COMMONWEALTH OF AMES

COUNTY OF POUND

MYRA RUBIN SANDERS, Executrix of the will of Joseph A. Rubin, deceased, Plaintiff v. IRA M. BENNETT, Defendant	)))))))	Civil Action File No. 1284 ANSWER

1. Defendant admits that he is a resident of the city of Gray, in the Commonwealth of Ames, and that he was present at Karron's Jewelry Shop, 613 Third Avenue, Gray, Ames, on the day and night of March 6, 19Y2. Defendant has insufficient knowledge or information to form a belief as to the truth of the remainder of the allegations contained in paragraph 1 of the complaint.

FIRST DEFENSE

2. Defendant denies the allegation in paragraph 2 of the Complaint that he was engaged in burglarizing the said Karron's Jewelry Shop. Defendant further denies the allegation in paragraph 2 that he is liable for any assault and battery which may have been committed upon Joseph A. Rubin by another person. Defendant has insufficient knowledge or information to form a belief as to the truth of the remainder of the allegations made in the Complaint.

SECOND DEFENSE

3. The defendant was present at the said Karron's Jewelry Shop on the night of March 6, 19Y2, only because he was compelled by one Philip Ricker and by another person, not known to the defendant, under threat of serious bodily harm or death both to the defendant and to his betrothed, Marsha Mather.

/s/ Arthur E. Sutherland
Arthur E. Sutherland
Attorney for Defendant
1010 Scott Tower
Gray, Ames

Assignments in Trial Practice

IN THE SUPERIOR COURT OF THE COMMONWEALTH OF AMES

COUNTY OF POUND

MYRA RUBIN SANDERS, Executrix of the will) of Joseph A. Rubin,) deceased, Plaintiff)		Civil Action File No. 1284
v.))		
IRA M. BENNETT, Defendant)		PRE-TRIAL ORDER

A pre-trial conference was held in this case, Richard H. Field, attorney for plaintiff, and Arthur E. Sutherland, attorney for the defendant, appearing, the Honorable PETER T. WHALEN, presiding:

STIPULATIONS

Now, therefore, for purposes of the decision and disposition of this cause but for no other purposes, the parties agree to the following stipulations of fact:

1. The plaintiff is the surviving spouse of Joseph A. Rubin and is the executrix of his last will.

2. Joseph A. Rubin died on May 30, 19Y2.

3. Dr. Robert Kline was family physician to Joseph A. Rubin for seven years prior to his death. Dr. W. N. Wilson performed an autopsy on the remains of Joseph A. Rubin on May 31, 19Y2. Dr. B. C. Harrison, a neurologist, treated Joseph A. Rubin in his last illness. All these doctors, if called to testify under oath, would testify that Joseph A. Rubin's death was caused by a gunshot wound. Dr. Kline would testify that the particular wound was incurred on March 6, 19Y2. The testimony may be offered at trial without calling any of the named doctors in person.

4. At the time of his death, Joseph A. Rubin was receiving on the first day of each and every month the sum of twenty-five hundred dollars ($2500.00) in payment of his interest as a retired partner in the firm of Cohen and Fairchild, stockbrokers, of Langdell and Gray in Ames.

5. Plaintiff has received no benefits from the same partnership since May 30, 19Y2, being entitled to none inasmuch as the rights of Joseph A. Rubin were to last for the remainder of his life and were terminated at his death by effect of the pertinent Partnership Agreement.

6. Dr. Robert Kline, a physician, and Dr. Wyatt Smith, a psychiatrist, if called to testify under oath, would both testify that

they had treated Joseph A. Rubin regularly prior to March 6, 19Y2, and on that date he suffered from no physical disability which might reduce his life expectancy below that of an average man of his age. This testimony may be offered at trial without calling either Dr. Kline or Dr. Smith in person.

7. The Commissioners' 1941 Standard Ordinary Table of Life Expectancy indicated that at the time of his death, the life expectancy of Joseph A. Rubin was 14.50 years.

8. As a result of the injury, last illness, and death of Joseph A. Rubin, the plaintiff incurred medical expenses of two thousand dollars ($2000.00) and funeral expenses of one thousand dollars ($1000.00), and such expenses are reasonable in amount.

9. On March 14, 19Y1, the plaintiff married Gordon I. Sanders.

10. Philip Ricker was convicted November 2, 1962, in the Superior Court of Ames for Pound County of receiving stolen goods. His sentence was suspended. He was convicted May 19, 1963, in the same court, of burglary and sentenced to six years in the state penitentiary. He was released on parole on May 20, 1966. Under a conditional sales agreement dated November 15, 19Y4, Ricker was the conditional vendee of a Buick automobile.

11. On July 1, 19Y5, the defendant, Ira Bennett, opened a savings account at the Gray Federal Savings and Loan Company. Periodic deposits were made and on December 29, 19Y3, the balance due him was nine thousand nine hundred and ninety-two dollars and sixty cents ($9,992.60). On December 29, 19Y3, he made his first withdrawal and between that date and February 19, 19Y2, inclusive, there were thirteen separate withdrawals which depleted the account completely.

12. There are two alternate highway routes between the cities of Gray and Thayer in the Commonwealth of Ames:

> (a) Route 22 through the city of Austin. Distance -- 149 miles.
>
> (b) Routes 30 and 136 through the towns of Powell, Morgan, and Thurston. Distance -- 154 miles.

13. On March 6, 19Y2, Marsha Mather was the registered owner of a 19Y3 Ford sedan. At 6:30 a.m. on March 7, 19Y3, her car was found by police officers deserted on a side road 200 feet off Ames Highway 27 between Gray and Langdell. The ignition keys were missing and no identifiable fingerprints were found.

14. The following diagrams have been marked as pre-trial exhibits. It is agreed that each exhibit is what it purports to be and that no further authentication of either will be required.

(1) Diagram of Karron's Jewelry Shop as prepared by Arnold Karron, Jr.
(2) Diagram of premises at 19 Westchester Road, Gray, Pound County, Ames.
(3) Diagram showing Third Avenue, Stone Street, Prince Street, and Queen Street.

15. Arnold Karron, Jr., is now in the Netherlands and is not available to testify at trial; subject to objections based on the rules of evidence his deposition may be read at trial.

ISSUES OF FACT LEFT FOR TRIAL

The following issues of fact are left to be determined at trial:
1. existence of conspiracy,
2. battery,
3. whether battery was within scope of conspiracy,
4. coercion, and
5. damages.

/s/ Peter T. Whalen

PETER T. WHALEN
Judge

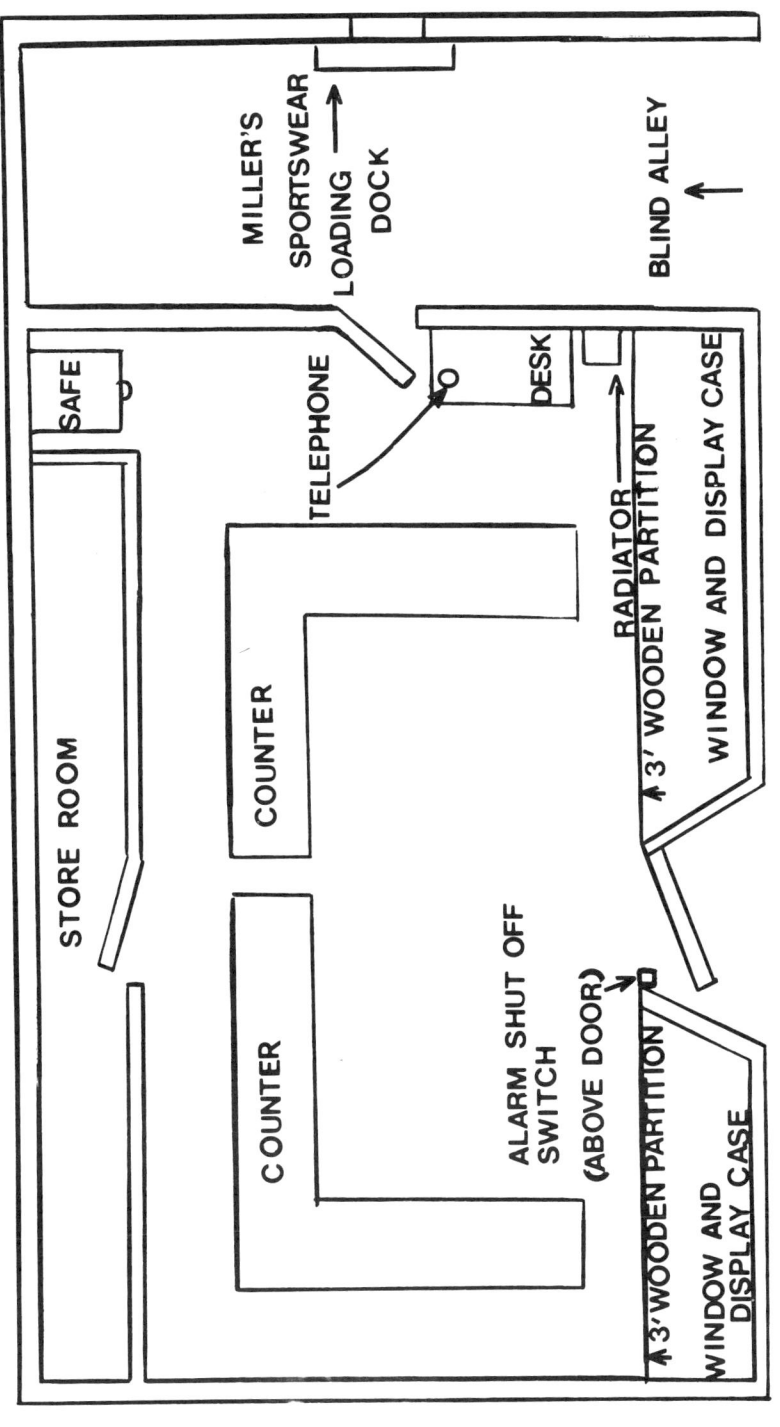

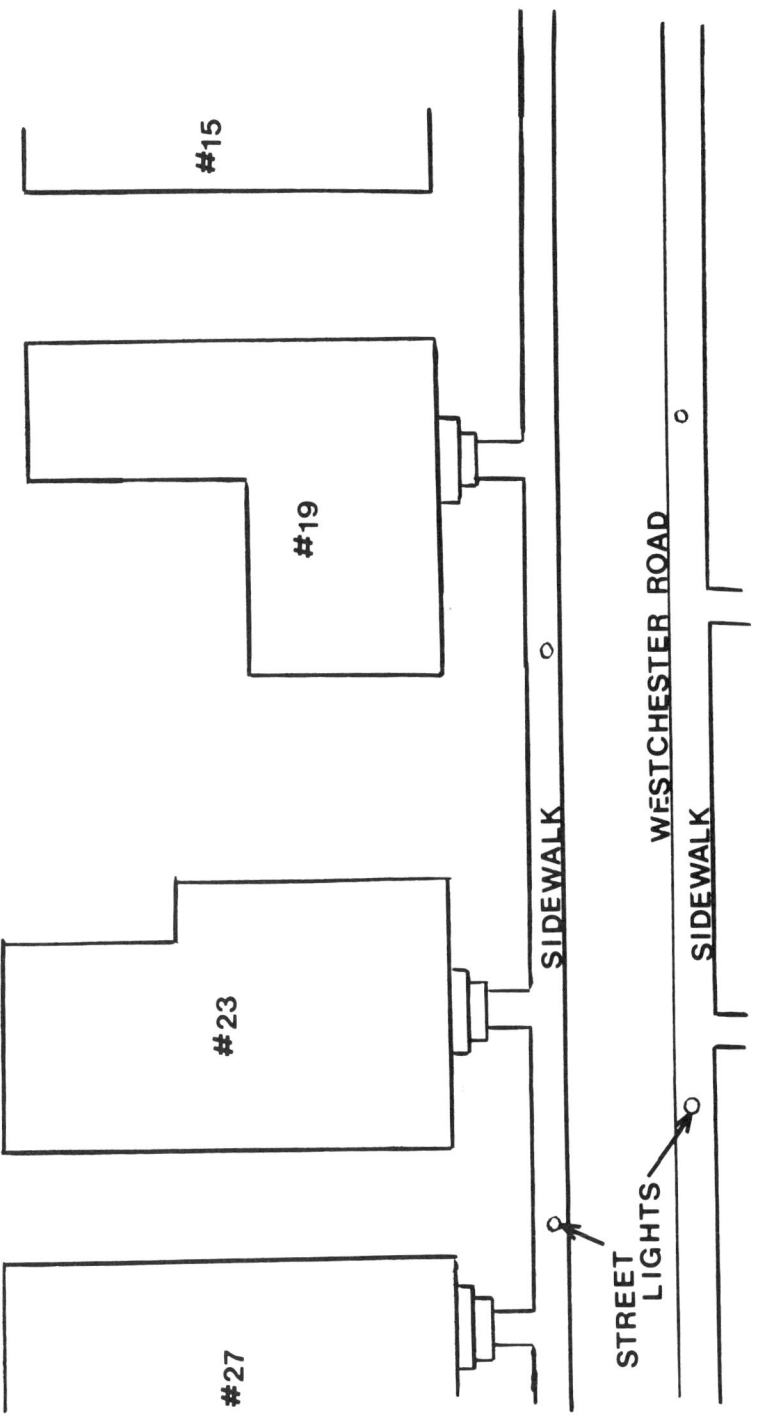

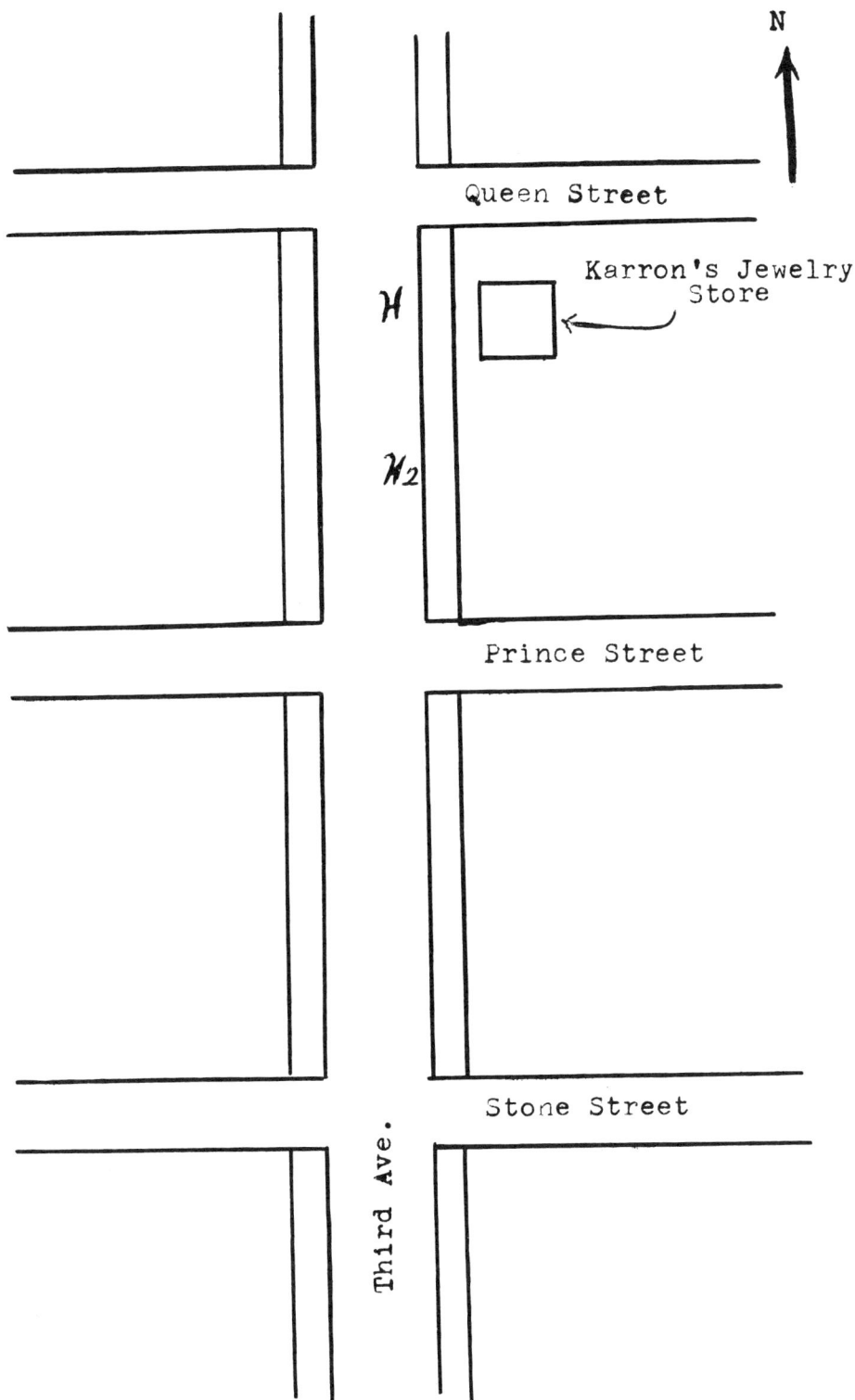

Assignments in Trial Practice

OPENING STATEMENT FOR THE PLAINTIFF

Mr. FIELD: Mr. Foreman, ladies and gentlemen of the jury, I am Richard Field. I am the counsel for Mrs. Sanders, the lady sitting at counsel table. The case you are about to hear is brought by her as plaintiff against Ira Bennett, the defendant, who is sitting in the middle of counsel table also, and who is represented by my friend Mr. Sutherland.

As counsel for the plaintiff, it is my duty at this time simply to tell you in a very general way what the plaintiff will endeavor to prove in this case and what witnesses we shall call. This is an action brought by Mrs. Sanders to recover for damages resulting from the death of her former husband, Mr. Joseph Rubin.

The circumstances which we will describe to you through witnesses were as follows: On the evening of March 6, 19Y2, Mrs. Rubin, as she then was, and her husband Mr. Rubin were airing their dog on Third Avenue in the City of Gray. As they were walking along, suddenly and with no warning so far as Mrs. Rubin was concerned, shots were fired and her husband fell to the pavement beside her, suffering gunshot wounds from which, as we will show you, he later died. This action is brought to recover damages for that death.

The defendant Ira Bennett was an employee of Karron's Jewelry Store, which was in the block where the shooting took place. We will show you that the shooting was done by an unknown, unidentified person who was one of the participants in a burglary of Karron's Jewelry Store. We will further show you that the defendant Ira Bennett was also a participant. We will, in fact, show you that Mr. Bennett was apprehended by the police officer in the store with some $150,000 worth of jewelry which he had removed from the safe, in his briefcase.

I believe his Honor at the appropriate time will instruct you that if Mr. Rubin was killed by a shot from this unknown person in the course of a burglary of the store in which Mr. Bennett, the defendant, was participating, Mr. Bennett is just as responsible for the death of Mr. Rubin as if he had himself fired the shot.

Many of the facts which I have outlined to you will not be contested in this trial. Some of them have actually been stipulated to, a device used by counsel to save his Honor's time and your time with respect to matters not genuinely in dispute. There are, however, issues of fact which are disputed in this case.

The defendant's main contention, as I understand it, is that, although he was actually in the store as I have described and actually had removed the jewelry from the safe, he did this because he was coerced into doing so by the unnamed gunman, and perhaps another. It is

Assignments in Trial Practice

asserted by the defendant that this is a sufficient defense to the facts.

You will, of course, hold your minds in suspended judgment on all these matters with respect to the law of the case until his Honor at the close of the evidence instructs you as to the law, and keep your minds in suspended judgment with respect to the facts until you have heard all the witnesses on both sides.

The plaintiff will call as her witnesses the plaintiff herself, Mrs. Sanders, and Officer Huggins, who was present at the scene. We shall also put in evidence certain stipulations that I have referred to and will read to you a deposition from the manager of the jewelry store, who is in the Netherlands and hence unavailable to be here. This deposition, which is his sworn evidence under oath, was taken in advance and in anticipation of the fact that he would not be here.

I shall now call Mrs. Sanders as the first witness.

MYRA RUBIN SANDERS, Sworn

- Q. (By Mr. Field) Will you state your name, please, Mrs. Sanders? A. Myra Rubin Sanders.
- Q. You are the plaintiff in this case? A. Yes.
- Q. Where do you live, Mrs. Sanders? A. At 1569 Beale Street, here in Gray.
- Q. Can you keep your voice up a little bit more so all members of the jury can surely hear you? You were the wife of the late Joseph Rubin? A. I was.
- Q. And Mr. Rubin has since died? A. He has.
- Q. When did he die? A. He died on May 30, 19Y2.
- Q. And at some subsequent time you married your present husband, Dr. Sanders? A. Yes.
- Q. Did you and Mr. Rubin have any children? A. We had no children.
- Q. Now turning your attention to the evening of March 6, 19Y2, what did you and your husband do that evening, Mrs. Sanders? A. We watched television until 10:30 and then we took our dog for a walk, as we usually did about that time in the evening.
- Q. Where did you and Mr. Rubin live at this time? A. At 713 Sixth Avenue in Gray.
- Q. Now will you tell us what you and Mr. Rubin did? A. We took the dog over onto Third Avenue. We usually went there because it was deserted at that time of night and the dog didn't bother anyone.
- Q. Was that part of Third Avenue in a shopping district? A. Yes. And I like to window shop.
- Q. About what time did you arrive on Third Avenue? A. I suppose about quarter of 11. I really don't know.

Mr. FIELD: It has, I believe, been stipulated, Mr. Sutherland, that these diagrams may be used.

Mr. SUTHERLAND: That is correct.

Q. I show you this diagram marked Pre-Trial Exhibit 3, Mrs. Sanders. North is on top of the map; Stone Street, Prince Street, and Queen Street are as marked. Will you indicate where it was that you were walking on Third Avenue -- from what direction to what direction?
A. We were walking from Stone Street toward Prince Street, north.
Q. And on which side? A. The right-hand side going north.
Q. That is on the right side of the map? A. Yes, on the right side.
Q. Will you tell us, please, what happened as you were walking along?
A. I saw a car which had been parked near the curb a little ahead of us --
Q. That is the curb on Third Avenue? A. Yes.
Q. And on the same side or the opposite side of the street? A. The same side we were on.
Q. And a little ahead of you? A. Yes, a little ahead of us.
Q. In what direction was the parked car headed? A. North. The same direction we were walking.
Q. Where was the parked car in relation to Stone and Prince Streets?
A. Almost in the middle of the block.
Q. What else did you observe about the car? A. It was headed in the direction we were walking, north. It had no lights on and it began to move very slowly north, and still the lights weren't put on. It went about a block, which would be between Prince Street and Queen Street, but nearer Queen Street, about three quarters of the way, I would say.
Q. Could you place it with reference to what is marked on the map as Karron's Jewelry Store? A. I can't be positive, but it was about there.
Q. That is, about opposite the Karron Jewelry Store? A. I would think so.
Q. Could you tell how many people were in the car? A. No.
Q. Will you go on with your description of what happened after you saw the car? A. The car stopped in the position indicated and someone got out and went into the building, and at about that time an officer came onto Third Avenue from Prince Street.
Q. And from which direction on Prince Street? A. Well, he turned right from Prince Street onto Third Avenue.
Q. Coming from the right or left side of the map? A. From the right side of the map.
Q. Thank you. A. In other words, he turned north.
Q. Yes. Go ahead, please. A. And he had gone only a few steps when someone came out of the building toward the car, which was parked there, and stopped for a few minutes and fired two gunshots.
Q. And then what happened, Mrs. Sanders? A. Then I felt Joe's grip on my arm tighten and he slumped to the pavement, and I bent over him and he was bleeding terribly, and I called to him and he couldn't--
Q. Bleeding terribly from what part of his body? A. From his head.

And he didn't answer, and I just don't remember much of what happened after that.

Q. Turning your memory back to a few moments before that, Mrs. Sanders, do you recall whether there were any other cars on Third Avenue as you were walking there? A. I didn't see any.

Q. Did you see any other pedestrians than the ones you have already mentioned? A. No.

Q. Now you have said that you don't remember much of what happened after your husband slumped to the pavement as you have described. Will you tell the Court and jury as much as you do remember, please? A. Someone came up from behind and offered to help, and I think he must have been the one who got the ambulance. Then an officer came back from -- I suppose it was the same one -- and took our names and addresses and he only stayed until the ambulance came.

Q. When the ambulance came, did you accompany him? A. I went in the ambulance. And there was another officer there, I think.

Q. You went where? A. To the hospital.

Q. How long was Mr. Rubin in the hospital? A. About three weeks.

Q. And thereafter what happened? A. He was told to be very quiet for a number of weeks and to resume activity rather slowly.

Q. At that time was Mr. Rubin engaged in business? A. No, he had retired.

Q. What was the general state of his health just before March 6, 19Y2? A. He was in very good health. He had had a recent check-up and his physical health was excellent. He did have a little nervous condition that played a part in his retirement.

Q. After he came home from the hospital and had been told to be careful, without going into any detail, Mrs. Sanders, what was the state of his health thereafter? A. He was in fair health, but he had headaches very frequently that bothered him a great deal.

Q. And these continued? A. They continued.

Q. With reference to his headaches, did something unusual happen in May? A. Yes. One morning toward the end of May he woke up with a very unusual headache, quite different from and much more severe than previous ones, and it was so bad I called our family doctor right away and he took him to the hospital again.

Q. What happened then? A. And he went into a coma and died a few days after that.

Mr. FIELD: I think that is all. You may inquire, Mr. Sutherland.

Mr. SUTHERLAND: And I think I have no questions, Mr. Field.

The COURT: Thank you, Mr. Sutherland.

Mr. FIELD: If Your Honor please, at this point I should like to read into the record certain of the stipulations made by counsel which appeared in the pre-trial order. For my purposes I shall not at this time read all of the stipulations unless Your Honor wishes them all read. I think there will be some which Mr. Sutherland may want later.

Mr. Foreman and ladies and gentlemen of the jury, as I stated in my opening, Mr. Sutherland and I have agreed to certain things; this means that no evidence will be offered, no witnesses on the stand will be asked to testify about these matters, and, as his Honor will instruct you when it comes time for you to deliberate on this case, you are to take them as agreed to be true. I shall now read them.

(Paragraphs 1-9 of the stipulations were read.) I shall for the time being omit stipulation ten. (Paragraph 11 was read.) Number twelve I will omit. Similarly number thirteen. (Paragraphs 14 and 15 were read.) I shall now offer testimony from Mr. Karron's deposition.

I shall ask my associate, Mr. Reardon, to sit in the witness chair and read the answers of Mr. Karron as I read the questions. First, Mr. Foreman and members of the jury, I will read the direct examination, which is the questioning of the witness by an associate in my office.

DEPOSITION TESTIMONY OF ARNOLD KARRON, JR.

(Questions read by Mr. Field and answers by Mr. Reardon)

Q. Are you Mr. Arnold Karron, Jr.? A. Yes.
Q. Where do you live, Mr. Karron? A. At 42 Fuller Street in the City of Gray.
Q. What business are you in? A. Since 19Y5 I have been manager of my father's jewelry shop -- Karron's -- located at 613 Third Avenue in Gray.
Q. Do you know an Ira Bennett? A. Yes, I do, he was employed by me as the assistant manager of the jewelry store.
Q. What caused the termination of your employer-employee relationship? A. Well, soon after the incident of Ira entering the store back on March 6th, we had a discussion about the incident and his gambling. I guess I tried to lecture him a little. Anyway, he got pretty huffed up about the whole matter and one thing led to another. He indicated that it would be best if he didn't continue on at the store and I agreed, so I gave him a month's pay and that's the last I saw of him.
Q. Were you friendly with Bennett socially? A. No -- I'm married and have three children while Ira was a bachelor, so we didn't really associate after business hours.
Q. Did Bennett ever mention financial problems or gambling to you? A. Yes, he did. The month before the attempted theft of jewels from the store, Ira asked for an advance on his salary. Since he gets paid at the end of the month, I saw nothing wrong with it. I was a little concerned, however, about the way he had been acting so I

asked him if anything was the matter. It was then that he told me about having lost some money gambling and needing an advance to make ends meet. I know how my dad feels about mixing gambling and the jewelry business, so I was a little upset over it.
Q. Could you tell us what Ira earned as an employee? A. Sure -- he made $18,000 a year until 19Y4 when he was promoted to assistant manager at $20,000.
Q. Do you know a Marsha Mather? A. No.
Q. Did Bennett ever mention the girl he was going with or the fact that he was engaged? A. No.
Q. Did Bennett ever mention coming down to the store at night to pick out a ring? A. No.
Q. Do you know a Phil Ricker? A. No.
Q. What was your policy about allowing Bennett to enter the store after hours? A. Well, I never forbade him to come in. He and I were the only ones with the key to the alarm or the key to the door. We occasionally would come down to the store at night to do some book work or let Mr. Mura, the watch repairman, in at night. Sometimes Ira and I would be in together, sometimes separately. I know of a few times he went in by himself at night to do book work and I never objected, so I guess I could be considered as giving him permission.
Q. Did he ever go in on personal business or to purchase something for a friend. A. Not that I know of.
Q. What type of alarm system did you have in the store? Would you tell us everything you can think of about it? A. We have an old type of burglar alarm with a large bell in the store. This bell is wired with the windows and doors of the store so that it goes off if they were broken open without first turning off the alarm. You can turn off the alarm only with a special registered H-shaped key. The lock to turn off the alarm is supposed to be pick-proof and this key, the insurance company tells us, can't be reproduced by any locksmith. The turn-off box is right above the front door to the store and we use the key to turn it off when we go in at night, or in the morning. Sometimes we open the front door in the morning without turning off the alarm in order to test it. It's pretty loud and can be heard for eight to ten blocks. The alarm can't be heard in the police station or at a detective agency as some of the newer systems can. It just rings loudly at the store.
Q. How do you set the alarm? A. The alarm is set before we close up each night. There's a switch in the back of the store and we set it and close the front door and the alarm is set. This switch can also be used to turn off the alarm from the inside.
Q. How many employees are there in your store? A. There are four of us all together.
Q. Who were the four on March 6, 19Y2? A. Myself, Ira, Phyllis Simms, our bookkeeper and saleslady, and Arno Mura, the watch repairman.
Q. Did Ira have the combination to the safe? A. Yes, I gave it to him when he was made assistant manager.
Q. What are the normal hours of operation of your store? A. 8:30 to

5:30.
Q. Who opened and closed the store? A. Usually Ira and I, but frequently one of us would do it alone, particularly when the other was on vacation.
Q. Do you remember who closed it on the night of the attempted theft? A. No.
Q. Was there a gun in the store? A. No.

Mr. FIELD: And I would like you to stop, Mr. Reardon, after the first word, because I should like to object to the balance of the answer.
A. No.

MR. SUTHERLAND: May I be heard, if Your Honor please?

The COURT: Surely.

MR. SUTHERLAND: I have made no objection to this dramatization of the deposition. It occurs to me, however, that inasmuch as my friend had launched upon this deposition, I should be allowed to complete the reading rather than to labor for the jury a fragment of it and omitting others which tend to favor my client.

The COURT: The only matter before me is whether this is admissible. I rule it is not and it may not be read.

Mr. SUTHERLAND: May the remainder of the excluded question go into the record as my offer of proof?

The COURT: It may. (The remainder of the excluded answer was as follows: "I don't believe in attempting to defend the store. I'd rather rely on police and insurance.")

Mr. SUTHERLAND: My exception.

The COURT: Your exception will be noted.

Q. Can the doors of the store be locked from the inside and the alarm be set while someone is still in the store? A. Yes.
Q. Would you describe the lock on the front door? A. Yes, it has a latch --it's the type that locks automatically when closed unless the button is pushed from the inside to keep it open.
Q. How long is the extension on the phone in the shop? A. It's fairly short, I'd say three or four feet because it just barely reaches the counter.
Q. Are there any street lights in front of the store? A. No, there are lights at each end of the block and two in the middle and opposite sides of the street - I'd say about in front of Miller's Sportswear, which is next to our store on the Prince side.

Assignments in Trial Practice

Q. When did you hear about the attempted larceny? A. About 3 a.m., after the police woke me up by calling my house.
Q. What did you do? A. I went to the store, locked up, set the alarm --then went to the police station to look at the jewelry and see if anything was missing.
Q. Was anything missing? A. No.
Q. How much was taken? A. I inventoried it at a cost value of $145,000 to $150,000.
Q. Was everything taken from the safe? A. No - only the top shelf was cleaned out. That's where the valuable stones and watches are. The less expensive stuff in the counter and window and on the lower shelf of the safe wasn't touched. We leave only a few inexpensive items in the counter or window over night.
Q. Did Ira know which shelf the valuables were on? A. Yes.
Q. Do you recognize this drawing marked Deposition Exhibit C?

    Mr. FIELD: Your Honor, it is agreed that Deposition Exhibit C is the same as Pre-trial Exhibit 1. A. Yes.

Q. What is it? A. A floor plan of my store and the nearby area.
Q. Is it accurate? A. Yes, I think so.
Q. Are there any night lights in the store? A. Yes, the insurance company required one on each side of the store. We have one over the safe and one in back of the left-hand counter as you walk in the store. Both are 100-watt bulbs.
Q. Do you think you could see into the store from outside, at night, well enough to see a person using the phone? A. Yes, unless he hid behind the desk.

    Mr. FIELD: That is the conclusion of the direct examination. I will leave the cross for Mr. Sutherland, if he cares to read it.

    Mr. SUTHERLAND: Will you please resume your seat, Mr. Counselor. If Your Honor please, I should like to read the cross-examination.

    The Court: Yes.

CROSS-EXAMINATION

(Questions read by Mr. Sutherland and answers by Mr. Reardon)

Q. Would you have objected to Ira's taking his fiancée to the store after working hours to pick out a ring? A. I don't think so - but I would have preferred knowing about it.
Q. Did you ever have anything stolen from the store while Ira was working there? A. Not that I know of and I would know if anything was missing.
Q. Didn't you have full faith in Ira's honesty, in other words, faith

Q. enough to leave him in complete charge? A. Well, yes.
Q. Did you frequently let him make cash bank deposits? A. Yes.

    Mr. FIELD: Now, if Your Honor please, I object to the following questions and answers.

    Mr. SUTHERLAND: Well, if Your Honor please, those questions and answers deal with certain arrangements within the store which were the subject of the direct examination. Direct examination brought out in considerable detail certain of the mechanical arrangements and these questions and answers carry further the point which my friend brought out by direct examination at the deposition.

    Mr. FIELD: If Your Honor please, the first of these two questions is purely argumentative and calls purely for a conclusion of the witness.

    The COURT: Your objection is sustained, Mr. Field. Do you desire an exception?

    Mr. SUTHERLAND: Yes, if Your Honor please. May the excluded question and answer go into the record as my offer of proof?

    The COURT: That will be done.

(The excluded question and answer were as follows:

Q. Isn't it true that if Mr. Bennett had wanted to preplan a larceny, he could have faked setting the alarm one night and could have left it off so someone else could have come in, thus allowing him to have an alibi for the time of the larceny? A. I guess so.)

    Mr. SUTHERLAND: So as to eliminate protracted argument, I waive the next question and answer.

    Mr. FIELD: The next question and answer are plainly inadmissible, but I have no objection if Mr. Sutherland would like to have it in.

(Mr. SUTHERLAND then introduced the question and answer, which appears next below.)

Q. Were you fully insured in case of any larceny? A. Yes.
Q. Was there any mention of gambling or need of an advance in pay prior to or after the one instance of February of 19Y2? A. No.
Q. Were there any rear exits from the shop that allowed one to leave without entering Third Avenue? A. No.
Q. Had any large order or purchase been received in the store just prior to March 6? A. No, we had about our normal inventory.

Assignments in Trial Practice

Mr. SUTHERLAND: That completes the cross-examination.

DANIEL R. HUGGINS, Sworn

Q. (By Mr. Field) Officer, what is your full name, please? A. Daniel R. Huggins.
Q. You are a police officer? A. Yes, I am.
Q. And have been for how long? A. Fourteen years.
Q. Of the Gray Police Department? A. Yes.
Q. What is your present position in the police department? A. Detective Sergeant.
Q. On March 6, 19Y2, what was your position in the police department? A. Patrolman.
Q. On the evening of March 6, where was your beat? A. I was in the downtown area of Gray, the 16-block area bounded by Third and Seventh and Prince and Market streets.
Q. You were on duty on the evening of March 6? A. Yes, I went on duty at 10 o'clock.
Q. Where were you about 11 o'clock of that night, officer? A. I was on Prince Street, checking the stores.
Q. In what direction were you walking on Prince Street? I think we need to have the other diagram again (placing Pre-Trial Exhibit 3 on the blackboard). A. I was on Prince Street walking towards Third Avenue.
Q. Where on Prince Street, on which side of Third Avenue? A. It was on the right side of the map.
Q. Walking then in a westerly direction on Prince Street? A. Yes.
Q. Thank you. As you were walking along Prince Street checking the stores, as you have said, I will ask you whether or not you observed anything on Third Avenue? A. As I was coming up Prince I noticed a car very slowly going along Third Avenue. That is not unusual at that time of night; a lot of people are window shopping.
Q. Going in which direction on Third Avenue? A. It was heading north on Third Avenue.
Q. That is in the direction of Queen Street? A. Yes, towards Queen.
Q. Did you observe any other traffic on Third Avenue at that time? A. No, it is a very quiet street.
Q. Was there any other traffic on Prince Street at that time? A. No, sir.
Q. Is this a common condition of things in that area? A. Yes.
Q. At that time of night? A. Quite common.
Q. What did you do thereafter? A. Well, I didn't pay much attention to the car; I just continued on my way until I got to the corner of the street and as I turned the corner--
Q. Which way did you turn? A. To my right.
Q. All right. A. I noticed the car had stopped approximately in front of Karron's, the door on the right-hand side was open, the engine was running, and the car lights were out. That was rather suspicious for that time of night so I quickened my pace and started

to go heading toward the car.
Q. Just stop there for a moment. Can you identify the make and type of car? A. Yes, it was a 19Y3 Ford.
Q. Sedan? A. Yes.
Q. All right, continue. Tell us what happened. Were you able to see who, if anyone, was in the car? A. No, I couldn't tell.
Q. All right. Now tell us what happened. A. Well, as I say, I rounded the corner and headed towards the car when I noticed the door open. I quickened my pace and started to run, and just as I did that a person came out of the doorway and headed towards the car. I called to him to halt and he fired two shots at me.
Q. What did you do then, officer? A. Ducked in the doorway.
Q. What happened after that? A. Well, I heard a woman scream, but that was way in the background, and I continued on.
Q. How long did you remain ducked in the doorway? A. Until I drew my gun.
Q. Just enough to draw your gun? A. To draw my gun.
Q. Then what happened? A. I headed for the car and it started to pull away quite rapidly.
Q. What happened to the car? A. It continued on down Third and then went around Queen Street.
Q. When you emerged with your gun drawn, would you indicate on the diagram approximately where the car was when you emerged with drawn gun. A. Oh, between --
Q. Will you step over and show us, please. A. Approximately there (indicating).

    Mr. FIELD: Now may we for the purpose of the record mark an "H" at that point, Mr. Sutherland, as indicating where he says the car was at that time?

    Mr. SUTHERLAND: Yes, indeed.

Q. And thereafter what happened to the car? A. The car -- there were no lights on it at that time so I couldn't get the license number; it just turned and went right down Queen Street, right down the street.
Q. How far were you from the Prince Street corner at the time you stepped out from the doorway? Can you indicate approximately where you were? A. Well, just about approximately there (indicating).

    Mr. FIELD: I will mark that "H 2," if I may (doing so).

Q. And I take it that at no time you were able to identify how many people there were in the car? A. No.
Q. What happened after the car disappeared? A. I ran on down the street and I noticed the door of the jewelry store open.
Q. Then what did you do? A. I stepped right inside, just glanced over it, and I noticed Ira Bennett crouched down by the counter.
Q. What lights were on in the jewelry store at that time? A. The

regular night lights that are always on.
- Q. Do you recall where they were? A. Yes, I patrolled that beat for some time. There is one over the safe and there is one over the opposite side of the store.
- Q. Now, you said after you went in and looked around you saw the defendant Ira Bennett? A. Yes.
- Q. Where did you see him? A. Right by the desk, between the desk and the counter area there.
- Q. Could you see him from the street? A. Yes, it was glass --
- Q. Did you see him yourself from the street? A. No, I didn't see him until I stepped in the door.
- Q. Will you tell us what happened after you saw him? A. Well, I saw him crouched there. I told him to stand up and asked, "What are you doing there?"
- Q. You said, "What are you doing there?" A. Yes.
- Q. Did he make a reply? If so, what? A. He said, "I work here."
- Q. By the way, had you ever seen him before? A. Yes, I had seen him in the store.
- Q. Did you know him to be an employee of the store? A. Yes, he was familiar in the store.
- Q. Did you know his name at that time? A. No.
- Q. Tell us what you did. A. I handcuffed him to the radiator and made sure he wasn't armed.
- Q. Which did you do first? A. Handcuffed him first.
- Q. Was there any further conversation? A. No.
- Q. What did you do after you handcuffed him to the radiator, as you have described? A. Called headquarters.
- Q. Where was the telephone? A. On the desk, as indicated.
- Q. At the point as indicated on the diagram marked Pre-trial Exhibit 1? A. Yes.
- Q. Was that telephone in good working order? A. Yes
- Q. You had no difficulty in putting the call through? A. None.
- Q. And you called, in effect, for help? A. Yes.
- Q. After you made that telephone call, what did you do? A. There was a bag beside Mr. Bennett and I moved it down by the safe, just glanced in it, and I seen there were jewels and I just put it there and went right out to the street.
- Q. What kind of a bag was it? A. A briefcase.
- Q. A briefcase, and you looked inside and saw there was jewelry? A. Yes, jewelry; that's all I could tell.
- Q. Did you say you put it in the safe? A. By the safe.
- Q. What did you do then? A. I wanted to check on the scream so I went and ran down Third Avenue.
- Q. Tell us what happened after that. A. I ran down Third Avenue and I noticed a man lying there with a woman kneeling over him.
- Q. How far down was that? A. Approximately halfway down the next block.
- Q. Where you had been, the block between Prince and Stone? A. That is right.

Q. Go on, tell us what you did. A. I knelt down and saw the man was bleeding and the woman was rather upset and crying, so I said, "I will get an ambulance right away," and she said something to the effect that an ambulance had been called, so I just got their names and I went right back to the store to my prisoner.
Q. Did you leave the door unlocked or open when you went out? A. I pushed the button so I could get back again.
Q. That is, you released it? A. Yes.
Q. So this knob or lock was then unlocked? A. Yes.
Q. Then what happened? A. The prowl car came.
Q. How soon was that? A. Oh, within a minute.
Q. Within a minute? A. Yes, we can get a prowl car in a minute to any part of the downtown district.
Q. That is, it came within a minute from the time you called? A. Yes.
Q. That would be when with reference to your return to your prisoner? A. Oh, a very short time, less than a minute; 30 seconds.
Q. After the prowl car came, what did you do? A. The other officers – one went to check on the man that was injured, and I released him from the radiator and put the handcuffs back on again, and then we checked the jewels in the case, just looked at them again and made a telephone call to Mr. Karron, the owner of the store.
Q. How many officers were in the prowl car? A. Two.
Q. The car, I take it, is radio equipped? A. Yes.
Q. What were the names of those officers? A. Dwyer and Nunn.
Q. After you made the call and the car came, what did you do? A. I took the prisoner down to headquarters.
Q. In the car, I take it? A. Yes.
Q. Did you have any further conversation with him before you left, sir? A. No.
Q. Have you told us all the conversation that you had with him at the time of your first entry when you found him crouching, as you have described? A. Yes, sir.
Q. I ask you whether or not in any form of words he said anything at that time about having been forced or coerced into doing this? A. Not then. He said something about it in the prowl car on the way.
Q. And you are completely sure that he didn't say anything about it the first time? A. Yes, positive.
Q. Did he say anything in the store in any form of words about any fear for the safety of the young lady he was engaged to? A. No.
Q. Or for fear of the safety of any other person? A. No.
Q. You are certain about that? A. I am positive.
Q. After you were in the prowl car on the way to the station, where did you sit and where was Mr. Bennett? A. We were both in the back seat.
Q. And one of the officers, I take it, was driving? A. Yes.
Q. Did you have any further conversation on the way to the station? A. At that point he was rather nervous and all that, and then he made some remark to the effect that "I was forced to do this, I didn't want to do it," something to that effect. I didn't believe him.

Assignments in Trial Practice

    Mr. SUTHERLAND: If Your Honor please, may that go out?

    The COURT: The statement of the witness "I didn't believe him" will go out. Ladies and gentlemen of the jury, you will disregard that statement.

Q. Was there any further conversation there, anything he said or you said after he made this remark? A. I said something like "Nuts" to the story.
Q. Did he say anything further? A. No.
Q. What happened after you got to the station? A. We brought him in, turned him over to the Sergeant, and the case, the jewel case, was turned over to the property clerk. He took care of it then.
Q. And he was booked, I take it? A. Yes, he was booked.
Q. I ask you whether or not you heard him say anything to the Sergeant at the time he was booked? A. I don't believe so.
Q. Well, specifically whether or not you heard him say anything similar to what he had said to you about being forced to do it? A. I believe he may have. I was busy booking the person.
Q. Did Mr. Bennett at any time name or describe in any way any other person who had been engaged in this operation? A. No.
Q. Did you have any further connection with the case after that? A. Well, when he was indicted, I didn't see him then.

    Mr. SUTHERLAND: Now may I ask my friend to state that the officer was wrong and that Mr. Bennett was never indicted?

    Mr. FIELD: I agree that the officer is in error when he states that Mr. Bennett was indicted. But I ask Your Honor to instruct the jury that they are not to consider this as bearing on their verdict in any way.

    The COURT: The jury will disregard what they have heard about indictment or lack of indictment.

    Mr. FIELD: That is all. You may inquire, Mr. Sutherland.

<u>CROSS-EXAMINATION</u>

Q. (By Mr. Sutherland) Sergeant, you told us a few moments ago that you had no connection with the case except for a matter that you mentioned after the events of March 6th. Is it not the case that on March 7th you made a written report to your superiors in the police department? A. Yes.

    Mr. SUTHERLAND: May I ask that this be marked for identification?

    The COURT: Yes.

(Typewritten document shown by Mr. Sutherland to the witness marked A for identification.)

Q. Would you glance at Exhibit A for identification and tell the jury whether this is the report to which you have referred? A. Yes.

Q. Was your recollection of the events of that evening better on the early morning of March 7th than it is now? A. I believe so.

Q. So that when you said to your superiors in the police department, "On the way in Bennett told us that he had not wanted to break into the store but that he had been made to do so by some hoodlum and that his girlfriend was still held as a hostage," that is a correct account of the events, is it not? A. Yes.

Q. So that it is a fact that in the car on the way to the station the defendant, Mr. Bennett, spoke of the word "hoodlum" and said that his girlfriend was still held as hostage? A. Yes.

Q. And this was the point at which you said, "Nuts," as you testified in direct examination, is that correct? A. Yes.

Q. At this time, Sergeant, you had been a police officer for how long? A. Five years.

Q. You had been, in the course of your official duties, familiar with kidnapping as a mode of compulsion by hoodlums? A. Yes.

Q. This is a fairly common practice of thugs, isn't it? A. I don't believe it is a common practice, but it has happened.

Q. It has happened with reasonable frequency, hasn't it, in the history of crime? A. Yes.

Q. When you went into the station house with the defendant on that evening did you report to any of your superiors on that occasion the statements that Mr. Bennett told you, that a young woman was held as a hostage by thugs in order to compel him to get into the store? A. Well, as I stated before, he was telling the Sergeant that, but I didn't -- I didn't pay attention because I really didn't feel it was true.

Q. Wasn't your reason for not reporting this the fact that Mr. Bennett was reporting it in your hearing? A. Partly.

Q. Partly, and so when you testified on your direct examination in response to my friend's question about Mr. Bennett's statements, "I believe he may have," your recollection now is quite definite that Mr. Bennett did complain that his fiancée -- A. I only heard part of the conversation. I would have when I had finished booking the person, I would have immediately contacted the Sergeant, but in the course of talking it over I would have said something to him, not in the sense of reporting it, I would just have said that he said he was compelled, but by indicating that I didn't believe him, but naturally the full decision would have been left to the Sergeant.

Q. Is it the case then that you did say to the Sergeant that Mr. Bennett complained of coercion and complained that his girlfriend was held as a hostage? A. No, I did not.

Q. You did not tell the Sergeant that? A. No.

Q. And you say your reason for not telling the Sergeant was two things:

first that you heard Mr. Bennett say it and, second, that you disbelieved Mr. Bennett, is that correct? A. Yes.
Q. Your practice as an officer is to report only those things which you believe?

Mr. FIELD: I submit that is an unfair question. He had already said he would have reported it to the Sergeant if he hadn't heard Mr. Bennett do so.

The COURT: Do you press the question?

Mr. SUTHERLAND: No, I don't press it.

Q. Sergeant, when you were in the jewelry store, when you first entered the store after the shots had been fired and you saw Mr. Bennett crouched by the counter, will you tell me again just where you saw him? I was unable to see the diagram from where I was sitting. A. Right between the desk and the counter, in that area there.
Q. Indicating the space at the front of the store on the right-hand side as you face the rear of the store? A. That is right.
Q. And to the right of the counter? A. That is right.
Q. Is there a glass window in the front of Karron's Jewelry Store, Sergeant? A. Yes.
Q. And the store is completely open to the street so that the passerby can look inside? A. Yes.
Q. Is the safe in full view from the street? A. Yes.
Q. And the light over the safe was lit so that the safe was fully open to view? A. It was.
Q. If you stood outside on the sidewalk in the evening you could easily see the safe and anybody opening it? A. Yes.
Q. I think you have testified that there were two 100-watt lights, am I correct, in that store? A. Yes.
Q. One was over the safe? A. Yes.
Q. The safe is taller than the desk where the telephone rests, is it not? A. Yes.
Q. So that the open door in the safe would be clearly visible from the street? A. Right.
Q. How long were you in the jewelry store from the time you entered after hearing the shots to the time that you left it after handcuffing Mr. Bennett to the radiator? A. It would have to be an approximation.
Q. Yes, of course it would have to be an approximation. A. Between two and three minutes.
Q. Two or three minutes. During that time you searched Mr. Bennett for weapons? A. Yes.
Q. And found none? A. That is right.
Q. He had no weapons whatever on him? A. No weapon.
Q. You saw none around him? A. No.
Q. You looked around him when you were handcuffing him to make sure

there was no weapon in reach of him? A. That is right.
Q. Was the door of the safe open when you came in? A. Well, I came in pretty fast, but I believe it was partially open.
Q. Stood ajar? A. It is rather difficult to be positive, I mean.
Q. Surely it is possible to be positive as to whether the door of the safe was open or not. A. Yes.
Q. Did you look in the safe to see whether or not anything else was in the safe? A. No.
Q. You did not? A. No.
Q. So that, Sergeant, after this passage of time your testimony now is that you are a little uncertain about the length of time you spent in the store and you are a little uncertain as to whether or not the door of the safe was open or not. A. I don't think anyone could say exactly how long they were in the store or know if the safe was open. I just glanced at it. My attention was concerned with the man more than the safe, so any length of time would tend to obscure your memory.
Q. You testified very definitely on your direct examination that the only words uttered by Mr. Bennett during the minutes that you were in the store were three words, "I work here." Are you entirely sure that those were the only three words uttered by Mr. Bennett during the minutes that you were in the jewelry store? A. I didn't say they were the only three words. It was just, "What are you doing to me? Why are you handcuffing me? I work here."
Q. Ah, he did say other things besides, "I work here"; he said, "What are you doing to me" and "Why are you handcuffing me?" A. Something to that effect.
Q. You aren't quite sure just what he did say? A. No, I can't remember whether he did just say these words at that time.
Q. Surely; and I just have been saying that your memory of exactly what was said is naturally, Sergeant, a little bit uncertain; am I correct in that? A. No, I remember quite well. It was just to the exact way the words were said. He might have said, "I work here" or "Don't you know me, I work here," or something like that, but nothing else but that.
Q. Am I not correct, Sergeant, in saying that you are not quite certain what he did say there? A. You mean the exact wording of that particular sentence; I am not positive of the exact wording.
Q. And he may have said two or three other sentences; that was your testimony a moment or two ago, was it not? A. No, that was all he said.
Q. Would you say that Mr. Bennett was calm and collected when you saw him? A. No, he was quite nervous.
Q. He was quite nervous. Well, you were a little bit excited at having been shot at, am I correct? A. Yes.
Q. No fun to be shot at, is it? A. No.
Q. You had pulled your own gun and were ready to shoot back, isn't that so? A. I was expecting trouble.
Q. You were expecting trouble at any minute? A. Yes.

Assignments in Trial Practice

Q. You were alert for trouble? A. Yes.
Q. Does your memory improve under these circumstances? A. I think you remember most of the details pretty well.
Q. You remember most of the details pretty well, but not all of them pretty well am I correct? A. I would say yes.
Q. So that it remains possible, doesn't it, Sergeant, that you don't remember everything that Mr. Bennett said to you during the time that he was in the store and he was in an excited state and you were in an excited state? A. I remember everything he said, but I can't say the exact words, but I mean the essential sentence, the fact that he was getting, trying to get across was that "I am an employee, I work here," but that was all he mentioned, that one fact that "I work here."
Q. Didn't he say, "What are you taking hold of me for?" You said that. A. Said something to that effect, "Why are you doing this to me, because I work here."
Q. In any event, some kind of a protest at your seizing him? A. Yes.
Q. Was the door of the store open or closed when you went in? A. It was open.
Q. It stood open? A. Yes.
Q. When you went out you closed it? A. I just snapped the button like that.
Q. You personally telephoned to Mr. Karron's from the store? A. No, one of the officers that was left behind.
Q. In your presence? A. No.
Q. So when you testified that an officer telephoned to Mr. Karron this is something that you don't know personally? A. Just the fact that back in the station we discussed it.
Q. You and the officer left behind? A. A routine procedure, when one officer remains in the store, to make a call like that, a fire or a burglary or anything like that.
Q. So when you testified a few moments ago that an officer had made a given call, you now testify that this was your assumption because that is what always happens when officers are under these circumstances, am I right? A. It is routine procedure, police procedure, yes.
Q. So you don't know what happened when you testified to this a few moments ago; this you testified to because you say it is routine. A. And the fact that I spoke to the officer back in the station.
Q. The same officer that was left behind in the store? A. In the morning when we were making our reports.
Q. Oh, I see, next morning you got this from the officer then. Now is there anything else in your testimony that you gave us today, Sergeant Huggins, that you got from the reports of other people or that you are not quite sure of? A. I don't believe so.

    Mr. SUTHERLAND: All right, thank you very much.

REDIRECT EXAMINATION

Q. (By Mr. Field) Regarding the words that you do not exactly remember, as you told Mr. Sutherland, do you remember for sure whether or not anything in any form of words was said about his being coerced while in the store? A. I am positive he made no reference whatsoever to that.

Q. Or about his girlfriend being a hostage? A. No reference whatsoever. I am positive.

Q. You told Mr. Sutherland that you didn't believe Mr. Bennett. Why didn't you? A. Well, where I had walked in on a robbery and had handcuffed this man and he had made no statement then, I mean to my way of thinking, the first thing I would have done was say "My girl friend is in danger. Never mind me." He made no reference to that, and no reference in the car right away until we were almost in the station, and then all of a sudden he made this reference to her. I just didn't believe it.

    Mr. FIELD: Thank you, that is all.

    Mr. SUTHERLAND: That is all.

    The COURT: Thank you.

    Mr. FIELD: That is the plaintiff's case, if Your Honor please. We rest.

    The COURT: The plaintiff rests.

    Mr. SUTHERLAND: Now, if Your Honor please I offer the following motion:

The defendant moves that the jury be instructed to return a verdict for the defendant on each and all of the following grounds:

1. There is insufficient evidence from which the jury could find that the defendant conspired with the unknown person who is alleged to have injured the plaintiff's decedent.

2. As a matter of law even if there were sufficient evidence from which the jury could find the existence of a conspiracy, the injury to the plaintiff's decedent was outside of the scope of such a conspiracy.

    The COURT: The motions are denied. Exceptions may be recorded.

    Mr. SUTHERLAND: Would Your Honor wish that I proceed to open?

    The COURT: You may proceed.

OPENING STATEMENT FOR THE DEFENDANT

Mr. SUTHERLAND: Mr. Foreman and ladies and gentlemen of the jury, I shall be very brief in outlining the testimony which shall be adduced before you on behalf of the defendant, Mr. Bennett. We shall show you by testimony of Mr. Bennett and the testimony of the young lady to whom he was engaged that he was a man of unblemished reputation, that he had been employed in a highly trusted situation for a long time, entrusted with the handling of valuables by his employer and indeed that confidence continued after the occurrences or events of that night, which resulted in the death of Mr. Rubin. And we make no attempt here to make light of the loss which Mrs. Rubin, as she then was, or Mrs. Sanders, as she now is, suffered by that event.

We shall show you that on the evening in question an ex-convict, a man who had done time for theft and a thug whose name is unknown, but who is a gunman, in fact, the gunman that did the killing that night, at gunpoint kidnapped the defendant; that the ex-convict whose name was Ricker kidnapped Mr. Bennett's fiancée to whom he had just become engaged; that under threats of death to Mr. Bennett by the gangsters and threats of death to his fiancée, Mr. Bennett went to the jewelry store and used the key which his employers had given to him to use; went into the store and had under this coercion put the jewelry in a briefcase at the time when fortunately the police arrived and broke up the crime.

Under these circumstances I shall ask his Honor to instruct the jury that the coercion to which he was subjected, that the threats of death by the gangsters are justification for him and render it legally impossible for you to bring in a verdict against Mr. Bennett.

I shall not detain you longer. I gather, Your Honor, that the witnesses will be called after the luncheon adjournment.

The COURT: Yes. Before we adjourn, Mr. Foreman and members of the jury, for the luncheon recess, may I ask you to bear in mind that you are sitting as judges of the fact in this important case. It is necessary for you therefore to keep your minds entirely open. I ask you not to discuss what has taken place in this courtroom today by way of testimony and that you defer your discussion, if you should be eating together, until after all testimony is over and the case is in your hands.

If you are at a loss concerning what to discuss, you may discuss the lawyers, the judge, and others. We will meet again at 2 o'clock.

AFTERNOON SESSION

The COURT: You may proceed.

Assignments in Trial Practice

Mr. SUTHERLAND: May it please the Court, I would like to call Mr. Ira Bennett, the defendant.

<u>IRA M. BENNETT, Sworn</u>

Q. (By Mr. Sutherland) Your name is Ira M. Bennett? A. Yes, sir.
Q. You are the defendant in this case? A. That is right, sir.
Q. You have lived in this city all of your life? A. Yes, sir.
Q. You are engaged to a young lady named Marsha Mather? A. Yes, sir.
Q. And she is sitting in the courtroom now, is that correct? A. Yes, sir, right there (indicating).
Q. You went to high school in this town? A. Yes, sir.
Q. After that what did you do? A. I was in the army for three years.
Q. What was your army experience? A. I was a clerk at the Headquarters at Fort Dix, New Jersey.
Q. Will you keep your voice up, if you please, so that the jury can hear you, Mr. Bennett? A. Yes, sir.
Q. After you got through with your Fort Dix experience what was your next move in life? A. I obtained a job at Bushings Credit Jewelers in one of their stores.
Q. You stayed with Bushings until when? A. 19Y5 when I came with Karron's.
Q. You stayed with Karron's until sometime in March of 19Y2? A. Yes.
Q. Your concluding position at Karron's was what? A. I was assistant manager of the store.
Q. What were your duties as assistant manager? A. It was a fairly small sized store and I had general charge of the store, taking care of the customers, the employees, opening and closing, taking care of some of the books, making bank deposits, just about regular charge of the business.
Q. The boss, if I may put it so, was Mr. Karron, Jr.? A. That is right, sir.
Q. And there was yourself and two other employees? A. Right, sir.
Q. And the bookkeeper and the watch repairman? A. That is right.
Q. Did you ever meet a man named Phil Ricker? A. Yes, sir. I was introduced to Phil Ricker at a cocktail party at Marsha Mather's house in December of 19Y3.
Q. What part of December? A. Before Christmas, December 22nd, it was, I guess, December 22nd.
Q. Did you have any great amount of talk with him at that party? A. No, sir. It was just a casual introduction.
Q. Did you ever see this man Ricker again? A. I believe that I saw him once again when he came into my car on the night of March 6.
Q. Did you ever see Mr. Ricker on any occasion besides the time when there was a party at Miss Mather's house and the episode that you are going to tell us about on the evening of March 6th? A. No sir. I had never seen him before and I have never seen him since.
Q. Did you have any talk with him at Marsha Mather's house? A. None that I can remember. I remember being introduced to him and a lot of people were there at the time. It just passed by and that was

the end of it.

Q. Until after the episode of March 6th had you ever heard of Ricker's having a criminal record? A. No, sir. I knew nothing about him.

Q. What was your pay at Karron's Jewelry Store during the period of December, January, February of 19Y3 and 19Y2? A. I was getting $20,000 a year.

Q. You had a key to the store? A. Yes, sir.

Q. You were trusted with the combination to the safe? A. Yes, sir.

Q. Will you tell us something about the interior of Karron's store, if you please, and with particular reference to the two doorways which appear in the display map marked Pre-trial Exhibit 1? A. There is the front door and there is a door right by the telephone going out into a space labeled "Miller's Sportswear Loading Dock," and "Blind alley."

Q. Is there any way out to any street from the inside of Karron's store other than Third Avenue? A. No sir. No matter which door you go out you would always come out on Third Avenue.

Q. After you met Marsha on the evening of December -- what date was that? A. December 22nd.

Q. Did you see her again? A. Yes, sir. I saw her quite often from then on, several times a week. We would go out to a show, dancing, so forth. We went out very often.

Q. You took her out a good deal, is that right? A. That is right.

Q. You and she had a good time, is that right? A. Very good, yes, sir.

Q. There has been some talk about gambling in a deposition of Mr. Karron read here. Would you like to describe any of your recreations in that connection? A. Well, unfortunately, I had started going to Warren's Raceway fairly often, a trotter and running raceway, and betting on the horses. I wasted my life's savings on that.

Q. Your savings amounted to how much? A. $10,000, about.

Q. Those were pretty well spent between going around places with Marsha and losing money at the race track? A. That is right, yes, sir.

Q. There has appeared in Mr. Karron's deposition something about your getting an advance on your pay at Karron's Jewelry Shop in the latter part of February. How much of an advance did you get at that time? A. I got $250 at that time.

Q. On the evening of the 5th of March something happened of interest to you and Marsha. What was it? Will you describe that event? A. We became engaged that night. We had gone out to dinner and a show and we were having some drinks before taking her home. I asked her if she would marry me. She said she would. Immediately then she said something, "I will have to tell Phil that I can't see him any more." I knew that she had been going out with other men but I didn't know that she was going out with one man to the extent that she would have to tell him that she couldn't see him any more. I became a little anxious that we could clinch the deal, and I asked her to come down to the jewelry store the next morning so that we could

pick out a ring.
Q. She said that she would have to tell Phil? Did she say Phil who? A. I asked her. She said, "You remember Phil Ricker. You remember, you met him at the party."
Q. Did she say any more about Phil? A. No. And I didn't ask her. That was going to be the end of Phil.
Q. All right. Now, when you asked Marsha to come down to the store and pick out a ring on the next morning, that would be March 6th? A. Yes, sir. That would be March 6th, yes.
Q. What did Marsha say? A. She said that she had a fitting engagement. She was a model at that time. She had an engagement. I was rather sore that she couldn't make it. I asked her to come down in the afternoon right after lunch. She said that she was having pictures taken at that time.
Q. She was a professional model? A. Yes, sir.
Q. And she was being called on to be photographed for some modeling? A. That is right, yes, sir.
Q. What happened next? She said that she had to be fitted in the morning and photographed in the afternoon, what happened next? A. She suggested that maybe as soon as she was finished with this camera session that she would come down to the store. I thought that that would be O.K. Then I remembered that I had to make a delivery late that afternoon when we closed the store.
Q. A delivery of what? A. We make deliveries to certain, special customers on items that they need on a certain special day. One of these customers ordered a certain special set of rings.
Q. Who ordered this special set of rings? A. Mrs. Van Fleet.
Q. Where does Mrs. Van Fleet live? A. Town Falls.
Q. That is how far from the city? A. That is about 20 miles from Gray.
Q. This errand to take these jewels to Mrs. Van Fleet on that afternoon was something which Mr. Karron had discussed with you or directed you to do? A. Yes. This was the usual state of affairs when we had a special item to get out within a certain time. The people usually wanted it for an engagement or anniversary and they wanted it on a certain date. Mrs. Van Fleet wanted this on a certain date.
Q. All right. Now, you explained this to Marsha, what happened next? A. I told her that I couldn't make it then. Then I told her that if when I came back, if there was time, we might go to the store and if she was home I would stop by at her flat and go down to the store and open up and I would show her some rings.
Q. Did you suggest a time? A. I expected that I would be back in the vicinity of 9 o'clock. I didn't think that it would be much later than that.
Q. All right, anything else that night, the night of the 5th, the night that you became engaged? A. No. sir.
Q. The next day, tell us what you did, please? A. The next day I went to work as usual. The day went as usual and I closed the store at 5:30.

Q. When you say that you closed the store, you mean you were the last man out? A. Yes, sir.
Q. What was your routine in closing the store? A. Checking the store, closing the safe, making sure that no stuff that we keep in the safe overnight was left out on display, then setting the alarm, shutting off all the lights except the two night lights, and locking the door.
Q. The two night lights are 100-watt lamps, one over the safe and one on the left part of the rear of the store as you face the rear of the store, am I correct? A. That is right, yes, sir.
Q. After closing up the store, tell us what you did next, please? A. Well, I of course took the ring and earrings and drove out to Town Falls to Mrs. Van Fleet's to make the delivery. I was kind of hungry but didn't stop on the way out. I wanted to get rid of the jewels before I stopped for supper. I delivered the jewels and turned around and started back. I stopped for supper on the road and I arrived back and went immediately to Marsha's flat.
Q. Where does Marsha live? A. Marsha lives at 19 Westchester Road.
Q. What kind of a house is 19 Westchester Road? A. It was formerly a single residence but it is now made over. It has about four apartments in it.
Q. And you arrived at 19 Westchester Road at what time? A. Approximately 9:30.
Q. You were driving what kind of a car? A. My own car, a 19Y4 Oldsmobile convertible, yellow.
Q. Bright yellow? A. Yes, sir.
Q. You parked your car where? A. Just about directly in front of the entrance to Marsha's house.
Q. Did you see anything of Marsha's car? A. I faintly recall passing it when I parked. I believe it was parked at the time a couple of car spaces behind me, two or three car lengths.
Q. Was the street crowded at that time? A. No, sir. It was fairly deserted.
Q. You got into Marsha's house about 9:30? A. Yes, sir about 9:30.
Q. Tell us what happened then, if you please? A. Well, I rang for her and she was ready to leave. She got her coat and we immediately went downstairs. We walked down to my car. I opened the door to let her in and went around to get in on my side.
Q. She got in on the side closest to the curb? A. That is right, sir.
Q. And your side was the driver's side? A. That is right, yes, sir.
Q. Now, just tell what happened in your own words, please. A. I got into the driver's seat and closed the door. Before I could start, I think that I had my key out, then some man put his head in the window of the car, with a gun right in my face, right in front of my eyes.
Q. Which side of the car was this man on? A. He was standing in the street. He was on my left.
Q. On your left? A. That is right, sir. And he said, "You just better listen to me. Don't make any noise." I don't really remember his exact words because he had this gun right in my face.

He said, "If you want to get out of this alive you will do everything I say." Meanwhile, I heard Marsha say, "What is this, Phil?" I turned around and apparently this Phil Ricker, from what I could see of him in the car, he had pushed into the back seat. He didn't say anything. This man just said, "You better get out." And with the gun, he sort of pulled at me and I got out of the car.

Q. Now, your convertible has a pair of seats immediately behind the wheel and another pair of seats just immediately behind those, is that right? A. That is right, sir.

Q. It was in the latter pair of seats that Phil Ricker pushed himself, as you testified? A. Yes, sir from Marsha's side.

Q. Then what happened, if you please? A. He marched me back to where Marsha's car was.

Q. Would you describe where her car was with relation to house No. 15 on the street? A. I would say on this chart, it is a little bit to the right of the corner, or just after the corner of house No. 15. I am not sure. It was about three or four car lengths, two or three car lengths. It was not a long walk from my car to her car.

Q. And both cars were heading toward the left as you faced this map, which is Pre-trial Exhibit 2? A. Yes, sir, that is right.

Q. And the top was up on the convertible, the top was sheltering the convertible? A. Yes, sir.

Q. It was not folded down? A. No, sir, no.

Q. Will you please tell us what happened then? A. Well, when we got to Marsha's car he opened the door and pushed me in and said, "Slide over." I got in and slid over and then he got into the driver's seat.

Q. What kind of a car is Marsha's? A. A blue Ford sedan, 19Y3, I guess.

Q. Dark blue or light blue? A. Dark blue.

Q. You got into the front door or the rear door? A. No, I got in right behind the wheel and he said, "Shove over." We got in on the street side.

Q. What happened then, please? A. He got in and then he started the car and he put his gun in his lap.

Q. You say that he started the car? Did he say anything about a key? A. I didn't even think about it at the time. But, apparently, he had all the keys he needed because the car started.

Q. Was the car a manually operated gear shift car? A. No, sir. Marsha's car has an automatic shift.

Q. Tell us what happened? A. He started the car and pulled away from the curb and we started out down Westchester Road.

Q. Where was your car as you started out? A. Well, as we started we passed my car. It was parked in the same place where I had left it.

Q. What happened then, please? A. He started driving in a rather odd fashion, making a lot of turns, backtracking over his own route. He just kept driving like this. As soon as we started I asked him what this was all about, what he was going to gain by kidnapping me. I had never seen him before. He said, "We are going down to Karron's

to clean out the safe. We are going to get the jewels out of the safe."
Q. Will you please describe this man? A. He gave me a very big impression. He was taller than I was and he was very broad. It was very shadowy and dark. I think that he was dark complected but it was hard to tell because it was so shadowy. But he was a big man.
Q. You mentioned a weapon. Will you describe the weapon, please? A. Yes, sir. I believe it was a revolver because I saw the cylinder. It had a short barrel. That is about all that I remember. He just pointed it right in my face.
Q. You brought us up to the time when this man was driving Marsha's car around with you in it. Now, go on with your story, please. A. He said, "We are going down to Karron's and get the jewels out of the safe." I said, "This is impossible. Karron's is locked up." He just laughed. He said, "If you want to get Marsha out of this alive you will get into Karron's." He said, "Just use your keys the way you planned to do with Marsha." I guess that he knew somehow that we were going down for a ring that night.
Q. All right, go ahead with your story. What happened with you and this man? A. He kept making funny turns, backtracking, so forth. He drove over to a section of town that I am not familiar with. It is an industrial section with factories and offices and it was quite dark. While we were driving through that section he pulled into an empty lot. There were some cars and trucks parked on the lot. He pulled in between the two trucks. He stopped the car and told me to get out. As soon as I got out he got out himself and he had taken from the back seat a length of rubber hose.
Q. Did you ever see that rubber hose before? A. No, sir. I had never seen it.
Q. You had been in the car with Marsha a number of times? A. Yes, sir.
Q. You had never seen any rubber hose before? A. No, sir.
Q. All right, continue. A. He uncapped a gasoline tank on a truck right next to us. We had pulled in between these two trucks. He siphoned gas from the truck's tank into our tank, using this rubber hose.
Q. You were standing there at all times? A. Yes, sir.
Q. Where were you standing with relation to this man? A. He was standing right about at the rear of the car where the gas tank is. I was standing right about where the front door handle would be.
Q. What was in front of you or in front of the car? A. Apparently, there was a wall, just a blank brick wall of some building next door.
Q. And beside the car, Marsha's car, what was there? A. The truck that he was siphoning the gas from.
Q. On the other side of Marsha's car, what was there? A. I don't know. There was another truck there.
Q. Did you see any people in the lot there? A. No, sir. The whole neighborhood was deserted.

Q. Was there a light in this lot? A. No, sir.
Q. What about the lights on the car while you were in between the two trucks? A. He shut them off as soon as we stopped, he shut the lights off.
Q. All right. After this gasoline episode, continue with the story, please. A. Then he ordered me to get back into the car. He started driving around again. I guess he went downtown. Still, this turning corners, backtracking, so forth. Then he got on to Third Avenue and he started going uptown.
Q. Was there any conversation between you during all this time? A. He just -- I just remember telling him that he was crazy to think that he would get away with anything because it didn't seem to me that you could rob Karron's that way.
Q. What did he say? A. He just said to keep my mouth shut and to listen to what he said if I wanted to see Marsha back and if I wanted to live myself.
Q. You got to Third Avenue, describe what happened then? A. Well, I think just about when we turned on Third Avenue he said, "I am going to drop you off right near Karron's and I am giving you five minutes to get inside and clean out that safe and to meet me out here." And, again he threatened me and he threatened Marsha. He said if I didn't hurry and if I was not ready at the end of five minutes that he would come in and "cool" me.
Q. Come in and cool you? A. Yes, sir.
Q. What did you do? A. Well, when we got to -- can I point it out?
Q. Yes, surely, get up and indicate on the map. A. We had been going uptown on Third Avenue.
Q. When you say "uptown," do you mean moving in a northerly direction? A. Yes, sir.
Q. You were moving northerly on Third Avenue? A. Yes, sir.
Q. Go on with the story, please. A. He slowed down. I guess it was about Summer Street that he slowed down. He told me he was giving me the five minutes and he would be by. He dropped me off between Stone and Prince, closer to Prince, I would say. I walked down to Karron's. I know that he pulled away and I believe that he drove down the street.
Q. Do you know whether his lights were on or off? A. I couldn't say. When he dropped me off I didn't notice. I don't know. But when he drove away his lights were on.
Q. When he drove away his lights were burning? A. Yes, sir.
Q. Did you see whether he stopped the car at any point on Third Avenue? A. I didn't see him stop. But I wasn't paying particular attention because he seemed to mean business. And I had to get to the jewelry store.
Q. Describe what you did, if you please? A. I walked down to Karron's. I used my alarm key to shut off the alarm, right over the store. I used my key to get inside and I went over to the safe.
Q. Mr. Bennett, were you in fear? A. Yes, sir, very much.
Q. In fear of what? A. Fear of being killed by this man. He had a

gun and he kept waving it in my face and threatening me with it. He seemed to me to be the kind that would use it.

Q. Were you in fear of anything else? A. I was in fear for Marsha. I knew that Marsha was with Phil and apparently Phil was no trustworthy character, being in on this sort of thing.

Q. Had you heard any talk from this man with you about threats to Marsha? A. From him to me?

Q. Yes. A. Oh, from the very beginning, yes. He always said that if we wanted to get out of this alive, or if I ever wanted to see her again, that I had better listen to everything that he said.

Q. When you reached the store and went in, as you have testified, describe what you did exactly? A. I went in and went over to the safe.

Q. The safe is about how high? A. The safe is about as tall as I am, one of these big jewelry store safes. I started to open it. It must have taken me quite awhile because I was pretty nervous and shaky. The combination didn't work for two or three times. I finally got it opened and there was this leather briefcase right out over the safe. I started to throw the jewels from the safe into the briefcase.

Q. Can you estimate how long this took you? A. I couldn't say. I know it must have been a short time because he said that he would give me only five minutes. But it seemed like an awful long time.

Q. Then what happened next, please? A. Well, before I knew it, while I was still putting the stuff into the briefcase, I heard a car pull up outside. The door opened and this same man sticks his head in the door and said, "Someone is coming. You better hurry."

Q. The door opened? Had you closed the door when you went in? A. I guess I didn't leave it entirely open. I must have left it so that it didn't catch on the latch. But just a little bit ajar. So it had to open before someone could really look in.

Q. Was there any talk by this man to you at this time? A. He said, "You better hurry up, someone is coming."

Q. Who said that, "You better hurry up, someone is coming"? A. That man who had kidnapped me in Marsha's car.

Q. What did you do then? A. I frantically began throwing everything into the briefcase, sort of sweeping it into the briefcase. I started to run toward the door. Before I reached the door I heard shots.

Q. From what direction did you hear the shots? A. From the same direction that I heard the car.

Q. What did you do? A. I just ducked. I thought he was shooting at me.

Q. Just a moment until I turn to the map of the store again. When you ducked, where were you? A. Well, I don't believe that I had yet rounded that turn by the right corner toward the door, somewhere in between. I guess it was somewhere in the vicinity of that desk.

Q. Do you see a pencil mark, "X" I think, between the desk and the street end of the counter? A. Yes, sir, I do.

Q. Will you describe where you ducked with reference to that pencil mark "X"? A. Well, just around that pencil mark, right near the desk. I know I was right near the desk and the counter.
Q. The counter, that is about how high? A. About waist high, three and one-half feet, I would guess.
Q. Describe what happened then. A. Well, before I knew it the policeman ran in the door. I knew it was the policeman because he ran over to me. And this was Officer Huggins. He is the cop on that beat, right in the jewelry store area. I tried to tell him that he had better get somebody to safeguard Marsha because this man had gotten away and that he knew me and should not worry about me, that I worked in the place. He just took out his handcuffs and handcuffed me to the radiator.
Q. Will you tell us please, Mr. Bennett, whether you were excited or not at this time? A. I was about the most nervous that I ever was in my whole life.
Q. Had you ever heard any outcry from anyone? A. I think that after the shots I heard a scream and some more screaming.
Q. Could you locate where you heard the screaming? A. Somewhere out on the street. I had no idea where it was from.
Q. All right. Now, will you describe what happened after you were handcuffed to the radiator? What happened next? A. It wasn't but a minute or two that the same officer came back. Again, I tried to tell him about Marsha and that I was forced into this thing and that her life was in danger because that man in her car had gotten away. He didn't seem to pay any attention to me. He just said, "Bide your time," or something like that, or "Wait." It wasn't long after that when this police car came by and they took me away in that.
Q. Did you hear Officer Huggins testify that the police car came a minute or less if I heard him correctly? A. I don't know that it was that soon. I know that there was a period of time while I was handcuffed, from the time he was there, and then there was another period of time after he had come back.
Q. Would you tell us whether it was a long time or short time? A. It was a fairly short time.
Q. All right. Then, what happened to you next? A. Well, while going down the corridor I was trying to tell some of the others that Marsha was in danger and that this man got away. I tried to tell them but he just wouldn't pay any attention to me. As he testified, once he yelled out, "Nuts."
Q. When was it that he yelled out "Nuts"? Was that in the car? A. Yes, sir, in the car.
Q. Were you riding from Karron's Jewelry Shop to where? A. I guess to the police station.
Q. What happened to you in the police station? A. They started all this booking procedure. They took my fingerprints and I had to answer to a lot of questions. Then they took me into another room where they started more questioning of what had gone on that night.
Q. Did you say anything about your experience at Marsha's house? A.

Yes, sir. I told them just what happened. I was a little more calm at the time. I guess that after awhile they listened to me, I think. This officer was not there then anyway.
Q. Officer Huggins had left? A. Yes, sir.
Q. How long after you came to the police station did Officer Huggins leave? A. I couldn't say exactly. When I was being booked he was around there. But when I moved into one of these rooms he was no longer there.
Q. There came a time when you signed a statement for the police? A. Yes, sir.
Q. At what time was that? A. I guess about 7 o'clock in the morning, 6:30 or 7 o'clock in the morning.

(Single-page document, statement signed by Ira Bennett, dated 6:30 a.m., March 7, 19Y2 marked Exhibit B for identification.)

Q. Mr. Bennett, I show you Exhibit B for identification, and I ask you if that is the statement that you signed at the police station? A. Yes, sir it is.
Q. I call to your attention the indication of an hour at the upper right-hand corner of that statement? A. Yes, sir.
Q. I ask you if your recollection is any clearer now as to the exact time that you signed that statement? A. Yes, sir. It was 6:30 a.m.
Q. What did you do after you signed the statement? A. Well, they took me back to the desk sergeant and he said that I could go home, but not to leave town, that they would want me for questioning. That was about all and I went home.
Q. You went home to your own house? A. Yes, sir.
Q. Were you asked to post any bail? A. No, sir.
Q. When you got home what did you do? A. The first thing I did was to call Marsha.
Q. You called her where? A. I called her at her home but there was no answer. I called several times.
Q. Does Marsha live by herself? A. Yes, sir.
Q. In a flat which you described in the made-over house? A. That is right.
Q. How often did you call her? A. I guess that I must have called her every fifteen minutes.
Q. Did there come a time when you heard from Marsha? A. Yes, sir. She phoned me about 9:30.
Q. And you had a conversation with her on the phone? A. Yes, sir.
Q. After the conversation, as you understand it, she went somewhere? A. Yes, sir. I told her to go to the police. She told me what had happened to her and I thought that the police ought to know about it.
Q. Did you see anything more of the police in the period between then and the present time?

Mr. FIELD: I submit, if Your Honor please, all of this seems thoroughly irrelevant in this case.

The COURT: I shall exclude this line of questioning.

Q. Did there come a time when you went back to your place of employment? A. Excuse me?
Q. Did there come a time when you went back to Karron's Jewelry Shop? A. Yes, sir. I phoned him that morning that I couldn't come in. I needed to get some rest. I phoned him just at about opening time, I guess, and said that I wouldn't be in that day. He said that it would be O.K. and that he would see me tomorrow.
Q. When did you go back to Karron's Jewelry Shop? A. The next day.
Q. That was the Thursday? A. Yes, sir.
Q. Now, my friend over here has read a deposition of Mr. Karron concerning a conversation between you and Mr. Karron. Would you describe in your own words, from your own recollection what you recall about that conversation? A. Yes, sir. I came to work as usual that day. I was still pretty tired and shaky from that experience. Early in the morning Mr. Karron took me aside and started to lecture me and preach to me about my betting on horses, what it leads to and things like that which had nothing at all to do with anything that had happened that night before. I guess that I just got a little fed up and I am afraid that I lost my temper and said that it would be better if I left. He was rather nice about it and said that he would give me a month's pay. And I left the job.
Q. You have different employment now? A. Yes, sir.
Q. What is that? A. A car salesman at Souza's Auto Discount Lot.
Q. You have been working at that since the time of this episode. A. That is right, yes, sir.
Q. Now, Mr. Bennett, did you at any time conspire with or plan with, of your own free will, with anybody to engage in a theft of any kind from Karron's Jewelry Shop? A. No, sir.
Q. Have you found out since then anything about Mr. Phil Ricker? A. I have found out that he is a man with a prison record for theft, burglaries, so forth.
Q. Have you ever seen him since the events of that night? A. No, sir. I have never seen him since.
Q. Have you ever seen the man who took you on this journey that you testified about in Marsha's blue car? A. No, sir I have never seen him since, either.

Mr. SUTHERLAND: You may cross-examine, Mr. Field.

CROSS-EXAMINATION

Q. (By Mr. Field) Mr. Bennett, you were, I gathered, in rather serious financial trouble in February. Is that a fair statement? A. No, sir. I was not in debt.
Q. Well, you lost all of your savings, I believe you said? A. Yes, I

Assignments in Trial Practice

did, very foolishly.
Q. And you were in such a position that you found it necessary to ask for an advance of $250 in February? A. Yes, sir.
Q. And you got it? A. Yes, sir.
Q. Now, in your direct testimony you said that you got a $250 advance that time. Were there any other occasions when you asked for an advance? A. No, sir. I never asked for any advance. That was the only time I ever got an advance and the only time that I ever asked for it.
Q. So when you said "that time," it was, in fact, the only time? A. Yes, sir.
Q. I take it, Mr. Bennett, that you never had any experience in the disposal of stolen jewelry, have you? A. No, sir.
Q. You had been at the store at night, I suppose, a good many times before. A. Yes. I had been there several times.
Q. Incidentally, whose briefcase was it that you used to put these jewels in? A. This is one of these things that just lies around the store. I guess it was old Mr. Karron's briefcase.
Q. You mean old Mr. Karron, Sr.? A. Yes, sir.
Q. And it was around the store all the time? A. Yes, sir.
Q. You knew that night that it was around the store? A. Well, I mean that I noticed it when I came in.
Q. You told us that it was around there all the time? A. Yes, sir.
Q. Now, on the occasion of March 6th, when you were, as you say, set upon by this unknown hoodlum, the hour was about 9:30? A. Yes, sir.
Q. He came to the left side of your car, the driver's side? A. Yes, sir, that is right.
Q. And he put his head in the window, right? A. Well, yes, sir. He bent down so that he looked right directly to me.
Q. Well, did he put his head inside the window? A. This, I couldn't say. I know that he was very close and I was at the driver's seat. It might have been inside and it might not. I know that he was very close to me.
Q. And sometime you became aware of the presence of someone whom you recognized as Phil Ricker, he was also in the car? A. Yes, sir.
Q. Where did he get in? A. He got in on Marsha's side, on the street side.
Q. So he was sitting there, that made three of you in the front seat? A. No, sir. What he had done, you see, in the convertible the front seat pushes forward. That is what made me notice it when he got in and Marsha said, "What is going on, Phil?" I guess it was when she was pushed.
Q. Marsha was in the front seat? A. Yes, sir.
Q. And he pushed the seat with her in it forward enough for him to be able to get into the back, is that it? A. Yes, sir.
Q. All right, I see. And he said nothing? A. No, sir.
Q. And then this unknown hoodlum, as you say, sort of pulled you? A. No. I got out of my own free will. He had a hand on my shoulder

and he had the gun in my face. He ordered me out of the car and I got out of the car.
Q. But you got out of your own free will? A. Yes.

    Mr. FIELD: May I see the exhibit, Mr. Sutherland, the statement that has been marked B for identification, that statement?

Q. In your statement to the police, at 6:30 in the morning of March 7th, the very morning after this event you did say, did you not, "But he didn't answer and instead just pulled me out of the car and made me get into Marsha's car"? Did you say that? A. Yes, sir, I did.
Q. Is that wrong or right? A. No, sir, that is right.
Q. Then what you have testified to now was wrong? A. I know that I was manhandled by him.
Q. No, please, just answer my question. A. I would say that this is right, that he did pull me out of the car.
Q. So that what you have said now, that you did get out of the car of your own free will, that is a mistake? A. Yes, sir.
Q. Now, this gun that you have mentioned, you said that he put it in his lap when he got in to start the car, is that right? A. Yes, sir. Yes. And then I sort of lost track of that gun for a long time.
Q. Did it stay in his lap during this hour and a half that you were driving around? A. Yes, sir.
Q. In his lap all the time? A. Yes, sir.
Q. I take it that it was not in his lap when he got up to siphon the gas? A. He had no lap then.
Q. He had no lap then? A. No, sir.
Q. When absent the lap, he was siphoning the gasoline, where was the gun? A. I guess that he put it in his pocket.
Q. You guess? Did you see it? A. No, I didn't see it. I guess --
Q. Did you see him put it in his pocket? A. No, sir. He ordered me out of the car first.
Q. This gun was the thing that you were interested in as I understand it. A. Yes, sir. That is what scared me first.
Q. And you did not see it anywhere while you were stopped getting the gasoline? A. That is right, yes, sir.
Q. Did it get back into his lap after you started driving around again? A. No, sir.
Q. When did you see the gun again? A. I believe while we were driving down Third Avenue and he was giving me these threatening instructions, he took it out again.
Q. And waved it some more? A. He held it in his hand.
Q. Not in his lap at this time? A. No, sir.
Q. All right. Now, as I understand it, you had a certain amount of conversation with him. You asked what it was about and he told you that you were going to clean out Karron's safe. Then when you tried to tell him that the place was locked up he indicated to you that he

knew that you had a key and had planned to use it? A. That is right, sir.
Q. And, of course, you have no idea how he had acquired this information. A. No.
Q. So far as you know the only people who knew anything about this plan were Marsha and yourself, is that right? A. That is right.
Q. When you arrived at some point on Third Avenue, between Prince and Stone, he stopped the car? A. That is right.
Q. I don't think that you indicated precisely where it was. Would you be good enough to indicate precisely where it was, if you can remember? A. It was between Prince and Stone, closer to Prince, roughly a third of the way.
Q. Roughly a third of the way down the block, is that right? A. Yes, sir.
Q. And at that time, as I understand your story, he told you that he would give you five minutes to go in and effect the theft of this jewelry, is that right? A. Yes, sir.
Q. And you got out of the car, is that right? A. That is right, sir.
Q. Where was the gun then, do you know? A. He had it in his hand and he was laying it down when he had to use his hands to manipulate the wheel. But he had it out. The gun was out.
Q. All right. Did you say something about the car pulling away? A. Well, after he let me out --
Q. After you got out? A. Yes, I did, I got out.
Q. You started to walk along the street toward Karron's, is that correct? A. That is right, sir.
Q. And the car pulled away? A. Yes, sir.
Q. Did it go by you? A. I believe, yes, sir, he did pass me.
Q. He passed you? A. Yes, sir.
Q. What happened after he passed you? A. I don't know. So far as I know he continued on down Third Avenue. He might have made a turn. I was going into Karron's.
Q. That is, he had gone on beyond Karron's and was by it before you got to Karron's, is that right? A. He may have, I don't know. He was going very slowly. He may have been a little --
Q. We don't want testimony on what may have been. We want your very best memory of what you recall seeing. A. He was past Karron's when I was at Karron's.
Q. All right. Did you see him turn a corner? A. No, sir. I didn't see him. But I wasn't noticing the car.
Q. All right. Now, when you went into Karron's you have told us that you must have left the door ajar, is that correct? A. Yes, sir.
Q. Did you intend to close the door firmly or did you not intend to close it firmly? A. I don't know that I had any other intention but to hurry to that safe.
Q. That is, as you recall it, you took no particular notice of whether you were closing the door or not? A. No, sir.
Q. You did not deliberately plan to close the door with the snap lock so that no one else could get in? A. No, sir.

Q. You just don't remember what your thoughts were? A. Yes, sir.
Q. But you do remember from the fact that this hoodlum got in that you didn't secure it completely? A. That is right.
Q. Now, when you got in, you went directly to the safe, is that correct? A. Yes, sir.
Q. You knew, I take it, in a general way, what to expect to find in the safe? A. Yes, sir.
Q. Yes. And you knew where the valuable jewelry was kept in the safe? A. Yes, sir.
Q. Where was it? A. On the top shelf.
Q. And the things of lesser value were kept on the lower shelf? A. Yes, sir.
Q. And when you, under coercion, as you say, from the unknown hoodlum, when you began to empty things into the briefcase from the safe, you did pick up the most valuable things to empty into the briefcase, did you not? A. I started at the top shelf.
Q. You started at the top shelf and you finished with the top shelf, did you not? A. Well, up to the time when the interruption came, yes, sir.
Q. Anyway, you did pick the most valuable jewelry to put into the briefcase, right? A. Yes, sir.
Q. All right. Now, the next thing you knew about the car, you heard it pulling out, as I understand it? A. Yes, sir.
Q. And you heard it coming, I take it, from the southerly direction, northerly on Third Avenue, toward Karron's? A. Right, yes, sir.
Q. This car which you had last seen going northerly, away from Karron's, is that right? A. That is right sir.
Q. And then this unknown hoodlum, as you say, he came in and told you to hurry? A. That is, right.
Q. Incidentally, there was, to your knowledge, a telephone right here on this desk, was there not? A. Yes, sir.
Q. You knew it was in good working order? A. Yes, sir.
Q. You knew, did you not, that the police cars in the City of Gray are radio equipped? A. Yes, I guess so, I knew that.
Q. You knew in fact, did you not, that it was greatly publicized and that they took great pride in the fact that they had a set-up whereby they could get very quickly to any place in the downtown area? A. Yes, sir, I have heard of that.
Q. Well, after this hoodlum, as you say, after he went out, you heard a couple of shots? A. That is right.
Q. Then you immediately ducked? A. That is right.
Q. Had the door been left open by the hoodlum whom you say went out? A. I think that it was in about the same position that it was in before.
Q. And where do you say that you ducked? A. I ducked right where I was when I heard the shot, which is right between the desk and the counter.
Q. All right. Now, when the hoodlum told you to hurry, where were you? A. I was still at the safe.

Assignments in Trial Practice

Q. And after he told you to hurry, what did you immediately do before the shots came? A. I guess I had something in my hand, if I remember. I had something in my hand, and I just dropped that in the case and started to run, closing up the briefcase as I started to run.
Q. That is, you took one more of these valuable jewels that you had and put it in your briefcase? A. I had it in my hand and I put it in the briefcase and then started to run.
Q. And closed the briefcase and started to run toward the door? A. Well, I was closing it as I ran.
Q. When you got to this point you heard shots and you ducked? That is right.
Q. Making yourself as inconspicuous as possible? A. Yes, sir.
Q. Incidentally, the wooden partition that separates the display case from the main store is about three feet high, is that right? A. Yes, sir, that is right.
Q. And you had ducked to a point so that you were less than three feet from the floor? A. Well, I was also hiding behind that counter because the shots were coming from that other direction.
Q. You thought that the shots were coming from over on the right, do you say? A. Well, over on my right.
Q. Are you sure that is where you were? A. Yes, sir.
Q. Were you sure of it before you heard the officer testify that that is where he found you? A. Well, I was quite sure. I remember that he had handcuffed me and there was the radiator which was very close. I remember also that I was between the desk and the counter.
Q. You had not then taken the place of obviously greater safety, behind the desk? A. No. When I heard those shots I just dropped.
Q. And you stayed dropped until the policeman came in? A. Yes, sir.
Q. Without moving? A. Yes, sir.
Q. Crouching? A. Yes, sir.
Q. Were you looking in the direction of the door? A. I was just looking at the window. I could just see out of it. I wasn't sticking my head out anywhere. I was just hiding behind that counter.
Q. Do you remember which way you were facing? A. I believe I was facing toward the window, the front.
Q. All right. And when you saw the police officer first, where was he? Where was he when you first saw him? A. I heard him come in. I believe, I am not sure, but I believe that he came in front of me.
Q. You heard him come in? A. I heard him come in.
Q. Then you saw him when he got over in here, is that right? A. Yes, sir. I believe that he came up in front of me.
Q. Tell us again, if you will, please, your very best memory of exactly what you did and what he did, what you said and what he said? A. Well, when he came in I was crouched, more or less lying there, with the briefcase very close by. I had dropped that. When he came in he looked at me and looked at the briefcase. I started to explain to him.

Q. Tell us, what did you say, as best you can recall? A. I said to him, "Don't worry about me, I work here. I wanted to reassure him that he had no worry about me. He took out his handcuffs and he put one on me and then he began looking for another place to tie me to.
Q. Did he search you for weapons? A. Yes, sir, he did.
Q. And you didn't have any? A. No, sir.
Q. All right, go on with anything else that was said and tell us when it was said. A. I told him that Marsha was in trouble, because this man had obviously gotten away.
Q. This is what you told him or what you were thinking about? A. No, sir, I told him.
Q. You said, "Marsha is in trouble and this man is getting away"? A. No, sir, I said, "My fiancée, Marsha, her life is in danger. I was forced to do this." I just blurted it out. I was very nervous at the time, sir.
Q. All right. Is that all? A. I guess more of the same, he didn't seem to be paying any attention to me. He clapped me to the radiator and went out.
Q. And when he came back before the police car came you had another such conversation. I believe that your testimony is that you were saying very much the same thing, is that right, sir? A. That is right, sir.
Q. And again he had no comment to make, is that correct? A. That is right, sir.
Q. When the squad car came he removed the handcuffs and released you from the radiator, then rehandcuffed you and took you to the station? And on the way to the station you again made these same statements for the third time? A. Yes, sir.
Q. And in roughly the same language? A. Yes, sir.
Q. And the third time the officer said, "Nuts"? A. Yes, sir.
Q. He had not said that the first time or the second time but only the third time, as I understand your testimony? A. I don't remember him saying anything about the first or second time, just bide my time.
Q. You remember him telling you to bide your time? You said that in direct examination? A. Something like that, yes It was inconsequential and in no way related to what I was pleading to him.
Q. All right. Now after you were released by the police you tried to get in touch with Marsha? You told us that? A. Yes, sir.
Q. You didn't succeed in reaching her until 9:30 or thereabouts in the morning? A. Yes, sir.
Q. Did you have any further communication with the police when you found that she was missing? A. When I found --
Q. When you found that she was not in her apartment did you communicate with the police? A. No, sir. I had told them ----
Q. No, please. Did you communicate with them? A. No, sir.
Q. Finally at 9:30 she called you, is that correct? A. That is right, sir.

Q. And you told her to go to the police, is that it? A. That is right, sir.
Q. Have you given the full conversation? A. No, sir. She had described to me the fact that she had been riding around with Phil and that Phil dropped her off somewhere. I don't remember the details of it. I was pretty tired at that time.
Q. You were tired? A. Yes, sir.
Q. And so she had given you a kind of summary of what she had done in these eventful hours since you had separated, is that it? A. Yes, sir.
Q. Then you told her to go to the police? A. That is right, sir.
Q. For the purpose, I take it, of helping you? A. Yes, sir.
Q. You told her to go right away? A. Yes, sir.
Q. How long did you talk with her on the telephone? A. I would guess about a quarter of an hour. I don't know.
Q. About a quarter of an hour? A. Yes, sir.
Q. Having told her to go, did you tell her what to say to the police at all? A. I told her to tell her story, just what happened, what she had told me.
Q. You didn't see her in person before she saw the police, did you? A. No, sir.
Q. When did you next see her? A. I guess I saw her -- I saw her that same evening. I think that we went out that evening.
Q. You were not too tired for that? A. I had slept the whole day.
Q. Now, Mr. Bennett, turning back for just a moment to the episode in Karron's Jewelry Store, did you really think that this hoodlum that you say had driven by Karron's going north, when you entered the store, did you really think that he would come back and shoot you before you could call the police? That is, he having told you that he would give you five minutes, did you really think that? A. I am afraid that I didn't do any clear thinking at that time. He had left me with an impression, I was scared and nervous. You see all those small streets there, he could have turned around and been in front of the store in two minutes. I was there in this lighted-up store, with nothing between me and the street. I was a sitting duck in that store.

    Mr. FIELD: I think that is all.

REDIRECT EXAMINATION

    Mr. SUTHERLAND: No questions, Your Honor.

    If Your Honor, please, I should like to read part of the stipulation, the pre-trial order, paragraphs 10 and 13, two paragraphs which were not read by my friend.

    (Paragraphs 10 and 13 were read.)

Assignments in Trial Practice

MARSHA MATHER, Sworn

Q. (By Mr. Sutherland) You are Miss Marsha Mather? A. That is right.
Q. And you live in the City of Gray? A. Yes.
Q. You are engaged to marry Mr. Bennett, who was the last witness, the defendant in this case? A. Yes, I am.
Q. Your calling is that of a professional model, is that right? A. Yes.
Q. And has been for how long? A. Well, I have been modeling ever since I got out of high school.
Q. At the time of the events we have discussed tonight, on March 6, 19Y2, you were living where? A. I was living on Westchester Road, No. 19.
Q. Westchester Road is a highway about 60 feet wide? A. No, it isn't a highway, it is one of those old streets in Gray with those old brownstone houses on both sides.
Q. It is a street about 60 feet wide with a sidewalk on each side? A. Yes.
Q. Do you live at 19 Westchester Road now? A. Not any more, no.
Q. Where do you live now? A. Now I am living on Normandy Road.
Q. Did you ever meet the man named Phil Ricker? A. Yes, I did.
Q. Tell us, please, what the circumstances of your acquaintance with Mr. Ricker were? A. It was just after I started modeling and one of the girls in the modeling studio introduced me to him. I started dating him but not very often, about once a month. We were just good friends. This went on until I read in a newspaper he was in trouble with the police. I didn't know he was that kind of a person.
Q. What kind of trouble was he in with the police? A. It was something to do with a burglary, something had been stolen.
Q. Did you ever know him as going to prison? A. Yes, sir, that was in the papers.
Q. Did you ever communicate with him while he was in prison? A. No, sir, we weren't dating seriously.
Q. When did you next see Mr. Ricker? A. I met him on the street in Gray, oh, some time in 19Y3.
Q. Can you give us some idea as to what part of 19Y3 it was? A. Around Thanksgiving time, I think.
Q. Did you see him after that? A. Yes, I did. He asked me if I would date him. At first I said no, because of this trouble I heard about. But he said it was something that was all over, and he was sorry for it, and I believed him. So I began to date him and dated him quite a bit.
Q. At some time around December 22nd, 19Y3, you had a party in your apartment, is that correct? A. Yes, sir.
Q. A number of friends were there? A. Yes, sir, quite a few.
Q. And Mr. Bennett was there? A. Yes, sir, he came with a date, one of my girlfriends.
Q. Did you introduce Mr. Bennett to Mr. Ricker? A. Yes, I think I

Assignments in Trial Practice

might have, someone did.
Q. Did you ever tell Mr. Bennett about Mr. Ricker's criminal record? A. No.
Q. You and Mr. Bennett saw a good deal of one another during that winter, did you not? A. Yes, right after the party he called me and began asking me to go out with him.
Q. And you went about with him, had a good time? A. Yes, we did.
Q. Did you ever go out to the Warren Raceway with him? A. He took me out one afternoon but I didn't care for it and never went back with him.
Q. He lost some money that afternoon? A. Yes, he did.
Q. How much? A. I don't know how much he lost all afternoon because after he lost the first three races I got pretty disgusted.
Q. Now, there came the evening of the 5th of March, can you tell us what happened that evening? A. Ira asked me to marry him.
Q. What did you say to Ira? A. I said yes.
Q. This happened where? A. It happened at a little lounge we used to stop in at the end of an evening.
Q. There was some talk that evening concerning Phil Ricker, was there not? A. When Ira asked me to marry him I was so excited I began to think of people to call the next day. I thought of Phil and said I would let him know I wouldn't be seeing him any more.
Q. Was there any talk about a ring? A. Yes, there was.
Q. What was the talk about a ring? A. Ira was very anxious to give me one but I had engagements in the day and couldn't see him the next day.
Q. Business engagements? A. Yes, I had a fitting in the morning for a fashion show the next week, and in the afternoon I had to be photographed and I didn't know how long that would be, so I couldn't be with Ira the next day.
Q. Was there some talk about going to Karron's Jewelry Store after work? A. Yes, there was. Ira said he wouldn't be back in the city until 9:30 and he could see me then and we could go to the store to pick out a ring. I said that would be fine because it would give me a chance to rest and change.
Q. Did he explain why he wouldn't be back until about 9:30? A. Yes, he said Mr. Karron asked him to make a delivery of some jewelry in another city.
Q. The next day you talked to Mr. Ricker? A. Yes.
Q. Did you have any talk with him that day over the telephone? A. Phil called me the first thing in the morning and asked me to go out with him that evening.
Q. Give the talk between yourself and Mr. Ricker. A. I told him I couldn't see him that evening or any other evening because I had become engaged. He was quite upset about it and asked me all kinds of questions about Ira. I knew he was much more serious toward me than I was toward him. He asked me what kind of a ring I was getting and I said Ira was working in a jewelry store, I don't know. I said I don't know because we are going down to the store that same

evening and pick it out.

Q. Can you give us any more information about your conversation with Mr. Ricker? A. No, he suggested taking me out to dinner and then I said I couldn't go because I was meeting Ira to go to the store. I explained to him Ira wasn't coming by for me until 9:30 because Ira was going to be out of the city.

Q. All right, that evening, tell me what happened then? A. Well, Ira came just about the time he said he was, about 9:25 or 9:30. I was ready and waiting for him. We went down out of my apartment. His car was parked almost outside my door.

Q. What kind of car did he have? A. An Oldsmobile convertible, a yellow Olds convertible.

Q. Was the top down or was it up covering the seats at this time? A. It was winter so it was covering them.

Q. On which side of Westchester Road was his car parked? A. The side closest to my apartment.

Q. Headed in what direction? A. Headed off to the right.

Q. When you say to the right on the map do you say toward the W or toward the E? A. Toward the W.

Q. When you say to the right you mean looking away from the house? A. Yes, as you come out of the house.

Q. Westchester Road is a two-way street or a one-way street? A. Two-way.

Q. What happened now after you came out of your house and went down to get into Ira's yellow automobile? A. Well, Ira opened the door on the passenger side for me and I got in. Then he walked around the front of the car and opened his door and he got in. He had the keys in his hand and was just putting them in the ignition when I felt the door open on my side. I looked up and saw Phil.

Q. Phil Ricker? A. Yes.

Q. May I interrupt you a moment, your car was parked in Westchester Road that evening? A. Yes, just a little way down in back of Ira's car.

Q. And your car at the time was a dark blue -- A. 19Y3 Ford sedan, yes.

Q. And who had the keys to your blue Ford, sedan? A. I, of course, had one set, and the week before Phil, Phil Ricker, asked to borrow my car because his was in the shop with some kind of engine trouble. I gave him the other set of keys and he returned the car by just leaving it outside the shop where I was working that day. I took it home and I never did think of asking him for the other set of keys.

Q. Now, I think you said Phil Ricker opened the door on your side? A. Yes, and he pushed into the back seat.

Q. He opened the door and pushed into the back seat of Ira's convertible, tell us next what happened in your own words. A. He opened the door. I was sort of sitting on the edge of the seat and I went forward as he pushed in. He got in the back seat. I was facing out to the sidewalk and he whispered in my ear if I made any noise Ira would get it. I looked toward Ira and I saw him opening the door and there was a man standing out on the street with a gun pointing it toward Ira. I said, "Phil, what is going on, what are you doing?" He just said keep your mouth shut or Ira would get it.

Q. What about the street lights on Westchester Road, what kind of lights are there? A. They are average for a residential street, not the bright lights you find downtown.

Q. Are the street lights located where the round black spots are on the map? A. Just about, yes.

Q. We are referring to the map showing 19 Westchester Road? A. Yes.

Q. Will you tell us what you saw then with respect to your own car? A. Well, when this other man, the man with the gun, made Ira get out of the car Phil got out and as he was getting into the car on the driver's seat I looked out the back window and saw this other man, and I saw him with Ira, with a gun. I saw him open the door of my car.

Q. Who is "him"? A. The man with the gun. I just began to see them get in my car and I turned around and began to question Phil about what was happening, where the man with the gun was taking Ira. He just started the car, didn't say anything.

Q. Which car started first, Ira's car or the Ford? A. I don't remember, I just know I looked back when Ira's car was starting, when it was started by Phil. I looked around then and my car wasn't there any more.

Q. Will you tell us about what happened from then on? A. Well, Phil drove directly to the corner of Belaire and Simpson streets.

Q. How far is that? A. Usually it is a ten or fifteen minute drive, but I wasn't paying too much attention to streets at the time. I was too frightened.

Q. Did you have any conversation with Phil during this drive? A. Yes, I was asking him what was happening, what happened to Ira.

Q. What did he say? A. He just said to keep my mouth shut and I would find out.

Q. When you got to this corner what happened? A. We just stopped and we both sat there. I asked him some questions and he said if I keep my mouth shut for about five minutes and be a good girl nothing would happen to Ira or to myself.

Q. Did he mention anything about a jewelry store? A. No.

Q. Did he mention anything about a wedding present? A. He said something to the effect Ira and his friend, Phil's friend, were going to get me a nice wedding present, but he said it very sarcastically.

Q. How long did you and Phil stay there on the street corner? A. I remember Phil kept turning the radio on to get time checks. He kept looking at his watch and I kept looking at mine too. At 12:30 he seemed very upset. He started the car and I had no idea of where we were going and he kept telling me to keep my mouth shut. I found out later by watching the road signs he was taking the route to Thayer.

Q. Thayer is a city how far from Gray? A. Just 150 miles.

Q. You did get to Thayer, I assume? A. Not until 5:30 in the morning.
Q. What happened when you got to Thayer? A. As soon as we got to the city he drove to the Penn Railroad Station. There is a taxi stand there. He left the keys with me and said if I wanted to I could drive back to Gray, but if I called the police I would never see Ira again. I had been so frightened that night I would do anything he told me to do. I turned around and started back to Gray, but while I was still in the city I stopped the car at one of those phones in the street and I tried to call Ira but there was no answer.
Q. About what time was this? A. About 25 minutes to 6, in the morning.
Q. Then what did you do? A. I got on the highway and started back to Gray.
Q. Did you stop on the way? A. I had to stop for gas, yes.
Q. What time did you get to Gray? A. I got to the outskirts of town about 9:30 in the morning and pulled into a station that had a pay phone on the cement part outside and I called Ira from there.
Q. You reached Ira on the telephone? A. Yes, I did.
Q. There was some conversation between you? A. Yes, he told me what had happened to him and he told me the police had been looking for me and he had been so upset about me.
Q. Did you tell Ira where you had been? A. Yes, I told him what happened to me.
Q. Was there any talk about where you were going? A. Yes, as soon as he told me the police were looking for me I realized the best thing for me to do was to get right to the police station and tell them what happened and maybe they could get Phil.
Q. You did go to the police station? A. Yes.
Q. What time did you get there? A. A little after 10 in the morning.
Q. This was the central police station? A. Yes, the one right downtown in Gray.
Q. How long did you stay at the police station? A. I was there all day. They were very nice to me. After they found out what happened to me they started asking me questions. When it got a little later they sent out for something to eat and wanted me to rest a little. Some other men came in, they were not in uniforms, but they asked me questions too. I don't know who they were, but some man typed up what I said and I signed it.

Mr. SUTHERLAND: If Your Honor please, I would like to have this statement marked for identification.

(Statement of Marsha Mather dated March 7, 19Y2, marked Exhibit C for identification.)

Q. Miss Mather, I show you Exhibit C for identification, and I ask you whether that is the statement that you signed as you have testified, which a man typed out at the police station? A. Yes, it is.
Q. Miss Mather, have you ever since that night seen or heard anything

Assignments in Trial Practice

of Phil Ricker? A. No, I haven't.
Q. You heard the stipulation that your car was picked up on a side road in the country, is that correct? A. Yes.
Q. Did you hear anything more from the police? A. Yes, as a matter of fact, a detective still comes to see me every two weeks to a month and asks me if I have heard from Phil Ricker.
Q. And you tell you have not? A. That is right.
Q. Miss Mather, did you ever at any time contrive or plan or conspire with Mr. Ricker or anybody else that they and you, or that you and Ira Bennett, or that you and Ira Bennett and they would engage in a robbery or any other kind of a crime at Karron's Jewelry Store or anywhere else? A. No, sir, I did not.

    Mr. SUTHERLAND: All right, that is all.

CROSS-EXAMINATION

Q. (By Mr. Field) Miss Mather, you became engaged to Mr. Bennett on the evening before the events we are discussing, as I understand? A. That is right.
Q. When you reached him on the following morning he asked you to go to the police station to help him? A. No, not in so many words. I don't know who suggested it, but as soon as I knew the police had been looking for me I suggested that I go.
Q. In any event you went to the police station? A. Yes.
Q. And you would still like to help him? A. Naturally.
Q. You are very much interested in his being successful in this litigation, is that right? A. Yes.
Q. Of course. You have described something about your acquaintance with Mr. Ricker, and you have told us you were not dating him seriously, is that right? A. Yes.
Q. You never were dating him seriously, is that what you want us to understand? A. That is true.
Q. It is true, isn't it, that from Christmas time on you were seeing either Mr. Ricker or Mr. Bennett practically every night? A. Yes.
Q. And a good deal of the time was spent with Mr. Bennett and a good deal of your time was spent with Mr. Ricker? A. I was seeing those two only.
Q. Just those two, practically every night? A. Yes.
Q. And you did not, as I understand it, tell Mr. Bennett about seeing Mr. Ricker, did you? A. No.
Q. And you didn't tell Mr. Ricker about seeing Mr. Bennett, did you? A. They were both fully aware they were not the only one I was seeing.
Q. You didn't tell them about it, did you? A. No.
Q. They both knew you were not going exclusively with one of them? A. That is right.
Q. I take it neither of them knew there was only one other man in the field, is that correct? A. It is true.

Q. You did know Mr. Ricker had had some trouble with the law and had served some time in prison? A. From the newspaper, yes.
Q. And he told you so? A. I asked him about it when I read it in the newspaper.
Q. Yes, he admitted it, didn't he? A. Yes.
Q. And you still thought him to be a nice fellow, you continued to see him several times a week? A. Yes.
Q. From that time on, after you knew he had served some time in prison? A. Yes.
Q. Did you also know he was a married man? A. The first time I found that out was at the police station, the day after the events.
Q. You believed up to that time he was unmarried? A. That is true.
Q. You thought you knew him pretty well by March 6th, did you not? A. Yes.
Q. And this Phil Ricker you saw that evening was an entirely new Phil Ricker, is that correct? A. It certainly was.
Q. There had not been anything in his conduct before which led you to believe he wasn't a perfect gentleman? A. He always appeared so to me.
Q. Did you ever meet any of his friends or associates? A. I never met any of his friends.
Q. You never saw this hoodlum who has been described as being part of this enterprise, to your knowledge? A. Not to my knowledge. I didn't see his face at the time.
Q. When you informed Mr. Ricker of your engagement you say he was upset? A. Yes, he was.
Q. And he asked you all kinds of questions about Ira Bennett? A. True.
Q. And you thought the least you could do, since you became engaged to somebody else, was to tell him all you could, answer his questions about Ira? A. Yes.
Q. And you told him about the jewelry store, where he worked, and you told him you and Ira planned on going to the jewelry store that evening to select a ring? A. Thinking of Phil's inquiries as being friendly, of course, I answered them.
Q. You thought his inquiries were friendly? A. Yes.
Q. Now, Miss Mather, do you know the newsboy who used to deliver the HERALD to you every day when you lived at Westchester Road? A. I don't know him except to say hello to him and give him his money each month.
Q. Do you know his name? A. Jimmy Adams, or Anderson, something like that.
Q. Did you see Jimmy Adams, on the evening of March 6, do you remember? A. No, I didn't, I left the money for him under the mat at my front door. I often do that.

    Mr. FIELD: Jimmy, stand up, please.

Q. Do you see him now? A. Yes.
Q. Is that Jimmy Adams? A. Yes, it is.

Assignments in Trial Practice

Q. You recognize him? A. Yes, I have never seen him dressed up before.
Q. Do you recall seeing him that evening? A. No.
Q. You didn't wave your hand to him as you went by in your car when it started? A. Not if I didn't see him, no.
Q. After you went for this long ride with the new Phil Ricker and you wound up in Thayer, he let you out? A. He got out.
Q. I beg your pardon, he got out of the car? A. Yes.
Q. This was 5:30 in the morning? A. Yes.
Q. You did not immediately go to the Thayer police, did you? A. He told me not to, and I was too frightened.
Q. You didn't telephone back to Gray immediately, did you? A. No, I did not.
Q. When you got back to Gray you did not communicate with the Gray police until after you had finally reached Ira, is that right? A. Until I had spoken to him.
Q. Until you had spoken to Ira at 9:30. Now, you say that this episode so excited you that you would do anything he told you, is that what you said, Miss Mather? A. That is not really what I meant.
Q. I just asked you if that is what you said? A. Yes.
Q. How long did you remain so excited you would do anything he told you to do? A. As long as I remained so frightened about what they would do to Ira.
Q. You were so frightened of this new Phil Ricker that even after he had long departed, you were still continuing to do what he told you to do or not do what he told you not to do, is that right? A. While I was with him.
Q. You tell us you were frightened about what was going to happen to Ira while you were with him? A. While I was with him I was frightened about what was going to happen to me. After he left me I began being frightened about what was going to happen to Ira.
Q. Didn't you think the best way to help Ira was to get in touch with the police? A. If I had I would have.
Q. Then you didn't think it was the best way to help Ira? A. No.
Q. Ira is a fellow who wears glasses, is he not? A. Ira?
Q. Mr. Bennett wears glasses, doesn't he? A. Yes.

    Mr. FIELD: That is all, thank you.

    Mr. SUTHERLAND: If Your Honor please, the defendant rests.

    Mr. FIELD: The plaintiff has some rebuttal, if Your Honor please.

    The COURT: Proceed, Mr. Field.

    Mr. FIELD: Mr. Reardon will interrogate this witness.

<u>JAMES ADAMS</u>, Sworn

Q. (By Mr. Reardon) Jimmy, please tell the members of the jury your full name? A. James Adams.
Q. How old are you, Jimmy? A. I am 17, sir.
Q. Would you tell us your occupation at the present time? A. I am a freshman at Gray City College.
Q. You just started this year? A. Yes, sir.
Q. Tell the ladies and gentlemen of the jury what you were doing for a living or what you were doing generally in March, 19Y2. A. I delivered newspapers at the time, sir.
Q. You were going to school also then. A. Yes, sir.
Q. Where did you deliver newspapers, Jimmy? A. I delivered newspapers in a block enclosed by Westchester, Potomac, Revere, and Harrison streets.
Q. Is that the same block shown on the exhibit now before you? A. Yes, it is.
Q. Jimmy, do you know Miss Marsha Mather? A. Yes, I delivered papers to Miss Mather.
Q. Can you see her in court now? A. Yes, she is sitting over there (indicating).
Q. In a gray suit? A. Yes, sir.
Q. Do you know an Ira Bennett, or do you know who Ira Bennett is? A. I do now, sir.
Q. Do you see him in the courtroom? A. Yes, he is sitting over at the front table.
Q. The front table, the defense counsel table? A. Yes, sir.
Q. Is there anything distinctive about him, can you point him out? A. Yes, he is wearing glasses.
Q. Thank you, Jimmy. Would you tell us if on March 6th you saw either Miss Mather or Mr. Bennett? A. I saw both of them, sir.
Q. Will you tell us about when you saw them? A. I believe it was around 10 o'clock.
Q. What were you doing at the time, Jimmy? A. I was collecting my monthly payments.
Q. What makes you so sure it was about 10 o'clock as opposed to 9 or 11 o'clock? A. I always made my collections in the evening, and I made it a point never to knock on anyone's door after 10 o'clock in the evening, and Miss Mather was at the end of my collections.
Q. You always finished up your collections at Miss Mather's house? A. Yes, sir.

Mr. SUTHERLAND: May I ask counsel for the plaintiff to permit the witness to testify?

Q. Where on this map, Jimmy, would you say Miss Mather and Mr. Bennett were at the time you saw them? You can get up and point to the place. A. They were in a car pulling out beside the street light when I was walking toward No. 19, I was coming from No. 23.
Q. Jimmy, where was the car when you first saw it? A. It was parked in front of Miss Mather's house.

Assignments in Trial Practice

Q. When you saw Miss Mather and Mr. Bennett, were they in the car? A. Yes, sir.
Q. Were they in a position where you could see them clearly? A. As they were driving away they passed in front of the street light here.
Q. Where were you then, Jimmy? A. I was crossing the sidewalk between the two houses, about ten feet from them, and they went driving away.
Q. In terms of your distance to me, with reference to where I am standing, would you say it was as far as that full distance or shorter than the full distance? A. I would say it was the full distance.

    The COURT: Will you resume your seat, Mr. Adams, please.

    Mr. REARDON: You may sit down, Jimmy.

Q. You say you were on the sidewalk at the time you saw them? A. Yes, sir.
Q. Were they along the curb or out in the road? A. They were just pulling away, probably about three feet from the curb.
Q. Are you sure, Jimmy? Who was closer to the curb when you saw them in the car, Miss Mather or Mr. Bennett? A. Miss Mather was sitting in the passenger's seat.
Q. Was that closer or was the outside of the car closer to you? A. She was closer to me; they were driving southbound on Westchester.
Q. Who was closer to you? A. Miss Mather.
Q. Jimmy, this is quite important so think for a moment before you answer. Are you as sure Mr. Bennett was in that car as you are sure Mr. Bennett is sitting right here now?

    Mr. SUTHERLAND: If Your Honor please, I think that is an improper question.

    The COURT: Excluded.

Q. Jimmy, how certain are you that it was Mr. Bennett you saw in the car?

    MR. SUTHERLAND: My objection, Your Honor.

    THE COURT: I shall exclude it.

Q. Jimmy, what makes you believe it was Mr. Bennett you saw in the car?

    Mr. SUTHERLAND: I object, if Your Honor please.

    The COURT: Your question as it is now phrased is what makes you believe it was Mr. Bennett?

Mr. REARDON: I will withdraw the question, Your Honor.

Q. Jimmy, had you ever seen Mr. Bennett before this evening? A. Yes, I had, sir.
Q. This is before March 6? A. Yes.
Q. Where had you seen him? A. I saw him several times, perhaps six to a dozen times, either coming out of Miss Mather's house or parked in front of the house.
Q. What kind of car did Mr. Bennett drive, are you familiar with his car? A. I believe it was an Olds convertible.
Q. Do you recall the color of this convertible or didn't you notice that? A. It was a light color, I am not sure if it was yellow, white, or cream.
Q. Did you notice the convertible every time Mr. Bennett was there, or just this particular time? A. I perhaps noticed it, I don't recall if I noticed it every time he was there.
Q. Could you tell us about the lights on this street at night, is it brightly lighted, poor or dark? A. It was fairly brightly lighted. The house lights were on at the time and the street lights were average. The house lights were on too.
Q. The house lights were on? A. Most of the house lights were on.
Q. Did they shed any light on the street at all? A. I would say they show a little bit.
Q. Would you say your vision into the convertible was poor, fair, or good? A. I had good vision, I believe.

Mr. REARDON: No further questions.

CROSS-EXAMINATION

Q. (By Mr. Sutherland) Mr. Adams, did you see any other cars on Westchester Road that evening? A. Not that I noticed, sir, there may have been but I didn't notice them particularly.
Q. You considered Miss Mather a friend of yours? A. Well, I knew Miss Mather, I wasn't that well acquainted with her.
Q. Do you know whether she had a car or not? A. I don't know for certain, no.
Q. Did you ever see her in a car? A. I may have, but I didn't connect it with her.
Q. Did you ever see her in a blue Ford sedan? A. Not that I recall, sir.
Q. In what other cars do you remember seeing people who you know on Westchester Road at any time when you were delivering or collecting for your papers that evening? A. I can't say for certain, sir.
Q. There may have been some other cars on Westchester Road? A. Might have been.
Q. At what point was the yellow car when you first recognized Mr. Bennett? A. When I first recognized Mr. Bennett the car was just about opposite the street light, pulling away from the curb.

Q. You did not recognize Mr. Bennett when you first saw the car stopped along the sidewalk? A. No, sir I couldn't see in the car.
Q. You couldn't see in the car, the windshield was between you and the driver's seat? A. Yes.
Q. Does this convertible have those little glass wings alongside the windshield? A. I don't recall that.
Q. It could or could not? A. It could, yes.
Q. Do you recall when you first saw Miss Mather, she was sitting back against the upholstery or was she leaning forward? A. I believe she was sitting back against the upholstery but I couldn't say for certain.
Q. You don't remember that? A. No, sir.
Q. Is it possible for you to be wrong about the identification of a man you see driving away from the curb on a dark night? A. Well, I have seen Mr. Bennett several times, sir, and I am almost certain it was he.
Q. You are almost certain? A. Yes, sir.
Q. Now, the car when you saw it was moving away from you toward the center of the road, was it not? A. Yes, sir.
Q. So the longer you looked at it the further it was going away from you, isn't that right? A. Yes, sir.
Q. When you say you are almost certain, you could be wrong about your identification of Mr. Bennett? A. I am almost certain, I am not quite positive, but say 95 percent certain.
Q. Is there much of a chance you could be wrong? A. Not much of a chance.
Q. Some chance, is that right? A. Sir, I am as sure it was Mr. Bennett as I am sure he is sitting over there.
Q. Had you seen Mr. Bennett in this yellow car before? A. Yes, I had, sir.
Q. And you knew the yellow car was Mr. Bennett's car, did you? A. Yes, sir.
Q. Since you have been in college have you studied the question of the association of individuals and things? A. Sir, I have only been there a month.
Q. Well, have you ever noticed that in some cases you think of a human being in connection with some familiar article, and you always think of the two of them together? A. Would you repeat that, sir?
Q. Do you often think of some person you know and some things that are familiar to you, and associate the two of them together? A. I often associate them together, but in this case if I saw the car perhaps I associated them and perhaps I did not.
Q. Perhaps you associated them and perhaps you did not, is that your answer? A. Yes, sir, sometimes I didn't pay too much attention to the car.
Q. So as a matter of fact, Mr. Adams, on this evening the yellow car had an influence on your conclusion as to the actual individual driver of that car? A. I don't believe it did.
Q. You don't believe it did but it is possible? A. Possible, yes.

Mr. SUTHERLAND: Thank you.

REDIRECT EXAMINATION

Q. (By Mr. Reardon) Jimmy, did you have any special reason for noticing this car or these people who were in it as it went by? A. I noticed both of them.

Q. Did you have any particular reason for noticing the people in the car? A. Yes, sir, it happens that most of the people on my block are older couples who live on the block and I have a certain amount of interest in younger people.

Q. Did you generally notice any men with Miss Mather, who were in a car with her? A. I usually looked to see who was with her, yes.

Q. Did you notice whether the man you saw in the car that night, the man you have identified as Ira Bennett, whether or not he wore glasses? A. Yes, I believe he wore glasses.

Q. Did you notice whether Miss Mather saw you that night as she drove by?

Mr. SUTHERLAND: Now, if Your Honor please, I don't see how Mr. Adams can arrive at a conclusion concerning the mental operations of Miss Mather.

Mr. REARDON: I would suggest, Your Honor --

Mr. SUTHERLAND: I suppose the right question would be as to what Miss Mather said, what Miss Mather said and did.

Mr. REARDON: I will rephrase the question, Your Honor.

Mr. SUTHERLAND: May I ask counsel not to lead his witness.

Q. Jimmy, did you notice anything Miss Mather did, anything she did in the car as she drove by? A. Perhaps she waved to me but I couldn't say positively.

Q. You think she waved to you or is it just possible? A. I remember waving to her and I think there is a chance she waved back to me. The car was pulling away at the time.

Mr. REARDON: Thank you, Jimmy.

Mr. SUTHERLAND: If Your Honor please, I ask that the words, "to me," be stricken out because they represent this young man's conclusion, and a conclusion as to a mental operation of Miss Mather. "There is just a chance she waved back to me," does not seem appropriate.

The COURT: I don't think it is quite necessary to engage in that for the simple reason that Mr. Adams said perhaps she waved but dwell on it. However, if you would prefer and if it will make you happier I will strike it.

    Mr. SUTHERLAND: I would prefer to strike it, Your Honor.

    The COURT: It may be stricken.

    Mr. FIELD: That concludes the rebuttal testimony, Your Honor.

    Mr. SUTHERLAND: Now, if Your Honor please, I wish to renew my motions made at the end of the plaintiff's case.

I move, if Your Honor please, that the jury be directed to return a verdict for the defendant on each and all of the following grounds:

That there is insufficient evidence from which the jury could find that the defendant conspired with the unknown person who is alleged to have injured the plaintiff's decedent.

Second, as a matter of law even if there were sufficient evidence from which the jury could find the existence of a conspiracy, the injury to the plaintiff's decedent was outside of the scope of such a conspiracy.

    The COURT: The motions are denied.

    Mr. SUTHERLAND: Exceptions, if Your Honor please?

    The COURT: The exceptions may be noted.

    Mr. FIELD: If Your Honor please, the plaintiff moves that the jury be directed to return a verdict for the plaintiff in the amount of $23,000 damages on the following ground:

The evidence establishes as a matter of law that the defendant conspired with an unknown person wrongfully to take jewelry from Karron's Jewelry Shop; that a battery was committed on Joseph Rubin by said unknown person in the furtherance of said conspiracy; and that as a result of such battery, damages were suffered by the plaintiff as executrix and as surviving spouse in the stipulated amount of at least $23,000. The coercion alleged by the defendant, even if proved, cannot negate the existence of the conspiracy. Furthermore, the coercion alleged by the defendant, as a matter of law, has not been established by the evidence.

    The COURT: Thank you, Mr. Field. The motion is denied.

APPENDIX B

IN THE SUPERIOR COURT OF THE STATE OF AMES

IN AND FOR THE COUNTY OF AUSTIN

STATE OF AMES,)
)
     Plaintiff)
 v.)
)
 DAVID LOUIS DEVEREAUX,)
)
     Defendant)
)
	No. CR-7419
	
	 INDICTMENT (ARC 690.2)

The grand jury charges:

That on or about the 23rd day of January (last year), in the state of Ames, David Louis Devereaux murdered Edward Pfizer.

A true bill.

Elizabeth Caetta, Foreman

Chadwicke Bourne, County Attorney,

By *Susan Rand*
Deputy County Attorney

<u>Defendant's plea:</u> not guilty.

Prosecutor's Memorandum to File

The defendant is a medical doctor who is charged with having injected a dying cancer patient with a fatal dosage of potassium chloride to accelerate the patient's death. Clearly we are dealing with a matter of first-degree murder. However, because the patient was so near death, we may have a problem of proving the cause of death and therefore should consider charging the defendant with attempted murder as an included crime or even an alternate crime under Ames Rev. Code § 690.75. Under this statute and the general common law view, we can get a conviction of attempt even if the evidence supports a conviction on the full charge of murder, State v. Miller, 252 A.2d 321 (Me. 1969), although there is authority to the contrary, that failure to commit the substantive crime is an essential element of attempt. See Lewis v. People, 124 Colo. 62, 235 P.2d 348 (1951).

A more difficult problem is whether we can obtain an attempt conviction in the event the patient was dead when the doctor tried to kill him. That is, it would have been impossible for the doctor to commit murder upon a corpse; therefore, it may be impossible for him to commit the crime of attempted murder. The issue has never been satisfactorily resolved. It is discussed in La Fave and Scott, Criminal Law § 60 (1972), wherein representative cases are set forth.

Against our position would be the case of People v. Jaffe, 185 N.Y. 497, 79 N.E. 69 (1906). Jaffe purchased certain goods believing them to have been stolen, whereas in fact the goods had been returned to the proper owners and thus were no longer still technically "stolen" at the time Jaffe purchased them. Jaffe's conviction was reversed on the ground of impossibility, namely that he could not have succeeded in purchasing stolen goods because the goods were not stolen; therefore, he could not be guilty of the attempted purchase of stolen goods either. The court reasoned that his intent was to purchase particular goods and even though he thought he had a criminal intent, in fact he did not. To the same effect is State v. Guffey, 262 S.W.2d 152 (Mo. App. 1953), wherein the defendant was held not guilty of the attempt to take a deer out of season when he shot a stuffed deer believing it to be alive.

But supporting our position are several authorities, such as United States v. Thomas, 13 U.S.C.M.A. 278, 32 C.M.R. 278 (1962), and the Model Penal Code § 5.01(1). In Thomas, the defendant committed intercourse upon a girl he believed to be drunk, when in fact she was dead; he was held guilty of attempted rape. See also Gargan v. State, 436 P.2d 968 (Alaska 1968), in which the defendant was held guilty of attempted larceny when he broke into a washing machine coin box seeking money, but discovered that the box was empty.

It may be possible to draw a distinction between the cases based upon a difference between factual impossibility and legal impossibility.

That is, in Jaffe, it was thought that Jaffe's actual conduct, as well as that which he intended, did not legally amount to a crime, since he intended to receive property which was not in fact stolen. His mistaken belief that the property was stolen should not, it was argued, convert noncriminal conduct into criminal. In Thomas, however, the intent was to commit an act which would have been criminal if completed as planned, so the frustration was factual, not legal. This may be a distinction without a difference, or, at least, without a useful difference, in light of the generally announced policy served by punishment of the crime of attempt, which is the punishment of those who are doing their best to indulge in antisocial conduct and who should not be released merely because fortuitous circumstances frustrated their intentions. In any case, the facts of Thomas seem more apposite to our present case than do those of Jaffe.

Ames Revised Code Sections

§ 690.1. Murder. Whoever kills any human being with malice aforethought, either express or implied, is guilty of murder.

§ 690.2. First-Degree Murder. All murder which is perpetrated by means of poison or lying in wait, or any other kind of willful, deliberate, and premeditated killing, or which is committed in the perpetration or attempt to perpetrate any arson, rape, robbery, mayhem, or burglary, is murder in the first degree, and shall be punished by imprisonment for life at hard labor in the penitentiary; and the court shall enter judgment and pass sentence accordingly.

§ 690.3. Second-Degree Murder. Whoever commits murder otherwise than as set forth in § 690.2 is guilty of murder in the second degree, and shall be punished by imprisonment in the penitentiary for life, or for a term of not less than 10 years.

§ 690.4. Degree Determined. Upon the trial of an indictment for murder, the jury, if it finds the defendant guilty, must inquire, and by its verdict ascertain and determine the degree; and the court must enter judgment and pass sentence accordingly.

§ 690.75. Criminal Attempt. A person commits criminal attempt when, with intent to commit a specific crime, he performs any act which constitutes a substantial step toward commission of that crime.

§ 690.76. Charge of Crime Includes Criminal Attempt; Alternative Conviction. A person charged with commission of a crime may be convicted of criminal attempt as to that crime without being specifically charged with the criminal attempt in the accusation, information, or indictment; but such person cannot be convicted of both criminal attempt and the completed crime.

Assignments in Trial Practice

Transcript of Record

(Summarized in part.)

The State's Direct Case

THE COURT: Mr. Bourne, you may proceed.

MR. BOURNE: Your honor, the state calls as its first witness Mrs. Irene Gossage.

(Refer to materials in Assignment 11B, as instructed.)

MR. BOURNE: The state next calls Detective Lieutenant Allen B. Ruger.

ALLEN B. RUGER, Sworn

Q. Please state your name and occupation. A. My name is Allen B. Ruger. I am a lieutenant in the Austin Police Department. I have been in the APD for 14 years, the last 3 of which I have been with the narcotics division.

Q. Have you been involved with any narcotics investigation relating to the Austin County Hospital, and if you have, would you please describe it briefly. A. Yes, I have been so involved. We received word from several informants, one of whom was the wife of the defendant here, Doctor Devereaux, that there was considerable drug --

    MR. GREACEN (Edward V. Greacen, co-counsel for the defendant): Objection.

    THE COURT: Overruled.

    THE WITNESS: -- that there was considerable drug usage and abuse among the staff of the county hospital. I therefore began investigating.

Q. Did you have at that time any information about any fatal injection of Mr. Pfizer? A. No.
Q. When did you conduct your investigation? A. Last May.
Q. Did you at any time during your investigation talk with the defendant, Dr. Devereaux? A. Yes.
Q. Please describe when, where, and who was present. A. Well, it was during the month of May -- on the 8th, according to my notes -- that I went to Dr. Devereaux's office at the hospital.
Q. Please report that conversation to the jury.

    MR. GREACEN: Objection, hearsay!

THE COURT: Overruled. You may proceed.

A. I introduced myself to Dr. Devereaux and told him that we had received information from his wife about drug abuse on the staff. I also told him that we understood that she had become upset because the people about whom she told it had found out that she had given us the information and were threatening to make trouble for her. To this Dr. Devereaux said, "I know she's up tight and has a problem, but I have a problem too, because Dr. Wintel has something hanging over my head because I did something unethical."

Q. Did he say anything else? Did he explain his remarks? A. No, he did not say anything by the way of explanation, but he did say he would talk to his supervisor about the problem he had.

Q. No further questions. Cross-examine.

MR. GREACEN: No questions.

(Witness excused.)

MR. BOURNE: The state now calls Dr. Orner W. Wintel.

<u>ORNER W. WINTEL, M.D., Sworn</u>

(Direct examination, summarized.)

My name is Orner W. Wintel, M.D. I am a medical doctor now in practice in Phoenix, Arizona. I specialize in pediatric medicine and was formally chief pediatric resident at Austin County Medical Center. I left there in August of last year.

While there, I knew Dr. Devereaux. During the month of May, or perhaps early June, I had a conversation with him about the drug abuse investigation at the hospital. I had heard his wife had contacted the police or was considering contacting the police and I told him so, and I further told him that if she had gone to the police or if he let her go to the police I would take steps to see that he himself was investigated. I told him that my wife, Georgia, had told me that he had used an IV push of potassium chloride in a terminal cancer case. I told him that if this drug investigation got close to me or Georgia I would blow the whistle on him. Devereaux told me then that whatever came to pass, "I'll take my comeuppance."

CROSS-EXAMINATION

Q. It's true, is it not, Dr. Wintel, that both you and your wife have used drugs extensively? A. Well, what do mean by "used" and what do you mean by "extensively"?
Q. Dr. Wintel, you personally have used marijuana, have you not? A.

Yes.

Q. And your wife used marijuana, did she not? A. Yes, she did.
Q. And also barbiturates in large amounts, isn't that true? A. Yes.
Q. In fact, isn't it true that your wife recently died because of an overdose of barbiturates? A. Yes, that is true.
Q. And is it not true that you forged another doctor's name to a prescription for a narcotic medication to feed your wife's habit? A. Yes.
Q. Have you discussed these facts with the county attorney or one of his deputies? A. Yes.
Q. And you have agreed to cooperate fully with him in the prosecution of this case against Dr. Devereaux, isn't that correct? A. Yes.
Q. And isn't it true, Dr. Wintel, that you have not been prosecuted for possessing marijuana or for forging prescriptions for narcotics? A. Yes, that's true.
Q. And that's thanks to the county attorney, isn't it? A. I guess so.

(Witness excused.)

MR. BOURNE: The state now calls for Dr. Nathaniel Engelen.

NATHANIEL ENGELEN, M.D., Sworn

(Direct testimony of Dr. Engelen, summarized.)

My name is Nathaniel Engelen, M.D. I am and have been a surgeon for 25 years, and am now chief of surgery at the Austin County Medical Center. In my capacity as chief of surgery I selected Dr. Devereaux for a surgical residency at the Medical Center and later appointed him chief surgical resident.

Near the end of last May or perhaps in early June, Dr. Devereaux came to my office and told me that he had a confession to make. He said that he had a patient with terminal cancer to whom he had given potassium chloride intravenously in order to stop the patient's heart. I asked him where he got the chemical and he said he had got it from the nurse. I also asked him if anyone was there when he gave the injection and he said no.

I asked Dr. Devereaux why he was telling me all this, and he replied that the night it happened he had gone home and told his wife in the presence of Mrs. Wintel that there was trouble with a nurse. Devereaux said he anticipated that the trouble would probably come out and he wanted me to hear it from him rather than from the nurse, a Mrs. Gossage.

I asked him if he would confess this to the priest and he said he would not. He told me he did not think he had done anything wrong, that it was no different from when kidneys are removed from donors or when respirators are disconnected and the heart stops. I asked Dr. Devereaux what Mrs. Gossage had said, and Devereaux said she told him "Don't tell me what you're going to use it for." Then Devereaux told me he had used 60 or 70 milligrams of potassium chloride, which is about 35cc's.

Later I looked over the charts of the patient, whose name was Pfizer, and found no record of the injection. The next morning I called Devereaux into my office and told him there was nothing in the record about the potassium chloride injection. He then said he would deny it. I then told him he would have to get himself a lawyer because he would have to defend himself. The following Monday I called Devereaux into my office again and told him I had to take him off duty. He asked whether it was for legal or ethical reasons. I told him it was for ethical reasons and he should consider this the termination of his position at Austin County Medical Center.

I recognize the medical chart you have handed me as that of Edward Pfizer, the patient involved in this matter. The chart shows that the patient was readmitted to Austin County Medical Center on January 19 of last year. Mr. Pfizer was admitted as a patient suffering from terminal cancer of the pharynx.

CROSS-EXAMINATION

Q. Doctor, referring to Mr. Pfizer's chart there, can you tell anything about the patient's condition when he was last examined prior to his having been pronounced dead? A. Yes. The chart indicates that on the night of January 23rd Mr. Pfizer's condition worsened. The chart says his respiration was unresponsive and he was in his agonal period -- that's the period preceding death -- his pupils were fixed; he was in a deep coma.

Q. The brain was then dead? A. The brain did not seem to be functioning. That is one of the criteria of death. The chart indicates that at 4 a.m. that day the drug morphine sulphate, which had been administered to minimize the patient's pain, was withheld because of the effects of the coma. There was no longer a need for it.

Q. He couldn't feel any pain? A. Yes.

Q. When you have no vital signs, doctor, what condition are you in? A. You're sick -- in shock or dead.

Q. What is shock, doctor? A. Shock is the beginning of the dying process, so Pfizer was at the time in the process of dying and we were retaining him only in custodial care.

Q. Doctor, I will repeat, when there are no vital signs, when there is no blood pressure, when there is no pulse and no respiration, what are you? A. You're dead.

Q. Doctor, turning again to the condition of the patient on his last night, would the patient have been lying face down or face up? A. Why, I'm sure he would have been supine, that is, face up. A patient in that condition would have to be face up, because his carotid artery had been exposed by cancer surgery, and it would also be difficult to give him any injections if he was lying face down.

Q. Then, doctor, if Mrs. Gossage, the nurse, described the patient's position as "prone," she would be indicating that the patient would be face down and she would probably be in error, is that correct?
A. Yes, I would say that is correct.

Q. Doctor, you have said that Dr. Devereaux confessed to you that he injected 60 to 70 milligrams of fluid into the patient, is that correct? A. Yes.

Q. How many cc's, or cubic centimeters, of fluid is that? A. About 35.

Q. Would this then mean that Dr. Devereaux would have had to use a 35cc. syringe? A. Yes.

Q. He could not have injected 60 to 70 milligrams of fluid in a 5cc. syringe unless he filled it at least seven times, is that correct?
A. Yes.

Q. In other words, if he had used a 5cc. syringe, he would have had to have given his patient at least seven injections in order to accomplish a total of 60 to 70 milligrams, is that correct? A. Yes.

Q. Dr. Engelen, what is the largest container of potassium chloride available at your hospital? A. I believe the largest single container is 20cc's.

Q. Then, doctor, even filling a 35cc. syringe would have taken two operations -- that is, draining the entire contents of one potassium chloride ampule and part of the contents of another separate ampule, is that correct? A. I would say so.

Q. Doctor, if the patient's blood pressure is quite low, what is the procedure for injecting that patient? Is it difficult to insert a hypodermic needle? A. Yes, it is difficult. In fact if the pressure is quite low, the physician would have to use a tourniquet to expand the blood vessel so that it would receive a needle.

Q. Would you then say, doctor, that referring again to Edward Pfizer's chart, that it would be virtually impossible to give him an injection of anything on the night of January 23rd, at least without the use of a tourniquet? A. Yes, I believe so.

Q. Doctor, would you say, then, that if the nurse testified that no tourniquet was used when the injection was made, that she would be lying?

MR. BOURNE: Objection, Your Honor!

THE COURT: Yes, sustained.

Q. Let us now discuss, doctor, the schedule of Doctor Devereaux on the night of Mr. Pfizer's death, that is, January 23. A. Yes.

Q. Do you know anything about a party being held by any of the staff at or near the hospital that night? A. No.

Q. Have you at my request brought with you hospital records recording the scheduled duties of Dr. Devereaux on the night in question? A. Yes.

Q. Would you consult them, please, and tell the court and jury what Dr. Devereaux's schedule was that night. A. He was scheduled for a straight 48 hours of duty.

Q. Who made the schedule, doctor? A. Dr. Devereaux made the schedule himself. You see, he was chief administrative resident and was in charge of making work schedules.

Q. Could he have given himself the night off? A. Yes.

Q. But he did not do so, did he? A. No, apparently not.

Q. What does "on duty" mean? A. It means that he is on call and responsible to respond to calls in the event of any need for a physician by a patient such as Mr. Pfizer or any of the other approximately 40 surgical patients in the surgical ward at that time. Many of the patients are, of course, in critical condition and may need a physician at any time.

Q. Directing your attention now, doctor, to the day you say Dr. Devereaux came to your office and "confessed." Isn't it true that Dr. Devereaux merely came to you in anticipation that you would soon hear from the wife of Dr. Wintel, and that Mrs. Wintel was merely attempting to divert attention from her and her own husband's drug abuse while at the hospital? A. No, that is not so. Dr. Devereaux made what I understood to be a genuine confession that he had in fact injected the patient to stop his heart.

MR. GREACEN: No further questions.

RE-DIRECT EXAMINATION

Q. Referring to the hospital schedule of physician's duties, Dr. Engelen, does it show any change in the scheduling for the night of January 23? A. Yes.

Q. Would you please describe that change. A. Well, originally, Dr. Devereaux had scheduled another physician to work with him on the night of January 23, but in a revised schedule Dr. Devereaux gave the other physician the night off and scheduled himself for duty that night.

Q. Doctor, is potassium chloride ever injected into a patient? A. No, it is not. It is only given in solutions by intravenous drip. The chart shows here that such a solution was originally ordered for Mr. Pfizer but it had been discontinued the same day that he was admitted to the hospital, which was five days before his death.

Q. Doctor, what is an "IV push"? A. Loosely, it could mean any intravenous injection; but it is more frequently used to describe the injection of a substance directly into an intravenous tube already operating and inserted into the patient's blood vessel.

Q. What would be a typical time, then, to use an "IV push"? A. It is not uncommonly used in cases of low blood pressure.

Q. Did Dr. Devereaux ever state to you, during his conversations with you about this matter, that Edward Pfizer was dead prior to his giving him the injection of potassium chloride? A. Definitely not.

RE-CROSS EXAMINATION

Q. Were you aware that a postmortem was conducted on Edward Pfizer? A. Yes.
Q. Did you participate? A. I was there as an observer.
Q. Who else was present with you? A. Dr. Avery Easton, the Austin County Medical Examiner, Miss Lois Cavender, who I believe was from the District Attorney's office, and then there were some detectives and other personnel from the Medical Examiner's office.
Q. I show you now an autopsy report marked Defense Exhibit A, and ask you if it reports the autopsy to which you have just referred. A. Yes.
Q. Does it contain protocol and findings? A. Yes.
Q. Is there a space there for cause of death? A. Yes.
Q. What is given as the cause of death? A. It's blank -- it doesn't say.
Q. There isn't any cause of death given there? A. It doesn't appear.
Q. It's not in the report? A. Right.
Q. Isn't it true that the original death certificate, signed by Dr. Devereaux, listed the cause of death as cancer of the pharynx? A. Yes, though there was an addendum added to it by Dr. Easton indicating that death was caused by the injection of potassium chloride.
Q. But Dr. Easton was not present at the patient's bedside at the time of his death, was he, doctor? A. No.
Q. Furthermore, Dr. Easton did not discover any particular potassium chloride in the body of Edward Pfizer, did he? A. No.
Q. Then isn't it true that Dr. Easton relied upon what you said Dr. Devereaux had said in those conversations you had earlier testified to? A. Well, --

   MR. BOURNE: Objection, sheer speculation by this witness.

   THE COURT: Sustained.

Q. Did Dr. Devereaux fill out a death summary? A. Yes.
Q. Isn't it true that he stated in that summary that Mr. Pfizer had ceased to breathe, had no blood pressure, and gradually went downhill until his death at 9:10 p.m. on January 23? A. I believe so.
Q. Referring again to the hospital chart, doctor, isn't it true that Mr. Pfizer had been receiving morphine sulphate from time to time to relieve his pain and anxiety? A. Yes.
Q. Is not morphine sulphate a narcotic, doctor? A. Yes.
Q. And could not the administering of so much of this narcotic drug have reduced Mr. Pfizer to his terminal status very rapidly? A.

Yes.

Q. Referring again to the conversation you say Dr. Devereaux had with you in which he made what you call a confession. Did you tell anyone at the hospital about that conversation? A. Yes, I reported it to Dr. Carlisle, who is the assistant to the hospital superintendent.

Q. Was there any further conversation with Dr. Carlisle about it? A. Yes, Dr. Carlisle told me that Dr. Devereaux's name had come up in connection with another investigation. He said that Dr. Wintel had mentioned Dr. Devereaux's name in connection with a euthanasia case.

Q. Did he actually use the word "euthanasia"? A. Yes, I believe he did.

MR. GREACEN: No further questions.

RE-DIRECT EXAMINATION

Q. At the time Dr. Devereaux came to you with his confession, had you heard anything at all about the other investigation at the hospital into drug abuse there? A. No, I had not. The first I heard of it was the next day, when I talked with Dr. Carlisle.

(Witness excused.)

MR. BOURNE: The state now calls Dr. Avery Easton.

AVERY EASTON, M.D., Sworn

(Direct examination of Dr. Easton, summarized.)

My name is Avery Easton, M.D. I am and have been a pathologist for 30 years. I have been for 20 years and am now the chief medical examiner for Austin County. As medical examiner I am a county official appointed by the Board of Supervisors to investigate the cause of death whenever there is any degree of doubt. I am to investigate the circumstances of the cause of death as well as the postmortem examination itself. In fact, if the circumstances were not allowed to be considered, I would have to testify in many cases that the cause of death is unknown or in doubt. I have testified at hundreds of murder trials over the years, and in most of those cases I have relied in part on the circumstances of the death in addition to the findings during postmortem.

A famous case in which a medical examiner based his finding on evidence extrinsic to the pathology itself was that in which Dr. Milton Helpern, chief medical examiner of New York City, testified in the trial of Dr. Carl Coppolino for murdering his wife, Carmela. Dr. Helpern had received information that Dr. Coppolino had obtained an unaccounted-for

supply of succinylcholine. This is a powerful muscle relaxer which can
be fatal and which becomes undetectable because it breaks down into
innocent chemical compounds immediately after injection. Dr. Helpern,
after receiving this information, searched for and found a tiny needle
puncture on the decedent. Then by applying some sophisticated
laboratory work at New York University, he established traces of the
drug in tissues which were immediately adjacent to the needle puncture.
If he had not taken advantage of the investigatory knowledge that the
drug had been shipped to the defendant, he would have had to list the
cause of death as unknown.

Similarly, the only doctor to be tried in the United States on a
clearcut euthanasia charge, Dr. Hermann N. Sander of New Hampshire,
called attention to himself by entering an air injection into the chart
of a patient whom he was later charged with murdering. Of course the
medical examiner will not base his conclusion on a confession alone,
such as Dr. Sander's entry on the chart. Nevertheless, the examiner is
entitled to look outside at the postmortem itself for the cause of
death. On the other hand, the extrinsic evidence pointing to a cause of
death may be disregarded if the autopsy itself provides an overwhelming
contradictory cause of death. For instance, in the present case, had
the patient's exposed carotid artery been ruptured, that would have
contradicted any finding of an injection of potassium chloride. Here,
however, the carotid artery was intact even though it was exposed and
posing the potential of rupture. Since it had not actually ruptured, it
could not be blamed for the death.

The body of Edward Pfizer was exhumed last August, seven months
after his death, and I then performed an autopsy on it. The district
attorney, Lois Cavender, Dr. Engelen, and some detectives and other
personnel from my office were present at the time, and I then listed the
cause of death as an injection of potassuim chloride, established by
investigation (homicide), and acute pulmonary embolism, diffuse
confluent bronchial pneumonia, carcinoma of the pharynx with metastasis
in the right neck, and advanced occlusive arterial disease.

Basically, potassium chloride is a salt, soluble in water and given
to patients to correct potassium depletion. The depletion may occur in
a patient on intravenous therapy and unable to take food orally. The
result may be muscle cramps, a general feeling of weakness and the
heartbeat may become irregular. Potassium chloride given either through
an intravenous solution or orally can help remedy these difficulties,
although it must be given in small amounts. An overdose of it can be
fatal, by virtue of its causing paralysis of the heart muscles, leading
to arrythmia, cardiac standstill, and finally convulsions, thus causing
the death.

The presence of potassium chloride cannot be detected at an autopsy,
however, because the potassium and chloride ions, which are the elements

of potassium chloride, are normally found in the body tissues. Even an autopsy performed immediately after death would not reveal its presence, unlike some alien substance, such as arsenic, which could be traced.

CROSS-EXAMINATION

Q. Showing you the death certificate, doctor, is this addendum yours? A. Yes.
Q. You are the one, then, who filled out the certificate showing the cause of death to be "injection of potassium chloride (homicide) established by investigation"? A. Yes.
Q. When you said "established by investigation" you meant you were relying on information which you did not find during the autopsy. Isn't that true? A. Yes.
Q. Isn't it also true, doctor, that the autopsy itself revealed absolutely no potassium chloride in Edward Pfizer's body? A. Yes.
Q. Thus there are no pathological findings of potassium chloride at all, isn't that true? A. Yes.
Q. Isn't it also true, doctor, that if you were asked to form an opinion as to the cause of Edward Pfizer's death relying solely on the pathology based upon the autopsy, you would be unable to form any opinion as to the presence or absence of potassium chloride and any relation it might have to the death? A. Yes.
Q. Then your conclusion that the cause of death was "injection of potassium chloride (homicide)" is strictly based upon investigation by other persons, is that not true? A. Yes.
Q. There was no scientific basis for your finding at all? A. Yes.
Q. Had you received your "investigation" information from the police and the district attorney? A. Yes.
Q. And from Dr. Engelen as well? A. Yes.
Q. Could you possibly make a finding of potassium chloride based solely upon the pathology of this case? A. No.

(Witness excused. State rests its case, and the defense moves to dismiss on the basis that there is no proof of the act of injecting the decedent, there is no proof of motive, there is no proof that the decedent was alive at the time of any act of the defendant, and the testimony of the nurse, Mrs. Gossage, should be ruled accomplice testimony and unreliable as a matter of law without corroboration. Furthermore, the testimony of Dr. Easton should be struck as opinion based on hearsay, and the death certificate addendum filled out by him should similarly be struck and a mistrial declared. The court denies all motions, ruling that they raise questions of fact, all of which are for the jury. The defense then proceeds with its direct case:)

THE DEFENSE CASE

MR. GREACEN: The defense calls Dr. Jacqueline Cunningham.

Assignments in Trial Practice

JACQUELINE CUNNINGHAM, M.D., Sworn

(Direct examination of Dr. Cunningham, summarized.)

My name is Jacqueline Cunningham, M.D. I am a deputy medical examiner for Austin County and was with Dr. Easton at the August autopsy of Edward Pfizer. Any of the ailments shown pathologically on the original death certificate might cause death, but I cannot say that any of them actually did cause death.

CROSS-EXAMINATION

Q. Would you agree with Dr. Easton that the cause of death was injection of potassium chloride? A. Well, yes, I would.

MR. GREACEN: Your Honor, I object! I want this witness declared hostile to the defense so that I can cross-examine her.

THE COURT: Objection overruled, but you may have re-direct as soon as Mr. Bourne is finished.

MR. BOURNE: We have nothing further of Dr. Cunningham, Your Honor.

RE-DIRECT EXAMINATION

Q. Now, Dr. Cunningham, you say you agree with Dr. Easton, is that right? A. Yes, essentially.
Q. But you will also agree that the autopsy revealed nothing about potassium chloride? A. Yes.
Q. So in fact, your agreement with Dr. Easton is based upon the same investigation he relied on, and not on the autopsy, is that right? A. Yes.

MR. GREACEN: The defense now calls Benjamin Copping, M.D.

BENJAMIN COPPING, M.D. Sworn

(Dr. Copping's testimony, summarized.)

My name is Benjamin Copping, M.D. I have been a pathologist for 44 years. I have performed over 30,000 autopsies. I am a professor of pathology and chairman of the department of pathology at the Austin University Medical School. I was formerly chief of pathology at Langdale General Hospital. Dr. Easton was one of my residents. He is a good man, and was one of my best students. I have written numerous articles in scientific journals and am a member of numerous medical associations.

I conferred for an hour and a half with Dr. Easton shortly before this trial and reviewed the gross findings of the death along with photographs and microscopic slides of specimen and tissue. Based upon this conference and examination, my opinion is that the cause of death of Edward Pfizer was cancer and pulmonary embolism, not an injection of potassium chloride. What happened specifically was that a hard blood clot developed in the leg, then carried up from the leg into Pfizer's pulmonary artery and stopped right there. That kind of embolism kills and it kills suddenly, and it is my opinion that it was the immediate cause of death in this case.

The addendum to the death certificate by Dr. Easton stating that the cause of death was an injection of potassium chloride as established by investigation, and homicide, is erroneous. There is nothing in the autopsy finding to support a statement by a medical doctor that death was caused by potassium chloride. In fact the addendum is erroneous because it is contrary to the findings of the autopsy and the information in the autopsy report. The medical examiner here did not see any evidence of potassium chloride. He is simply relying on somebody else's word, and I do not believe that a pathologist should do that. Thus, I would characterize the death in this case as due to cancer of the oral pharynx with complicating pulmonary embolism which caused immediate death.

A 5cc dosage of potassium chloride would not kill a person. That amount of potassium chloride is used in open-heart surgery frequently.

CROSS-EXAMINATION

Q. Doctor, did you actually yourself perform 30,000 autopsies? A. Actually, I perfomed 5,000 of them myself, and I supervised the other 25,000.
Q. Would an autopsy ever reveal an injection of potassium chloride, doctor? A. No.
Q. In considering the pathology of a death, you frequently rely on information given you by others, do you not, such as laboratory reports and the like? A. Yes.
Q. Have you not yourself signed death certificates even though you had not personally pronounced the death in cases where you relied on the patient's chart for your information? A. Many times.
Q. Isn't it true that the chart contains much information put there by other people, including a death summary by the attending physician? A. Yes. In fact I am usually told by the attending doctor what the cause of death was. Then I examine the patient's history myself and I write down what I think to be the cause of death.
Q. And if the doctor in the death summary stated that he injected the patient with potassium chloride to stop his heart, what would you put down as the cause of death?

MR. GREACEN: Objection, your Honor! Move for mistrial.

THE COURT: Denied. Proceed, doctor.

A. I would say to that attending physician that he should leave such matters to the medical examiner and that I would not sign such a certificate.

(Witness excused.)

MR. GREACEN: The defense calls Mrs. Marjorie Hudacek.

MARJORIE HUDACEK, Sworn

(Mrs. Hudacek's testimony, summarized.)

My name is Mrs. John Hudacek -- Marjorie Hudacek. I was a patient of Dr. Devereaux's last year. I was horribly injured in an automobile accident and was in the Austin County Medical Center. There was a time when I believed I was going to die and hoped that I would die, but Dr. Devereaux gave me the will to live. I am indebted to him for my life. He is a dedicated doctor and would not have it in his soul to harm anyone.

MR. GREACEN: The defense rests.

THE STATE'S REBUTTAL CASE

MR. BOURNE: The state calls as a rebuttal witness Dr. Thomas DeGowin.

THOMAS DEGOWIN, M.D., Sworn

(Dr. DeGowin's testimony, summarized.)

My name is Thomas DeGowin. I am a pathologist and have been a pathologist for 47 years, during which time I have performed approximately 25,000 autopsies. I was for 17 years chief medical examiner of Major City, Ames, and have now retired from that post and from active practice.

I reviewed the charts and other information concerning Edward Pfizer for two hours and I would agree with Dr. Copping that the pulmonary embolism had formed before death. But I would not say as he does that the embolism was the cause of death. In the first place, a man can survive with an embolism of this type, and in the second place, there is a difference between a cause of death and "the" cause of death. That is, something which could have killed a patient is not necessarily that which did kill this particular patient. The medical examiner has the duty to go beyond the autopsy to discover circumstances surrounding suspicious deaths. The medical examiner must always avoid the trap of seeing likely causes as real causes. Even the pathology itself may be misleading. I remember the case of a man whose autopsy revealed that he had serious heart trouble. However, the narrative of the events of his death showed that he had not suffered from chest pain immediately prior to death but instead had convulsions. Further investigation revealed an old head injury which was seen to be the precipitating cause of death, not the heart.

Therefore, I would agree with Dr. Easton's opinion that the cause of death was injection of potassium chloride into the vein of the deceased, based upon the circumstances. I would definitely not base this conclusion on the autopsy report alone. In fact, I could not come to a conclusion based upon the autopsy report alone. I would have to have the other information necessary to form an opinion before I would form it, and the autopsy alone in this case is insufficient. I personally find persuasive the testimony of Dr. Engelen that Dr. Devereaux came to him and confessed injecting the chemical. The chemical can cause fatal heart standstill when enough of it is given in that way and still not appear in the autopsy. Also, since the autopsy itself does not force me to a different conclusion, the totality of information is adequate to support a conclusion that the cause of death was the injection of potassium chloride. If Dr. Devereaux had not gone to Dr. Engelen and told him what he had done, the whole thing would have gone completely unsolved.

CROSS-EXAMINATION

Q. Would 5cc's of potassium chloride be a fatal dosage, doctor? A. No, it would not, but I would not give credence to the technical details of the nurse's testimony that only 5cc's were injected.
Q. Isn't it true, doctor, that the autopsy report itself gives no indication of any injection of potassium chloride, but it does give many other indications of other immensely serious pathological difficulties, any one of which could have been the cause of death? A. Yes, the autopsy gives no indication of potassium chloride, but I believe I have already explained the difference between a possible cause of death and the actual cause of death.

(Witness excused.)

MR. BOURNE: Your Honor, the state rests.

[Following are a hospital chart and a death certificate which may be presumed to have been used in the trial. Counsel here are invited to use them during performance of assignments relating to this case.]

Pfizer, Edward

AUSTIN COUNTY MEMORIAL HOSPITAL

Doctor's Order Sheet

DATE	TIME		
1/19	3:30 pm	① ABR ② NPO	
		③ Xray	
		④ Complete Blood Count	
		⑤ Urine	
		⑥ VDRL	
		⑦ 1000 cc 5% D/W I.V. @ 75 cc/hr	
		Follow ̄c 1000 cc N/S same rate	
		⑧ Electrolytes	
		⑨ SMA - 12	
		⑩ Morphine Sulfate 1/4 gr I.M. Q4H for pain	
		⑪ No Code 4	
		⑫ EKG	
		⑬ Vital Signs	
		⑭ I & O	
		⑮ Nembutal 1/2 gr @ H.S. PRN for sleep	Hand MD
1/20	9 am	Same as above — except ⑫	Hand MD
1/21	9 am	Same as above	Hand MD
1/22	9 am	Same as above	Hand MD
	1:10 pm	① Chest X-ray — stat	
		② Ampicillin 1 gr Q6H (I.V. Push)	
		③ Heparin 5000 units (I.V. Push)	Hand MD
	9 pm	1) Continue above	A. Devereaux MD
1/23	9 am	① Same as above	Hand MD
	2 pm	1) Continue above	A. Devereaux MD
1/24	9 am	No orders —	Hand MD

PROGRESS NOTES (Notes should be signed by Physician)

Date	Time	Note
1/19	3:30 pm	Elderly ♂ via ambulance c̄ history terminal cancer of pharynx. Patient is unable to swallow food or water. No pain.
		Exam ① BP 100/60 apical rate 120 & reg.
		② Lungs clear – heart regular – no murmur
		③ Abdomen soft – no masses
		④ EENT – multiple masses palpable in neck bilaterally. Throat inflamed
		⑤ Neuro Exam (-)
		Diagnosis ① Dehydration secondary to inability to swallow due to ca. of pharynx c̄ metastasis
		Prognosis: Grave
		Plan: ① Supportive care
		② Hydrate
		③ Consult c̄ surgery dept. Bland MD
1/20	9am	Vitals O.K. – continue c̄ same as above
		Hydration satisfactory
		Prognosis still grave Bland MD
1/21	9am	Vitals O.K. – Same as above – continue c̄ same
		Hydration O.K. – prog. same Bland MD
1/22	9am	Vitals O.K. – cont c̄ same as above
		Hydration still O.K. – prognosis same. Bland MD
	7:30 pm	Temp 103° – coughing, chest pains, chills. Diaphoretic
		X-rays = pneumonia bilateral
		Radiology suggests pos. pulmonary Emboli –
		Lung scan several Emboli – Pain in left lower extremity
		Diagnosis ① Bilateral bacterial pneumonia
		② Pulmonary Emboli – left lung
		③ Terminal ca.
		Orders written Bland MD
1/23	9am	Temp. spiking – 101° – Maintain same orders – Same diagnosis Bland MD
	10am	Temp down – agonal period – orders discontinued – pt. is comatose Bland MD
	12N	Pt. still diaphoretic but unresponsive, comatose – agonal period – terminal – will maintain supportive care only Bland MD
	9:05 pm	Called to see patient @ 9:05 pm. BP(-) No heart sounds, No respiration, pt. terminal, no Code 4 called. Pronounced death @ 9:15 pm.
		D.L. Devereaux, M.D.

NURSES NOTES

Date	Time	
1/19	3:35 pm	c̄ via ambulance
		pt complains of pain
		pain
1/20	am	pain in
	pm	pain z
1/21	am	pain - restless - D.
	pm	pain M
1/22	am	sleeping better A
	1 pm	pain - cough - called Dr. M
	2 pm	antibiotics started M
1/23	am	comatose Dr. in
	pm	patient very poor
	9 pm	pt comatose bad vital signs temp down call dr. H.

MEDICATIONS

DATE		1/19	1/20	1/21	1/22	1/23
DAY OF WEEK						
Morphine 1/4 gr Q4H	A.M.		4am 8am 12N	4am 8am 12N	4am 8am 12N	4am 8am
	P.M.		4pm 8pm 12M	4pm 8pm 12M	4pm 8pm 12M	
Nembutal 1/2 gr PRN @HS for sleep	A.M.					
	P.M.	10 pm			8 pm	
	A.M.					
	P.M.					
Ampicillin 1/2 gr Q6H IV Push	A.M.					1:30 7:30
	P.M.				1:30 7:30	
Heparin 5000 units IV Push	A.M.				1:30 7:30	1:30
	P.M.				1:30	
	A.M.					
	P.M.					
Nurse Signature	7-3					
	3-11					
	11-7					

GRAPHIC RECORD — RECORD IN BLACK

PFIZER, EDWARD

Date	1/19	1/20	1/21	1/22	1/23		
PO/PP Day							
Year AM/PM HOUR	4 8 12 / 4 8 12	4 8 12 / 4 8 12	4 8 12 / 4 8 12	4 8 12 / 4 8 12	4 8 12 / 4 8 12	4 8 12 / 4 8 12	4 8 12

TEMPERATURE F° Oral — scale 97–103, Normal at 99.

Pulse (X-apical, Δ-radial), Orthostatic — scale 30–220.

| Blood Pressure | / | 100/60 100/60 100/60 | 110/60 105/85 100/60 | 115/60 100/60 100/60 | 110/60 100/60 100/70 | 110/70 100/70 115/70 | 115/70 110/65 90/50 60/30 60/20 | / | / |

Ht. ___ cm Wt. ___ kg

GRAPHIC CHART

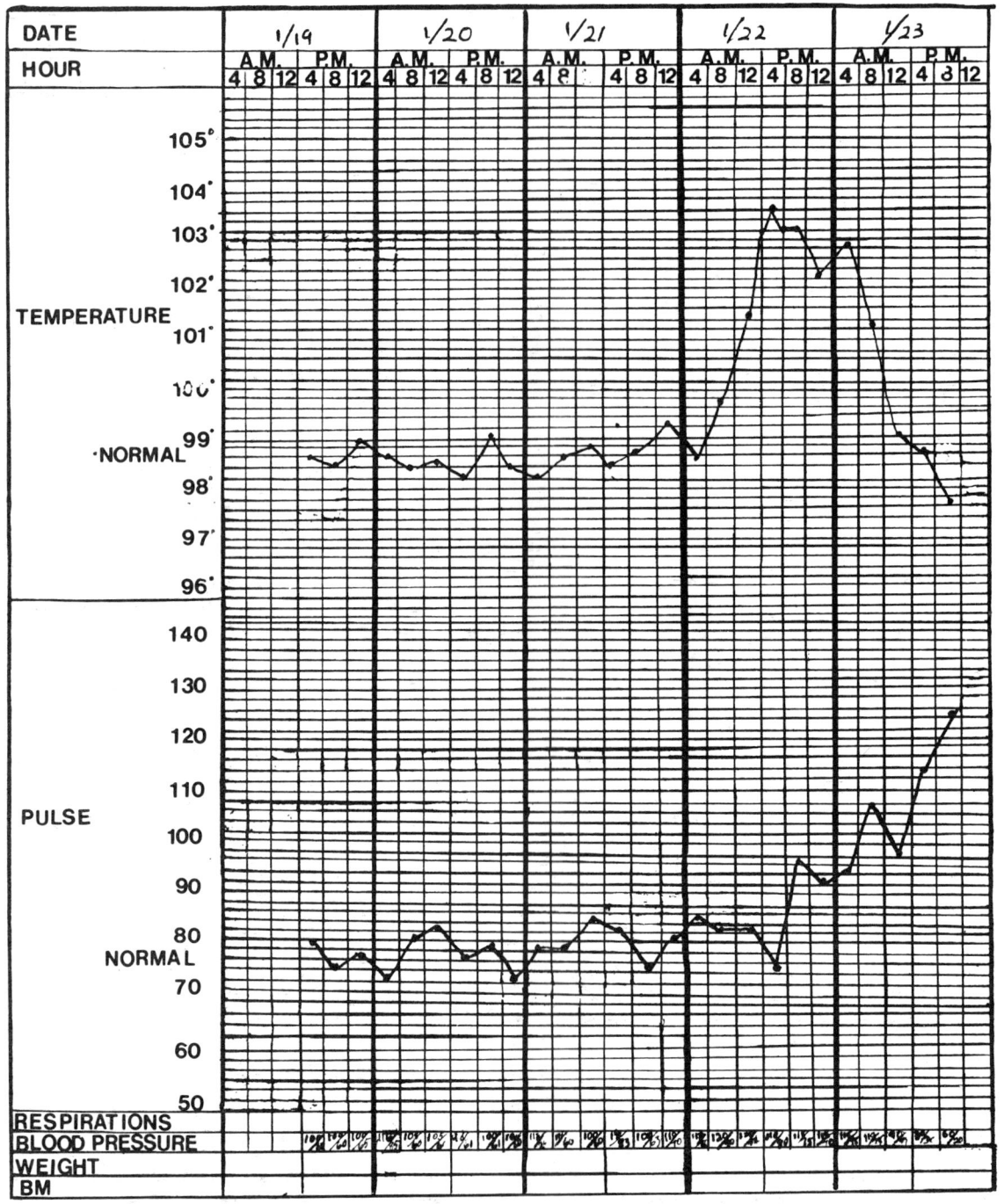

DIVISION OF HEALTH SERVICES – VITAL RECORDS BRANCH
CERTIFICATE OF DEATH

Registration District No. _____ Local No. _____

1. Name of Deceased (First, Middle, Last): EDWARD PFIZER
2. Sex: M
3. Date of Death (Month, Day, Year): 1/23
4. Color or Race: W
5a. State of Birth:
5b. County of Birth:
6. Date of Birth:
7. Age (In Years, Last Birthday): 53
8a. Place of Death-County: AUSTIN
8b. City or Town: AUSTIN
8c. Name of Hospital or Institution: AUSTIN CO. MEM.
8e. Inside City Limits: YES
9a. Residence - State: AMES
10. Citizen of What Country:
11. Married, Never Married, Widowed, Divorced:
12. Surviving Spouse:
13. Social Security Number:
14a. Usual Occupation:
14b. Kind of Business or Industry:
15. Was Decedent Ever in U.S. Armed Forces:
16. Father's Name:
17. Mother's Maiden Name:
18a. Informant's Name and Address:
18b. Relation to Deceased:

PART I. DEATH CAUSED BY:
19.
(a) Immediate Cause: BILATERAL PNEUMONIA
(b) Due to, or as a consequence of: CARCINOMA OF PHARYNX
(c) Due to, or as a consequence of:

PART II. Other Significant Conditions Contributing to Death but not related to cause given in Part I(a).
20a. PULMONARY EMBOLI
20b. Autopsy: NO
21. Was case referred to Medical Examiner:
22. Time of Death: 9:10 P.M.

23a. Name and Title of Certifier: DAVID L. DEVEREAUX - M.D.
23b. Address: AUSTIN CO. MEM. HOSP.
23c. Signature of Certifier: DL Devereaux MD
23d. Date Signed: 1/24

DHS 1872 FORM 8 REV. 7/79

Addendum: Cause of death: injection of potassioum chloride, established by investigation (homicide) and acute pulmonary embolism, diffuse confluent bronchial pneumonia, carcinoma of the pharynx with metastasis in the right neck and advanced occlusive arterial disease. Per autopsy 8/5. Avery Easton, M.D., Chief Medical Examiner, Austin Co.

Avery Easton, MD

Assignments in Trial Practice

APPENDIX C

General Instructions to Witnesses

1. Learn your story completely before talking to any of counsel. Your general background material is contained in the Assignment Book materials and in such Special Materials as you may have been given by the instructor. Avoid changing your story between interview and examination.

2. Do not have any discussion with counsel about any aspect of the case except in your role as witness. It is especially important that you do not interrupt an interview, or respond to an interruption by counsel, for "off the record" discussions. Violation of this rule almost invariably leads to misunderstandings between witness and counsel about what is "on the record" and what is "off the record."

3. Be prepared to answer any question concerning a matter about which you would reasonably have knowledge. Wherever appropriate you may simply assume your own background in answering personal questions.

4. If asked a question as to which it is reasonable for the person whose role you are taking not to know the answer, do not improvise a hasty story. A simple "I don't know" is least likely to complicate the situation.

5. Do not endeavor to create an unusual character in your performance as witness. A natural handling of the role of the witness best effects a profitable examination experience.

6. If your directions indicate that you are to cooperate with counsel, and counsel give you any instructions about such matters as volunteering answers or avoiding mention of something, try to oblige. Of course counsel should not ask you to change the facts. If they do so, either directly or by implication, react as you think the witness whose role you are taking would react. If your role is that of a witness who is flatly dishonest, or else willing to cheat a little on the truth, then follow counsel's lead.

7. Witnesses are infrequently find themselves sympathetic to one party and hostile to another. In answering a question on the witness stand, they may try to help or harm the questioners' case depending on where their sympathies lie. You should exhibit such partiality if you think your role calls for it.

8. Immediately after the interview, make notes of all incidents occurring during the interview that you think may be worthy of attention during the critique.

Assignments in Trial Practice

9. If you have any questions concerning the witness role or the supplementary facts, consult the instructor.

10. Dates of recent events in these materials are frequently stated in a dating code in which 19Y1 means one year ago, 19Y2 means two years ago, 19Y3 means three years ago, and so on.

11. Counsel have sometimes been supplied with copies of previous statements by witnesses. These have been typewritten for legibility, but all parts of such a statement except for the signature should be assumed to be in the handwriting of the person who obtained the statement from the witness. The signature should be assumed to actually be the signature of the witness.

12. Please return any Special Materials given to you by the instructor at the conclusion of the assignment.